THE
GREAT
AMERICAN
ADVENTURE
BOOK

THE GREAT AMERICAN ADVENTURE BOOK

BY JOSEPH DANIEL

DOLPHIN BOOKS   DOUBLEDAY & COMPANY, INC.
GARDEN CITY, NEW YORK 1985

A BUZZWORM BOOK

PRODUCED BY DANIEL PRODUCTIONS
2333 21st Street, Boulder, CO 80302

ART DIRECTOR: **JOSEPH DANIEL**
EDITORIAL & PRODUCTION STAFF: **SUSAN EASTMAN, SHERI STEELE,**
WENDY ROTHMAN, MARK DANIEL, VALARI JACK
RESEARCH: **PHIL BRITTIN**
CARTOGRAPHY: **JOY YULE**
TYPOGRAPHY: **LINDA BEVARD & DEBORAH HAVAS, HORIZON GRAPHICS & TYPE COMPANY**
COVER PHOTOGRAPHY: Glider, Cyclists, Sailboats, Dory in whitewater—**JOSEPH DANIEL,**
Diver with fish—**DAVE DE PUY,** Climber on summit—**GLENN D. FORTNER**

© 1985 by Joseph Daniel

Library of Congress Cataloging in Publication Data
Daniel, Joseph.
 The great American adventure book.
 "A Dolphin book."
 1. Outdoor recreation—North America—Guide-books.
 2. Outdoor recreation—North America—Equipment and
 supplies—Directories. 3. North America—Description and
 travel—1981-   —Guide-books. I. Title.
 GV191.4.D36   1985   917   84-26006
 ISBN 0-385-27942-6

PRINTED IN THE UNITED STATES OF AMERICA
FIRST EDITION

Dedicated to Naomi Uemura, the intrepid explorer who, in February 1984, was reported missing and is feared lost on the west face of North America's highest peak, Mount McKinley in Alaska. Uemura had just become the first climber to succeed in a solo attempt on the mountain in midwinter and was on his way back down when he was overcome by a severe storm. His unique ability as an explorer left behind a record of accomplishments that commands respect and awe, but it was his true love of adventure and his desire to live life to its very fullest that will be remembered in the hearts of all who knew him.

Photo: Joseph Daniel

TABLE OF CONTENTS

100 UNFORGETTABLE TRAVEL EXPERIENCES

WILDERNESS OUTFITTERS DIRECTORY

Photo: Joseph Daniel

THOUGHTS OF ADVENTURE

About half an hour ago I passed over the Grand Canyon at an altitude of 35,000 feet. I had been sitting in my seat fretting over my inability to write this preface—writers call it a block; I call it not being a writer—when I glanced out of my window and to my surprise and joy I was looking down into the same crack in the earth that I had floated down just a few short weeks before. The perspective from the air was fantastic and for the first time I understood geographically just exactly what I had been through. Floating down the Grand Canyon in wooden dories (similar to the way Major John W. Powell had done it for the first time over a hundred years ago) had taken us 18 days and had cleansed my mind and rejuvenated my spirit like nothing else I've ever experienced. Aboard a jet the trip took about 20 minutes, but it was enough to immediately set me thinking about adventure and what a powerful tonic it can be. This plane trip was actually a very fitting place to finish this book, as it was taking me to the high deserts of California to photograph a test flight of a very special aircraft (pictured at left), which, by the time you read these ramblings, may be on its way to reaching one of the last great milestones in aviation history—being the first plane to circumnavigate the world nonstop without refueling. Adventure at its purest!

The idea for this book was born, strangely enough, in a crowded bar deep in the bowels of New York City. A long overdue trip had taken me from my quiet Colorado mountains to the offices of Doubleday & Co. high up on the 43rd floor of a stone and steel mountain smack in the middle of Park Avenue. After spending a long morning finishing business I stopped to say hello to an editor and a sales manager I knew there and was soon persuaded to join them for lunch. They wanted to talk about several book ideas, and so we pushed through the mad rush of Manhattan to a favorite spot of theirs and fought our way to a small table. Necessity truly being the mother of invention, it doesn't really seem so odd that within such a crowded, hyper city—so far from the thunder of whitewater, the swish of skis in deep, dry powder snow or the intense quiet of a desert night—the talk soon turned to adventure. Chasing thrills was very much in vogue at that time, and it seemed like every other day you'd read about some crazy character parachuting off a high canyon cliff or scaling a famous building—usually to be met by law enforcement officers at the completion of the stunt. Members of a questionable organization known as the Oxford Dangerous Sports Club were jumping off bridges on long rubber bungee cords while a handful of sailors kept breaking each others' records for sailing across the Atlantic single-handedly in as small a boat as possible—would you believe 7 feet 9 inches!? An Italian climber had just recently conquered Everest alone and without oxygen, while in a secret hangar deep in the Mojave Desert a jet fighter pilot, survivor of 325 combat missions in Vietnam, was drawing plans for a plane he hoped would be the first to fly nonstop around the world without refueling. What was this elixir of excitement that had normally sane people trying to climb frozen waterfalls or hang glide off higher and higher peaks? Finding the answer to that, we mused, would be difficult. But then that was the whole point, adventure should be for adventure's sake and for no other reason. You don't need to justify it. Nor does it need to always be terribly dangerous or expensive or demand tremendous skill to succeed. It requires only the desire to do something different in your life, to reach out for some goal beyond the normal comforts of life and to taste, as it were, the thrill of a new experience.

That was over two years ago that we drank cold beers well into the afternoon, talking enthusiastically about the adrenalin rushes that could be had by kayaking through heavy whitewater or skiing down a 14,000-foot peak in the middle of summer. Eventually we struck a deal to do a book that would be a compendium of all that was offered by way of adventure in North America. I knew there were many fantastic experiences available to that special breed of person willing to really go for it, and a comprehensive guide to these adventures sounded like a great idea. But later that day, as I emerged into a dull grey landscape of stuffy air, snarled traffic and thousands of asphalt-bound cityfolk, I began to worry—what about these people? Was quality adventure readily available to the general public at a price comparable to what would be spent during an outing of similar length to Disneyland or Club Med? And are enough people really even looking for an alternative vacation, or is this adventure craze limited to the extreme examples we had been talking about? What about safety and expertise—would you have to be an expert at technical climbing or hold a pilot's license to fully appreciate, or even survive, a true adventure? Fortunately, as it turned out, these worries were quite unfounded.

The adventure travel industry in the United States and Canada has been booming in the past decade. Stories abound of small, private outfitters suddenly becoming full-scale adventure companies, doubling and tripling their number of clients within just a few years. Rafting the Colorado River down the entire 280-mile length of the Grand Canyon is one of America's premier adventures. In 1956 a total of 55 people experienced the thrill; in 1983 nearly 16,000 took the trip (and it would be a lot more if not for the Park Service limit). Several national magazines have started seasonal adventure guides—one even offers a companion television show on PBS—and *Time* magazine recently did a cover story[1] on the craze. It's become big business—Americans are hungry for adventure, and hundreds of outfitting companies are supplying the demand.

This is exciting news, but it creates many problems, not the least of which is commercialization. Big bucks can be made taking the tenderfoot on a wilderness "adventure," and often outfitters lose sight of their main goal—to provide a unique, quality experience to every person who longs for the opportunity to test themselves and their new environment and to instill a sense of appreciation and respect for the wilderness. Unfortunately, it's all too easy for outfitters to adopt an amusement park attitude by rushing as many clients as possible through the exact same trip time and time again with the primary goal of making money. The outfitter becomes merely a concession, and what potentially could be a great experience becomes mundane and uninspiring, lacking the mental and physical turn-ons of true adventure. This makes it more and more difficult for the small, independent outfitter who strives to keep his trips fresh and unique—often leading each outing himself—to even stay in business. It's very hard to compete with the big companies, or worse yet, the two or three commercial groups acting as booking agents for select outfitters. These agents promote their outfitters in large, full-color ads and booklets and operate with the discounts possible with large numbers of clients. There is nothing wrong with this in theory, and the outfitters being represented by these groups are, for the most part, reputable folks. The disadvantage comes with the little guy who cannot afford either the agent commission or the cost of splashy advertising and still charge a reasonable price for his trip. It's an unfortunate side effect of supply and demand, and it carries the very real dangers of monopoly. It is for this reason that I've made every effort to research the small, independent outfitter in the same fashion as the larger companies when selecting trips for this book.

Another problem that is potentially far more serious than those posed by the pitfalls of free enterprise is the development of an ecological catch-22. With the explosion in numbers of people rafting this river, skiing that trail or camping on those islands comes the inevitable question of impact. Most of the popular adventure travel being enjoyed by millions of Americans today occurs in wilderness areas. How many people can a certain wild area endure and yet remain wild?

[1] *Time* Magazine, August 29, 1983
[2] *The New York Times Sunday Magazine*, September, 12, 1982, cover story: "Preservation For Profit." © The New York Times Company. Reprinted by permission.

Enter the era of low-impact camping—no campfires; biodegradable soaps, papers and even food; strict requirements on handling human waste; rotation of camping sites; even mandatory permits. Many purists scorn these imposed strictures as contradictions to the very freedom that wilderness offers. They are, however, absolutely necessary—rules that should be strictly adhered to, or the desecration of natural areas will be swift and complete. Outfitters must accept an awesome responsibility—the preservation of our wilderness.

But what is preservation without appreciation? Those very people who, by sheer number alone, pose a grave danger to the wilds are also the last possible hope for a continued and protected wilderness.

A couple of years ago I was in Kenya, East Africa photographing a magazine story[2] on radical conservation strategies with writer Clifford May. It was there that I learned what appreciation and the need to place a value on wild areas and wild animals really meant. We had discovered that a growing number of African conservationists were rejecting traditional views of preservation in favor of a radical new strategy—one that could be applied in theory to our own problems here in America. May writes, "Such wildlife 'utilizationists' contend that attempts to introduce Western conservation values in places such as Africa were doomed from the start for reasons that should have been obvious: To the average rural African, wild animals are not a marvelous natural heritage but dangerous pests. Elephants and rhinos destroy the farmer's crops; lions, leopards and cheetahs threaten the rancher's cattle and children." May goes on to reveal that these people need to be shown that wildlife has a very real value and should be protected because of that—not because of some irrelevant philosophical argument on animal rights that carries little weight with people struggling just to stay alive in a country burdened with severe drought and overpopulation. Utilizationist theory argues that the way to save wildlife and wild areas in Africa is to make it pay for itself, to utilize it as a profitable, renewable resource—make it something of value to the common man. They propose several ways to do this: (1) Upgrade the facilities and zoological information available for tourists at wildlife parks and preserves. This would attract more tourists who would, in turn, spend more money. (2) Reinstate regulated, licensed hunting of nonendangered species. They argue that legal hunting has never accounted for a biologically significant offtake of game, and it is a far more efficient means of generating revenue than game viewing. (3) Crop and ranch Africa's indigenous game species as a food source in an attempt to prove that they can produce more protein per acre than cattle could for the same investment.

Now I'm not suggesting that we start marketing wild game or lead African-style safaris in our national parks. But I am suggesting that the more people who come to appreciate the wilderness from first-hand experience, the more people we have to protect it. And that number, if exposed to the wild in proper fashion, can never be too large. Unfortunately millions of Americans still suffer from a malaise potentially far more dangerous than the threat of elephants or lions. Through the power of mass media we are quickly becoming a society of armchair enthusiasts. Our minimum daily requirement of excitement can be quickly satisfied by merely turning on the tube, where we can thrill to Jacques Cousteau wrestling sharks on the bottom of the ocean or astronauts cavorting around in weightless wonder high above the earth. Television, magazines and even this book are guilty of creating a breed of vicarious adventurers. And, although that's better than no appreciation at all, it is still not enough. As Thoreau once said, "I went to the woods because I wished to live deliberately, to front only the essential facts of life, and see if I could not learn what it had to teach, and not, when I came to die, discover that I had not lived."

Joseph Daniel—October, 1984
Somewhere over the Grand Canyon

A FEW WORDS ABOUT EQUIPMENT

For most of the adventures listed in this book, you won't need to supply any special equipment other than yourself and your clothes. If camping or backpacking gear is required, most outfitters will rent you perfectly acceptable equipment; if anything specialized is needed like climbing ropes or waterproof duffels, they are usually provided. It is always a good idea, however, to call or write an outfitter prior to a trip and request an equipment list. This is particularly important for trips that involve extreme geographic or temperature changes. Many outfitters will automatically send you one upon reservation or deposit.

I have, however, provided a general pack list for those folks who prefer to use their own equipment or are considering buying some basic items. I compiled this list over many years of backpacking through the Rockies and I think it serves as a pretty good foundation for a variety of different types of outings. Feel free to photocopy it and use it whenever you're preparing for an adventure. You may want to add or subtract items depending on the length of your trip, what geographic and weather conditions you expect to encounter and your own needs and preferences. I have left a blank area under the FOOD heading to provide room for listing whatever type of food is needed on each trip.

In the last ten years the outdoor equipment industry has metamorphosed from a common and clumsy caterpillar to a beautiful and highly specialized butterfly. What was, for all comparative purposes, nothing more than a handful of innovative cottage industries is now a handful of major conglomerates complete with all the trimmings of big-time manufacturing. Every conceivable niche of need has been filled and it's rather hard not to find what you're looking for in a particular piece of equipment. But to KNOW what you're looking for is another question. Function and design have evolved so drastically that even seasoned experts rarely agree on the merits of this pack or that tent. It doesn't seem that long ago that there were some fairly specific rules regarding equipment; everyone had their favorite style or brand of hiking boot or sleeping bag, selected from a pool of perhaps half a dozen rather similar manufacturers, and the biggest controversy was the introduction of the internal frame pack. Well, folks, if you're not already aware, get ready for a little time-warp leap forward next opportunity you get for some wilderness window shopping.

We have entered a high-tech era in outdoor clothing and equipment. The different new materials and styles and the popular shift toward ultralight gear has made something as seemingly simple as selecting a raincoat a confusing mini-course in petro-chemistry and thermodynamics. Unfortunately I have neither the space nor the expertise to offer a comprehensive guide to selecting equipment. So, before you buy spend some time educating yourself on what's available. Talk to several different salespeople and if possible try to get advice from someone who uses a specific item professionally like a ski patrolman or forest ranger. Mountain shops, commonly staffed by serious climbers, may not offer the discount prices of a large sporting-goods chain or department store, but the knowledgeable help is often worth the difference. A great investment for anyone about to spend hard-earned money on expensive outdoor gear is a copy of Colin Fletcher's *The Complete Walker III*. It's a nearly 700-page how-to book on backpacking that many consider to be the bible of the sport.[1]

The most important thing to keep in mind when embarking on an adventure is minimizing discomfort and maximizing appreciation. An ill-fitting pack or leaky raincoat can make you feel lower than a snake in a wagon rut in no time flat. Being sure of your equipment and clothing needs will not only heighten the enjoyment of a wilderness venture but will give you the satisfaction of coping with mama nature—and that's a secure feeling.

---

[1] Published by Alfred A. Knopf, 1984, paperback $11.95, ISBN 0-394-72264-7.

PACK LIST

BASIC EQUIPMENT
—PACK
—SLEEPING BAG
—MATTRESS PAD
—GROUNDSHEET
—TENT w/rain fly
—WATER BOTTLE
—BOOZE FLASK
—FLASHLIGHT w/spare batteries
—CANDLE LANTERN w/spare candles
—SMALL ROPE
—KNIFE
—COMPASS
—MAP
—TROWEL
—BINOCULARS
—EMERGENCY KIT: first aid kit, sew & repair kit, water purification tablets, fishing kit, matches, flintstick, signal mirror, whistle, money, credit card
—SMALL DAY/HIP PACK
—PHOTO EQUIPMENT: camera, 24mm wide angle, 50mm macro, 135mm telephoto, 300mm telephoto, UV filters, small tripod, cable release, small flash, extra batteries, film
—FISHING EQUIPMENT: spin/fly combo trail rod, lightweight reels, trout flies, lures
—

CLOTHING
—BOOTS
—GAITERS
—MOCCASINS/SANDALS
—SOCKS
—LONG PANTS
—SHORTS
—SWIM SUIT
—LONG SLEEVE SHIRTS
—SHORT SLEEVE SHIRTS
—STRING VEST
—WOOL SWEATER
—PILE JACKET (Patagonia)
—DOWN JACKET
—RAIN PONCHO
—BANDANA
—GLOVES
—HAT
—
—

PERSONAL KIT
—SOAP/TOWEL
—SHAMPOO
—COMB
—TOOTHBRUSH/TOOTHPASTE/FLOSS
—VITAMINS
—INSECT REPELLENT
—SUNSCREEN/LIP BALM/LOTION
—RUBBING ALCOHOL/FOOT POWDER
—TOILET PAPER
—GLASSES/SUNGLASSES
—WALLET/KEYS
—WATCH
—JOURNAL/NOTEBOOK & PENCIL
—READING MATERIAL
—
—

KITCHEN
—STOVE (Svea)
—WINDSCREEN
—GAS BOTTLE
—EYE DROPPER
—FUNNEL
—WIND & WATERPROOF MATCHES
—COOK KIT w/2 pots & fry pan
—POT GRABBER
—SILVERWARE
—CUP (Sierra)
—CAN OPENER
—MARGARINE CONTAINER
—SPICE CONTAINERS
—TROUT SEASONING BAG
—TIN FOIL
—TRASH BAG
—SPARE PLASTIC BAGS
—SCRUBBER/SPONGE
—TOWEL
—BIODEGRADABLE SOAP (all purpose)
—
—

FOOD
—
—
—
—
—

Photo: Joseph Daniel

WILDERNESS PHOTOGRAPHY

Deciding whether or not to bring a camera on a wilderness adventure is as much a philosophical question as it is an operational one. Some people who spend a lot of time in the wild question the merits of photography in a wilderness situation. This may sound a bit like a contradiction in terms, but the argument condemns photography as actually getting in the way of total appreciation of a wild moment or scene. Being someone who makes his living with photography, I guess I should take affront with that line of thinking, but I have to admit that I've felt that way myself a few times. Standing with a dozen other people around a bewildered deer or jammed together at the perfect spot along the foot of a spectacular whitewater rapid—shutters a-shootin' and flashes a-flashin'— kind of makes one feel like a wilderness paparazzi. Or discovering yourself concentrating so hard on the technical execution of capturing that perfect moment, that try as you might you can't even remember what the scene looked like until you get your pictures back. Sometimes it seems easier and maybe a little purer to just leave the cameras at home. The fact still remains, however, that most of us enjoy pictures of what we do and where we go, and it's certainly our right to do so. I believe a certain etiquette should be observed when photographing wild areas so as to leave them undisturbed for the next person. But, I also believe wilderness photography is challenging, exciting and a great way to while away the hours—and the rewards you get from it far outweigh the frustrations of equipment or the time lost looking through the viewfinder.

To spare you from a boring, technical, and probably ineffective dissertation on photographic "how-to," I'm going to assume that most readers have a basic understanding of photographic principles. I'm also going to be referring only to the 35mm format because its low-cost availability, simple operation, multi-lens versatility, compact construction and overall quality of image size make any argument for Instamatic-type 110 cameras rather outdated.

When selecting photographic equipment for a wilderness trip, the only real considerations besides cost are weight and space. Since most adventures have restrictions in both categories, the solution becomes one of compromise. What is the least amount of equipment you can carry and still be as technically versatile as the situation demands? Let's start with the lightest and most simple system and work our way up in weight and versatility.

In the past few years a number of compact ultralight 35mm cameras have become very popular. They offer automatic exposure, automatic focus, and a reasonably sharp fixed wide angle lens, and they often come with built-in flash and automatic film winder. Prices range from $80 to $175. The drawbacks are that on some models the autofocus isn't that accurate, composition is often a problem since you're framing through a separate viewfinder and not a lens, and lack of an interchangeable lens system severely hampers versatility. However, if you want to take general scenics and candids yet travel as light as possible, this is probably the route to go. My favorite ultralight is undoubtedly the Olympus XA. It is very compact, you can manually focus it (which is a big plus), and the resolution quality of the lens is quite acceptable. You can also buy a small flash attachment that works fairly well. Other brands include Canon Sureshot, Minox 35mmGT, and Minolta AFC.

Next up the ladder are the simple, compact SLR's (single lens reflex) being marketed by most of the major brand names. The advantage with these is through-the-lens focusing, interchangeable lens systems, and a big jump in overall lens quality. Most of these cameras have both automatic exposure and a manual override (for those folks who want a little more creative control) and accept a wide range of accessories. Prices range from $150 to $300. Models include the Nikon EM and Olympus OMG. The only real drawback to these cameras other than plastic construction is that for just a little more money you can purchase what I call the professional level compact—a camera that will last you a lifetime and most likely be all you'll ever need for any photographic situation.

Photo: Joseph Daniel

These professional compacts are really one of the great things to happen to photography. They are small and light and yet are built to last. Many pros use them in favor of their heavier, more expensive main cameras. They accept all of the top-of-the-line lenses and offer all of the really important features, and yet they're inexpensive enough that if one overturns with you in Lava Falls or decides to take its own quick route down El Capitan, it's not going to put you into the poorhouse. Prices range from $200 to $400. The more popular models are Nikon FM and FE2, Canon AE1, and Olympus OMI.

Beyond the compacts we move up to the highly sophisticated top-of-the-line cameras from each manufacturer. Because of heavy weight and cost increases, these models don't really have a practical place in our discussion, so let's move on to building our system with additional lenses.

If you're going to bring along a camera and only one lens then make it a 50mm macro (close-up). With this you can shoot "normal" shots as well as effective close-ups of small flora and fauna. Spending a few hours in a high alpine meadow playing fashion photographer with the wildflowers is fascinating and an aesthetic turn-on.

But if you have the opportunity, add a wide angle (24mm-35mm) for panoramic shots and include as long a telephoto as your budget and back can support. It can be very frustrating getting your photos back from the processor and discovering that those "fantastic" shots of that rare species of warbler or that record bighorn, high on a rocky crag, are really just barely recognizable specks in the middle of the picture. I rarely go on any trip where I might encounter wildlife without my trusty (albeit heavy) 300mm telephoto, but lenses from 135mm on up can be very useful. Another option is a single zoom lens that collectively offers a wide range of focal lengths. Zooms unfortunately lack a bit in speed and resolution quality, but may make up for that in space and weight.

You will probably also want a small tripod and cable release to help steady your telephoto and to do interesting low-light long exposure shots very early or late in the day. Otherwise, the only other pieces of equipment that you might consider are a small flash for fill-lighting backlit objects and a motordrive (winder) for situations where you don't want to take the camera away from your eye even to wind it. I can see a real need for a motordrive if you're shooting kayaks doing tip stands in some nasty water, but for general use in the wild they're too heavy, far too noisy, and may require—as might a flash—that you bring extra batteries.

This forms about the maximum (and in my opinion also the minimum) amount of gear for an efficient, all-around wilderness system. However, you need to carry and protect it in something. I've run the gamut from wrapping lenses in socks to hiking with a regular shoulder bag to using a retro-fitted internal frame pack and I've never been quite satisfied. There has been, however, a recent surge in the development of packs and cases designed specifically for camera equipment with many interesting models ranging from fanny packs to expedition size backpacks. A few brands that show good promise include Lowe, Tough Traveler, and Atlan, but the prices are still pretty steep. A cautionary note: If you're going on an adventure that includes river running or any excessive exposure to water, you need to consider some type of waterproof protection for your camera. There are several rigid waterproof housings on the market, but they are cumbersome and awkward to use and don't accept a very wide variety of cameras. A better solution might be a product I recently used on a whitewater trip in the Grand Canyon called the Ewa-Marine bag. It's a flexible plastic housing with an internal glove for operating your camera and it worked like a charm for me. The manufacturers claim it's safe under water to 100 feet and they make models which accept any brand of camera as well as motordrive and flash. Worth checking.

And finally, film. Most professional photographers working in 35mm shoot only three kinds of film: Tri-X for black and white (normal ASA 400, but often "pushed" two or three stops faster), Ektachrome for color transparencies (slides) needing processing immediately (normal ASAs 64, 200, 400, 800 and 1600, all of which can also be pushed), and Kodachrome 64 (ASA 64), also for color transparencies but used when color and resolution quality is critical . . . in other words, for when you want the best results. In my opinion, Kodachrome 64 is the only film to carry for wilderness photography. It's sharper, brighter, and more stable than Ektachrome and with the new methods of direct slide printing available today it's easy to get great prints from your slides if you so desire. It is not easy to get good quality slides from the print film used by most amateur photographers. Besides, Kodachrome 64 is cheaper to buy and cheaper to process than print film—and if you're going to show the Joneses down the street your trip through the Boundary Waters Canoe Area, wouldn't you rather do it with slides projected ten feet high on the wall than with little snapshots?

Protecting film while on an adventure is a big concern. All film—particularly when it has been exposed but not yet developed—is sensitive to heat and humidity. Spend a little extra time making sure your film is kept out of direct sunlight or any type of enclosed container that might become hot from the sun. I generally keep my exposed rolls in the little plastic cans they come in (which are good protection against moisture) wrapped loosely in the middle of my pack which I try to leave in the shade when not hiking. Be conscious of the film in your camera, too. A camera left in the sun quickly heats up to a point too hot to touch—not healthy for camera or film!

A final word: A flippant remark commonly heard amongst pros, particularly those suffering from trigger finger, is that "film is cheap." Well, it isn't; neither is processing; but there is nothing more expensive than running out of film just when you've come across two magnificent bull elk dueling it out over a herd of cows. Bring as much film as you can carry; it'll keep if you don't use it. Just remember, there are no camera stores (thank goodness!) on top of Mt. McKinley, but there are endless photographs. Good shootin'.

 GATES-OF-THE-ARCTIC EXPEDITION

The Brooks Mountain Range is silent under its blanket of ice and snow. Deserted valleys, windswept snow sculptures, moonlit snowscapes and Northern Lights in the evening, tracks in the snow. The wilderness residents are watching you—moose, caribou, wolves, Canadian jays and ravens. Sourdough offers a unique opportunity for experiencing this wonderful wilderness area at a seldom-visited time of year by dogsled, the old and honorable means of visiting the winter arctic. Bettles is the staging area for the expedition. The dogs will be raring to go so hold onto your knit hat as you take off. Your destination is the Gates-of-the-Arctic area on the North Fork of the Koyukuk River. The Nunamiut Eskimos are at home here and still travel from their village of Anaktuvuk Pass to hunt and trap fur bearers. Routed primarily along an old trail, you camp at some of the same sites which Robert Marshall and Ernie Johnson used while exploring this "blank spot on a map" nearly five decades ago. Your camps are cabins and heated tents. The trip will terminate within view of the Gates-of-the-Arctic near the northern limits of the treeline. A ski plane will return you to Bettles, allowing a scenic overview of the immense expanse of the land that has been your home for over seven days.

LENGTH OF TRIP: 10 days
TOTAL COST: $1,200
DEPARTURE DATES: Feb.-April
TYPE OF PAYMENT ACCEPTED: Cash, t.c. cashiers

RESERVATIONS/DEPOSIT: $200 deposit when booking
CANCELLATION POLICY: Loss of deposit
DEPARTURE LOCATION: Bettles, AK   **NEAREST AIRPORT:** Bettles, AK
TRANSPORTATION INFORMATION: N/A
HEALTH, FITNESS OR AGE REQUIREMENTS: Good physical condition
TYPE OF WEATHER TO EXPECT: -30° - +30° F
BEST TYPE OF CLOTHING AND FOOTWEAR: Winter expedition gear
PERSONAL GEAR REQUIRED: Personal duffle, sleeping bag
SPECIAL GEAR/EQUIPMENT REQUIRED: List provided
WHAT NOT TO BRING: Alcohol during the winter
PHOTO POSSIBILITIES: Fantastic
FISHING POSSIBILITIES: Fantastic   **LICENSE REQUIREMENTS:** 10 days $15
BEST TYPE OF FISHING TACKLE: Provided for ice fishing
REPRESENTATIVE MENU—BREAKFAST: Bacon, eggs, toast
LUNCH: Trail lunch
DINNER: Steaks, potatoes, vegetables, dessert
CHORES/DUTIES GUESTS ARE EXPECTED TO HELP WITH: Fetch water, firewood, pitch camp
NAME OF OUTFITTER: Sourdough Outfitters
ADDRESS: General Delivery   **CONTACT:** David Ketscher
CITY: Bettles   **TITLE:** President
STATE: Alaska   **ZIP:** 99726   **TELEPHONE:** (907) 692-5252
NUMBER OF YEARS IN BUSINESS: 10   **NUMBER OF STAFF:** 4-8
SPECIALIZING IN: Wilderness trips in Alaska's Brook Range
SPECIAL PHILOSOPHY, CREDO, GOALS BEHIND BUSINESS: We are Christians and run our business in such a way to bring glory to God.

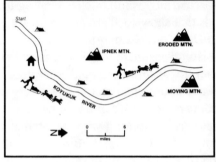

104   105

ABOUT THIS BOOK

Somebody once said, "You *really* learn how to ski in the summer and sail in the winter." I think they were talking about the power of "imagery" and how, even in the dead of winter, a good sailor can become better by curling up in front of a warm fire with a good sailing book and letting his mind wander. I've tried hard to capture that same power in this book by giving the reader a clear look at what adventure is available and how to capture it. However thorough I wanted this guide to be, though, was in the end controlled by the sheer nature of the beast. Trying to compile an accurate compendium of facts on a subject that by its very definition is often transient and elusive is quite difficult. Adventure is where you find it, or better, where you create it. Sure, there are specific outfitters who can take you down this river or up that mountain—but who does it best, and when is the best time to go, and what's a fair price? Offering a hundred trips by a hundred outfitters is such a subjective judgment call on my part that the reader should use this book as a helpful guide in planning an adventure vacation and certainly not as the final word on the subject.

The problem with most of the adventure travel guides available today is that they list their offerings by outfitter and not by specific trip. This leaves most readers in a bit of a quandary, for although they may be looking for an adventure under the general heading of, say, *River Running*, they'll soon discover that dozens of companies offer dozens of methods of running dozens of rivers. It's a bit like shooting in the dark if you're unfamiliar with differences among rivers. Most of these guides also lack comprehensiveness, as they require a fee of some type from the outfitter before listing the company. This might be in the form of a "service" fee or agent commission, or it might be pressure to advertise in the publication. In any case, it pretty well guarantees that every outfitter won't be represented, as many may not consider the fee worth the exposure.

I've tried to alleviate a lot of these problems by structuring this guide in a new way. First of all, to insure that the book remain comprehensive and commercial-free, none of the outfitters contacted for information or selected for any type of inclusion in the book was charged a fee. All that was ever required from any company wishing to be considered was some of their time and cooperation in providing necessary trip information, maps and photos. Secondly, I decided that the emphasis of the book should be on specific adventures and not outfitters. Although I went ahead and included an outfitter directory I reserved the bulk of the book for a selection of 100 specific adventures that I felt represented a good cross section of what the industry offers.

My method was as follows: A list was compiled of every outfitter who had advertised or appeared in any type of article or listing in any publication in the United States in the previous five years. It came to nearly 400 companies. Next, an initial one-page questionnaire was sent to all of these outfitters in order to get a better look at their company and its activities. An astonishingly large number of outfitters responded to this first query, and I was able to establish a pretty good picture of what the adventure industry in America looked like. I then threw out obvious fly-by-night operations, repeats, agents and any trips that were too expensive, too long, or required special strength or skill. In order that this book be useful to the largest number of people I felt it was important to limit the trips with certain restrictions. They couldn't cost more than a total of $1,500.00 (not counting travel cost to departure location), they couldn't be any longer than two weeks, and they had to be nontechnical enough that any average adult in good health could enjoy them. This left me with about 200 possibilities. The next step was quite a bit harder as I had to start deciding whether Outfitter A or Outfitter B might run a better trip. Since I obviously wasn't going to be able to actually go on every one of the trips, I needed more information to make my final choices. So, I prepared an additional 4-page questionnaire that asked in-depth questions about the outfitter's background, experience, special offerings, and the specific adventure I was interested in. I requested that each outfitter write a short text describing the particular trip, draw a map showing the route and provide some representative photos. It was from all this additional information that I made my final selection.

As you look through the book you'll notice that each trip is presented in a two-page spread. The title of the trip appears with a small graphic designating the type of adventure offered. The descriptive text is in the style we received it and has been changed only for editorial and space considerations. The bold headings are fairly self explanatory, but readers should be aware that prices and departure dates are subject to change and should be considered as generalized information. Most outfitters offer current price lists and brochures that will provide readers with any additional information needed. This is especially important on any adventure requiring special gear or clothing. Each spread also has a representative photograph from that specific adventure and a somewhat stylized map prepared from information supplied by the outfitter.

In the front of the book you'll find a section on equipment and on wilderness photography— two subjects that go hand in hand with total appreciation of the outdoor experience. Following the adventures is a listing of some of the better wilderness schools that offer instruction in a variety of specialized outdoor skills. The outfitters' directory is set up in alphabetical order by type of adventure and by state and province. It is cross-referenced so that the same outfitter may appear under several different headings if he provides different types of services in different areas.

All of this should start you off in the right direction when selecting your next adventure travel vacation. So have a good one!

WILD CAVE TOUR

Eyeing suspiciously the obviously abused coveralls, badly scratched hardhat and light issued to us by the guides, I wondered what this cavern exploring adventure was going to be like. Walking through the beautiful California Caverns Park to the cavern entrance, the guides gave us instructions on how to move through this unique environment. Going from the bright California sunshine into the cavern brought a hushed awe from our inexperienced group. As my eyes became accustomed, I was delighted to see white crystals all around us sparkling from our lights. As we followed our guides through a mind-boggling maze of passages and crawlways, we saw ever more spectacular flowstones and cavern formations, including a 15-foot-high frozen waterfall and a massive chandelier composed of thousands of sparkling crystals. As the going got tougher, I got down on my belly using my elbows to drag myself through the sticky clay, and through small holes seemingly too tight for people. We helped each other up slopes, over boulders, through tight passages and into rafts for crossing deep inky lakes, forming close bonds with people who were strangers just hours ago. When we emerged into the blue-white glare of the surface world later, we all appreciated a previously unconsidered luxury—sunshine!

LENGTH OF TRIP: 5 hours   **DEPARTURE DATES:** Daily June-October

TOTAL COST: $49   **TYPE OF PAYMENT ACCEPTED:** Any

RESERVATIONS/DEPOSIT: 25% deposit

CANCELLATION POLICY: 25% fee if cancelled less than 2 days in advance

DEPARTURE LOCATION: Cave City   **NEAREST AIRPORT:** San Andreas, CA

TRANSPORTATION INFORMATION: By arrangement from San Andreas; none from commercial airports

HEALTH, FITNESS OR AGE REQUIREMENTS: Good health, not pregnant, not excessively overweight, no heart problems, no mobility problems, 12 years and older

TYPE OF WEATHER TO EXPECT: Cavern temperature 57° F

BEST TYPE OF CLOTHING AND FOOTWEAR: Warm, comfortable, grubby; high-top boots

PERSONAL GEAR REQUIRED: Towels for shower, change of clothing, food to eat after expedition.

SPECIAL GEAR/EQUIPMENT REQUIRED: None

WHAT NOT TO BRING: Fancy clothing

PHOTO POSSIBILITIES: Not allowed inside cavern

FISHING POSSIBILITIES: None

REPRESENTATIVE MENU: Supply your own

CHORES/DUTIES GUESTS ARE EXPECTED TO HELP WITH: None

NAME OF OUTFITTER: California Caverns at Cave City

ADDRESS: P.O. Box 78   **CONTACT:** Linda Fairchild

CITY: Vallecito   **TITLE:** Assistant

STATE: California   **ZIP:** 95251   **TELEPHONE:** (209) 736-2708

NUMBER OF YEARS IN BUSINESS: 4

SPECIALIZING IN: "Wild cave" exploration trip through a spectacularly beautiful, natural limestone cavern.

SPECIAL PHILOSOPHY, CREDO, GOALS BEHIND BUSINESS: To present a cavern in its wild state and encourage a sense of adventure in visitors.

Photo: Bob Elliott

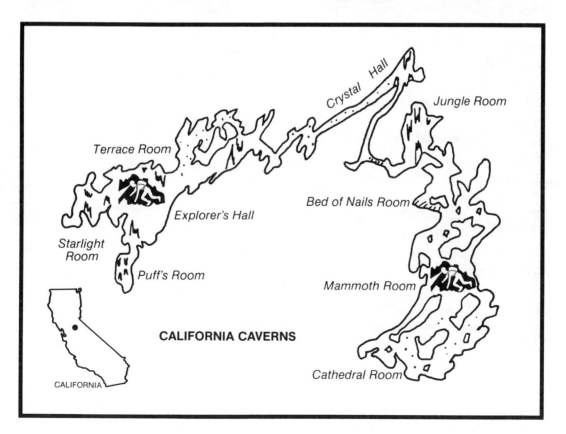

Crystal Hall

Jungle Room

Terrace Room

Bed of Nails Room

Explorer's Hall

Starlight Room

Puff's Room

Mammoth Room

CALIFORNIA CAVERNS

CALIFORNIA

Cathedral Room

🥾 SNOWMASS WILDERNESS TREK

We load our packs and cameras near the trailhead at Maroon Lake, a perfect vantage point for one of the most photographed mountain spectacles in North America. Leaving civilization behind, we enter the natural world in the shadow of the Maroon Bells and walk six miles of trail to our first camp beside Snowmass Creek. Rising with the sun the next day, we begin a beautiful day's hike in soft early morning light. We'll spend most of this afternoon setting up a base camp above Geneva Lake at 11,000 feet. The next three days are spent rock climbing, bouldering, climbing 14,000-foot Snowmass Mountain, shooting lots of film and relaxing in camp. On our fifth day, we reshoulder our packs and proceed 3.5 miles on high ground to camp at Avalanche Lake. A short hike next day brings us to our last and highest camp at Capitol Lake, situated at a 11,500-foot elevation, yet beneath the magnificent north face of 14,130-foot Capitol peak. On the seventh day we'll climb the classic Knife Edge route, an easy but spectacular route to the summit. Hiking out beside Avalanche Creek, we'll return to civilization carrying with us many special moments captured on film and in our memories of a wonderful trek in the heart of the Colorado wilderness.

LENGTH OF TRIP: 8 days

DEPARTURE DATES: August 4, 18, September 1

TOTAL COST: $525

TYPE OF PAYMENT ACCEPTED: Check, cash

RESERVATIONS/DEPOSIT: $250 up to 1 week before trip

CANCELLATION POLICY: Refund of payments minus cancellation fee

DEPARTURE LOCATION: Aspen, CO

NEAREST AIRPORT: Aspen, CO

TRANSPORTATION INFORMATION: Limo, bus, taxi

HEALTH, FITNESS OR AGE REQUIREMENTS: Good cardiovascular condition

TYPE OF WEATHER TO EXPECT: Warm days, cool nights, possible rain showers

BEST TYPE OF CLOTHING AND FOOTWEAR: Equipment list available

PERSONAL GEAR REQUIRED: Backpack, sleeping bag, pad, eating utensils, personal duffle

SPECIAL GEAR/EQUIPMENT REQUIRED: Ice axe

WHAT NOT TO BRING: Dog, radio, TV

PHOTO POSSIBILITIES: Fantastic

FISHING POSSIBILITIES: Good

LICENSE REQUIREMENTS: CO

BEST TYPE OF FISHING TACKLE: Trout flies

REPRESENTATIVE MENU—BREAKFAST: Eggs, hashbrowns, toast, jelly

LUNCH: Bread, cheese, pepperoni, dried fruit

DINNER: Soup, German sausage in brown gravy, mashed potatoes, bread, pudding

CHORES/DUTIES GUESTS ARE EXPECTED TO HELP WITH: Everything

NAME OF OUTFITTER: Sunrise Adventures

ADDRESS: 364 Weston Drive

CONTACT: Glenn D. Fortner

CITY: Durango

TITLE: Director

STATE: Colorado   **ZIP:** 81301

TELEPHONE: (303) 259-1137

NUMBER OF YEARS IN BUSINESS: 7   **NUMBER OF STAFF:** 5

SPECIALIZING IN: Mountain climbing, backpacking, skin diving

SPECIAL PHILOSOPHY, CREDO, GOALS BEHIND BUSINESS: We know the way.

Photo: Sunrise Adventures

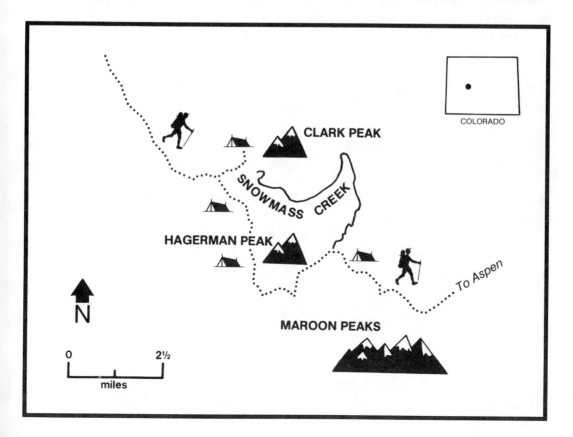

CLARK PEAK

SNOWMASS CREEK

HAGERMAN PEAK

To Aspen

COLORADO

MAROON PEAKS

N

0   2½

miles

# CARIBOU MIGRATION CAMP

"Caribou were coming toward me along an unbroken front perhaps a quarter of a mile wide. The sound was incredible. As they drew closer, the sound was drowned out by the grunting and coughing of the cows and the constant bleating of the calves. The intensity rose. The air was saturated with the energy of the sound. The herd enveloped me. Cows and calves, and bulls with long, velvet-coated antlers reaching high above their heads, rushed by a few yards away, as if I were not there. Individuals paused a moment or two to feed, then moved on. The animals filed past for nearly an hour, and I sat and watched the trailing column for another hour until it melted into the wavy tundra several miles away. It was over as suddenly as it began. Once again the land was still and empty. The only sight of the huge herds passing was an occasional nondescript shock of gray fur clinging to the low tundra."—*A Passage of Caribou* by Wilbur Mills. Each spring, 130,000 caribou from the Porcupine Caribou herd migrate across the Brooks Range. This one-week base camp in the Arctic National Wildlife Refuge affords a chance to witness caribou during the post-calving concentration and migration to Canada and to experience the arctic tundra ecosystem during its intense spring season.

LENGTH OF TRIP: 8 days   **DEPARTURE DATES:** June 18, 1984

TOTAL COST: $868   **TYPE OF PAYMENT ACCEPTED:** Check

RESERVATIONS/DEPOSIT: $200 deposit, full payment 60 days prior to trip

CANCELLATION POLICY: Refunds within 60 days of departure at our discretion

DEPARTURE LOCATION: Fairbanks, AK   **NEAREST AIRPORT:** Fairbanks, AK

TRANSPORTATION INFORMATION: Guests must buy air transportation to Barter Island. Charter air flight from there provided by outfitter

HEALTH, FITNESS OR AGE REQUIREMENTS: None

TYPE OF WEATHER TO EXPECT: Spring snow showers to 80° F

BEST TYPE OF CLOTHING AND FOOTWEAR: Down or synthetic jacket, rain gear required; Shoepac boots

PERSONAL GEAR REQUIRED: Sleeping bag, pad, backpack or duffle bag

SPECIAL GEAR/EQUIPMENT REQUIRED: None

WHAT NOT TO BRING: Suitcases, tents

PHOTO POSSIBILITIES: Fantastic

FISHING POSSIBILITIES: Poor   **LICENSE REQUIREMENT:** AK out of state $15

BEST TYPE OF FISHING TACKLE: Small backpacking rod, mixed lures

REPRESENTATIVE MENU—BREAKFAST: Pancakes, oatmeal, coffee, omelette

LUNCH: Crackers, cheese, spreads, jerky, peanut butter, nuts, other high energy foods

DINNER: Stroganoff, noodles, fresh baked bread

CHORES/DUTIES GUESTS ARE EXPECTED TO HELP WITH: Pitch/strike camp, dishes

ADDITIONAL SPECIAL INFORMATION: Physical examination recommended

NAME OF OUTFITTER: Wilderness: Alaska/Mexico

ADDRESS: Bissel Road   **CONTACT:** Ron Yarnell

CITY: Hunters   **TITLE:** Owner

STATE: Washington   **ZIP:** 99137   **TELEPHONE:** (509) 722-6164

NUMBER OF YEARS IN BUSINESS: 10   **NUMBER OF STAFF:** 3

SPECIALIZING IN: Backpacking, kayaking, nature camps, whalewatching, fishing, photography

SPECIAL PHILOSOPHY, CREDO, GOALS BEHIND BUSINESS: Enable participants to experience some of Alaska's and Mexico's most unique and beautiful wilderness areas

Photo: Wilderness; Alaska/Mexico

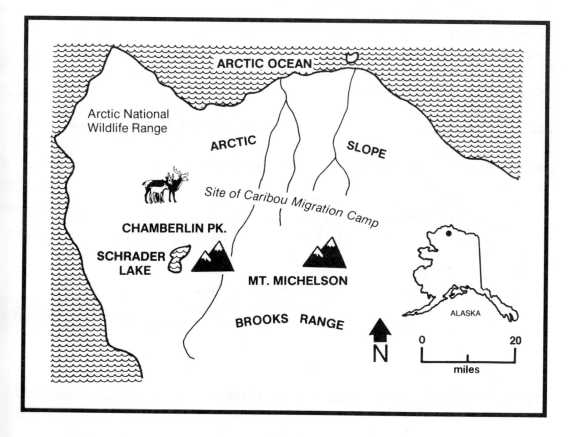

🚶 HUT TRAVERSE

We traverse the White Mountains of New Hampshire enjoying delicious meals, spectacular mountain scenery and the uniqueness of America's original hut system. Our 60-mile, 10-day summer trek begins at Carter Notch Hut, nestled amid clear mountain lakes and boulder-covered ice caves. From there we climb above treeline to the windswept Presidential Ridge. We stay at Madison Springs Hut, site of the oldest Appalachian Mountain Club Hut, which was built in 1888. We continue above treeline through delicate alpine vegetation, above deep glacial cirques and across rocky summits of some of New England's highest mountains, including Mt. Washington, to the Lakes of the Clouds Hut. We continue south above treeline along the exposed backbone to Mizpah Springs Hut. Our journey continues into the remote Zealand Valley. We spend a day enjoying cool waterfalls and peaceful white birches. After one day of rest, we again traverse the glaciated ridge through the krummholz to Galehead Hut, offering panoramic views of Mt. Garfield and through deep coniferous forests to Mt. Lafayette and Greenleaf Hut with its breathtaking sunsets and awesome view of the Franconia Ridge. We cross the notch and spend our last night at Lonesome Lake Hut.

LENGTH OF TRIP: 10 days

DEPARTURE DATES: July 2

TOTAL COST: $389 plus lunch/transportation

TYPE OF PAYMENT ACCEPTED: Check, cash

RESERVATIONS/DEPOSIT: $50 nonrefundable deposit with reservation

CANCELLATION POLICY: Nonrefundable deposit

DEPARTURE LOCATION: Pinkham Notch

NEAREST AIRPORT: Boston, MA

TRANSPORTATION INFORMATION: Concord Trailways Bus—$18.50

HEALTH, FITNESS OR AGE REQUIREMENTS: Good physical condition

TYPE OF WEATHER TO EXPECT: Anything (cold, foggy, hot, sunny)

BEST TYPE OF CLOTHING AND FOOTWEAR: Hiking boots, comfortable and warm clothes

PERSONAL GEAR REQUIRED: Backpacking equipment. (List available)

SPECIAL GEAR/EQUIPMENT REQUIRED: Backpack, sleeping bag, flashlight

WHAT NOT TO BRING: Glass containers, heavy objects, dogs

PHOTO POSSIBILITIES: Fantastic

FISHING POSSIBILITIES: Fair

LICENSE REQUIREMENTS: NH $24.00

BEST TYPE OF FISHING TACKLE: Fly

REPRESENTATIVE MENU—BREAKFAST: Cereal, eggs, pancakes, bacon

LUNCH: Bring your own

DINNER: Soup, salad, meat, potato, veggie, homemade bread, dessert.

CHORES/DUTIES GUESTS ARE EXPECTED TO HELP WITH: Setting tables, folding blankets

ADDITIONAL SPECIAL INFORMATION: Pillows and blankets provided. Participants must bring own lunches. Snacks may be purchased.

NAME OF OUTFITTER: Appalachian Mountain Club

ADDRESS: P.O. Box 298

CONTACT: Walter S. Graff

CITY: Gorham

TITLE: Programs Director

STATE: NH   **ZIP:** 03581

TELEPHONE: (603) 466-2721

NUMBER OF YEARS IN BUSINESS: 108

NUMBER OF STAFF: 28

SPECIALIZING IN: Hiking, backpacking, skiing, ski mountaineering, snowshoeing, orienteering, canoeing.

SPECIAL PHILOSOPHY, CREDO, GOALS BEHIND BUSINESS: Education, recreation and conservation.

Photo: Paul Mozell

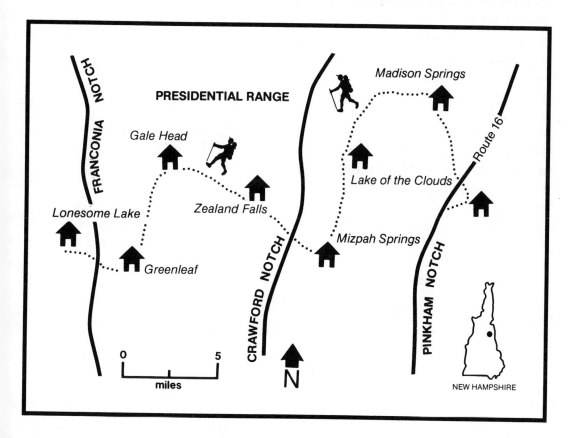

FRANCONIA NOTCH

PRESIDENTIAL RANGE

Madison Springs

Gale Head

Route 16

Lonesome Lake

Lake of the Clouds

Zealand Falls

Greenleaf

Mizpah Springs

CRAWFORD NOTCH

PINKHAM NOTCH

0   5

miles

N

NEW HAMPSHIRE

🚶 THE 5-DAY EXPERIENCE

A sense of humor and a sense of adventure with good health thrown in for spice are all that are required to participate in the 5-Day Experience. The mountainous hike begins at the WildWalk Lodge at Lake Tahoe where the staff warmly greets participants at the pre-trip meeting. The actual trek begins at perhaps the West's most photographic body of water, Emerald Bay. The hike winds into the Desolation Wilderness and rises 600 feet to offer a view of the Bay feeding into resplendent Lake Tahoe, surrounded by alpine peaks. The landscape along the trail was sculptured by ice and wind and is decorated with mountain waterfalls and multi-hued wildflowers. More than 30 alpine lakes will be witnessed during this journey through the longest continuous mountain chain in the United States. One campsite is pitched in the lunarscape around Lake Aloha, which is a shallow, 13-foot deep lake eclipsed by wind-swept terraces and haunting jagged lodgepole pines. At dusk, one almost expects the ephemeral shadow of a dinosaur to glide past the purple-lit waters. On the fifth day, civilization is once again reached on the shores of Echo Lake, and perhaps a sense of increased self-sufficiency and physical well-being have also been attained.

LENGTH OF TRIP: 5 days

DEPARTURE DATES: Mondays May 21-October 1

TOTAL COST: $199

TYPE OF PAYMENT ACCEPTED: Check

RESERVATIONS/DEPOSIT: $100 deposit 15 days before trip

CANCELLATION POLICY: Normally deposit forfeited, but depends on situation

DEPARTURE LOCATION: Wildwalk Lodge, S. Lake Tahoe, CA

NEAREST AIRPORT: Lake Tahoe, CA

TRANSPORTATION INFORMATION: Included

HEALTH, FITNESS OR AGE REQUIREMENTS: Good health

TYPE OF WEATHER TO EXPECT: Generally mild

BEST TYPE OF CLOTHING AND FOOTWEAR: Personal choice

PERSONAL GEAR REQUIRED: Personal duffle

SPECIAL GEAR/EQUIPMENT REQUIRED: Community gear provided by outfitters

WHAT NOT TO BRING: Radio, firearms

PHOTO POSSIBILITIES: Fantastic

FISHING POSSIBILITIES: Good

LICENSE REQUIREMENT: CA $2

BEST TYPE OF FISHING TACKLE: Spinning and fly

REPRESENTATIVE MENU—BREAKFAST: Hot cereal, fruit, coffee

LUNCH: Salami, trail mix, lemonade, fruit bar

DINNER: Chicken ala king, potatoes, instant cheesecake, vegetable, coffee, cocoa

CHORES/DUTIES GUESTS ARE EXPECTED TO HELP WITH: As much as guests want

ADDITIONAL SPECIAL INFORMATION: The following senses are required: adventure and humor

NAME OF OUTFITTER: Wildwalk

ADDRESS: P.O. Box 7718

CONTACT: Bob Cordaro

CITY: South Lake Tahoe

TITLE: President

STATE: California   **ZIP:** 95731

TELEPHONE: (916) 577-5506

NUMBER OF YEARS IN BUSINESS: 3

NUMBER OF STAFF: 5-10

SPECIALIZING IN: Backpacking experiences in Lake Tahoe's Desolation Wilderness and the Tahoe-Yosemite Trail

SPECIAL PHILOSOPHY, CREDO, GOALS BEHIND BUSINESS: We hope to encourage a sense of self-sufficiency and physical well-being

Photo: Wildwalk

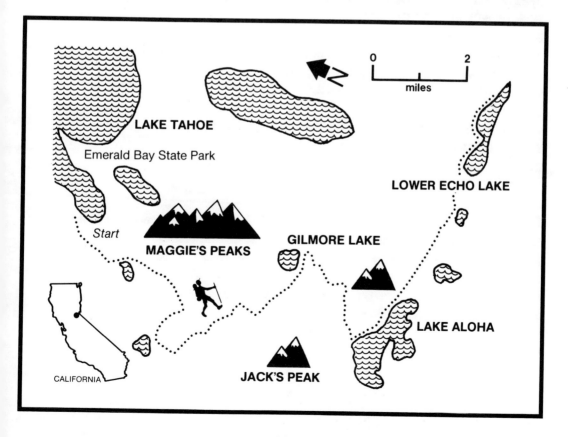

LAKE TAHOE

Emerald Bay State Park

LOWER ECHO LAKE

Start

MAGGIE'S PEAKS

GILMORE LAKE

LAKE ALOHA

CALIFORNIA

JACK'S PEAK

0   2
miles

N

ASSINIBOINE BACKPACKING

The perfect alpine vacation is a backpacking trip in the Canadian Rockies. The hike starts at the wild Kananaskis Mountain Range near Banff and zigzags up a rocky trail to the first campsite at 6,900 feet, an altitude change of 2,200 feet. What a vantage point from which to watch the surrounding peaks blush a rosy pink in the sunset! Higher elevations are reached the next day after hiking up to the snowy fields of Buller Pass. Elusive Rocky Mountain sheep may be glimpsed at this 8,110 elevation, and the Matterhorn of the Rockies, 11,870-foot Mount Assiniboine, looms ahead. Turbulent Smuts' Creek is safely forded by clutching a rope strung across its swift running water. Two days later, camp is established on the shores of Lake Magog at Assiniboine's base after crossing Wonder Pass over the Continental Divide. A rest day in this magnificent area allows exploration of alpine meadows carpeted with flowers or fishing in the streams and Lake Magog. It passes all too quickly, though, as the trek continues through the strange and eerie Valley of the Rocks and then up and over Citadel Pass, a demanding ascent. The rewards await at the summit because Golden Valley, named for the abundance of larches that turn gold each autumn, spreads below. The eight-day expedition is completed.

LENGTH OF TRIP: 8 days **DEPARTURE DATES:** July 23

TOTAL COST: $330 Canadian **TYPE OF PAYMENT ACCEPTED:** Check

RESERVATIONS/DEPOSIT: 50%

CANCELLATION POLICY: 90 days prior to trip: lose 50% deposit; 30 days prior to trip: lose entire deposit

DEPARTURE LOCATION: Banff, Alberta, CN **NEAREST AIRPORT:** Calgary, Alberta, CN

TRANSPORTATION INFORMATION: Bus

HEALTH, FITNESS OR AGE REQUIREMENTS: Good physical condition

TYPE OF WEATHER TO EXPECT: 50-70° F

BEST TYPE OF CLOTHING AND FOOTWEAR: Warm jacket, hiking boots

PERSONAL GEAR REQUIRED: Equipment list available

SPECIAL GEAR/EQUIPMENT REQUIRED: Sleeping bag

WHAT NOT TO BRING: Anything not on list

PHOTO POSSIBILITIES: Fantastic

FISHING POSSIBILITIES: Fantastic **LICENSE REQUIREMENT:** $3

BEST TYPE OF FISHING TACKLE: Fly rod

REPRESENTATIVE MENU—BREAKFAST: Juice, hot cereal, muffins

LUNCH: You supply own

DINNER: Soup, main course, dessert

CHORES/DUTIES GUESTS ARE EXPECTED TO HELP WITH: A daily crew is appointed

NAME OF OUTFITTER: Willard's Adventure Expeditions

ADDRESS: 110 Dunlop St. West **CONTACT:** Willard Kinzie

CITY: Barrie **TITLE:** Leader

STATE: Ontario, Canada **ZIP:** L4M 4S9 **TELEPHONE:** (705) 737-1881

NUMBER OF YEARS IN BUSINESS: 11

SPECIALIZING IN: Backpacking treks and base camp hiking

SPECIAL PHILOSOPHY, CREDO, GOALS BEHIND BUSINESS: That everyone participating has an exciting adventure

Photo: Willard Adventure Expeditions

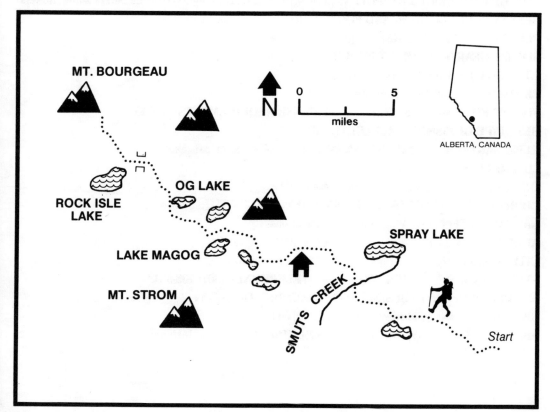

MT. BOURGEAU

N

0   5
miles

ALBERTA, CANADA

ROCK ISLE
LAKE

OG LAKE

LAKE MAGOG

SPRAY LAKE

MT. STROM

SMUTS CREEK

Start

🚶 ABSAROKA RANGE BACKPACK

Northeast of Jackson Hole and adjacent to Yellowstone National Park, this huge wilderness includes some of the most remote country in the lower 48 states. This week-long adventure will be in a rugged section of the Shoshone National Forest. The Absaroka is a volcanic mountain range characterized by thick forests, waterfalls, deep canyons, lakes, volcanic buttes topped by sweeping expanses of alpine tundra and abundant wildlife. A portion of this trip will be off-trail as we literally walk atop the Continental Divide. Also, September is a great time of year for backpacking—the mosquitoes are gone, there is a tinge of frost in the air, and the spine-tingling bugle of bull elk in the rut will assure you of a wilderness adventure that you'll never forget. Our trailhead is about 75 miles northeast of Jackson, Wyoming, and our trip will loop through the West DuNoir Creek drainage and along the Continental Divide. Parts of this trek will be at elevations over 10,000 feet. While suitable for beginners, the high elevations and rugged terrain make it important that all guests arrive in good physical condition. There is a limit of eight participants, who will be among an elite few to experience some of the most spectacular county in the U.S.

LENGTH OF TRIP: 7 days　　　**DEPARTURE DATES:** Sept. 8

TOTAL COST: $395　　　**TYPE OF PAYMENT ACCEPTED:** Check, cash, money order

RESERVATIONS/DEPOSIT: $75 deposit, full payment 10 days prior to trip

CANCELLATION POLICY: Varies according to situation

DEPARTURE LOCATION: Jackson, WY **NEAREST AIRPORT:** Jackson, WY

TRANSPORTATION INFORMATION: Taxi, limo

HEALTH, FITNESS OR AGE REQUIREMENTS: Good physical condition

TYPE OF WEATHER TO EXPECT: Variable—sunny days, cool nights, possible rain or snow showers

BEST TYPE OF CLOTHING AND FOOTWEAR: Equipment list available

PERSONAL GEAR REQUIRED: Equipment list available

SPECIAL GEAR/EQUIPMENT REQUIRED: Equipment list available

WHAT NOT TO BRING: Pets, radios

PHOTO POSSIBILITIES: Fantastic

FISHING POSSIBILITIES: Fair　　　**LICENSE REQUIREMENTS:** WY $5

BEST TYPE OF FISHING TACKLE: Fly fishing

REPRESENTATIVE MENU—BREAKFAST: Oatmeal, sausage, pancakes, eggs

LUNCH: Cheese, crackers, fruit

DINNER: Spaghetti dinner (very little freeze-dried)

CHORES/DUTIES GUESTS ARE EXPECTED TO HELP WITH: Self and community chores

NAME OF OUTFITTER: Wild Horizons Expeditions

ADDRESS: Box 2348　　　**CONTACT:** Howie Wolke

CITY: Jackson　　　**TITLE:** President

STATE: Wyoming　　**ZIP:** 83001　　　**TELEPHONE:** (307) 733-5343

NUMBER OF YEARS IN BUSINESS: 6　　**NUMBER OF STAFF:** 2

SPECIALIZING IN: Wilderness backpacking expeditions

SPECIAL PHILOSOPHY, CREDO, GOALS BEHIND BUSINESS: Instillation of a conservation ethic; nature interpretation; providing a quality wilderness experience.

Photo: Wild Horizons Expeditions

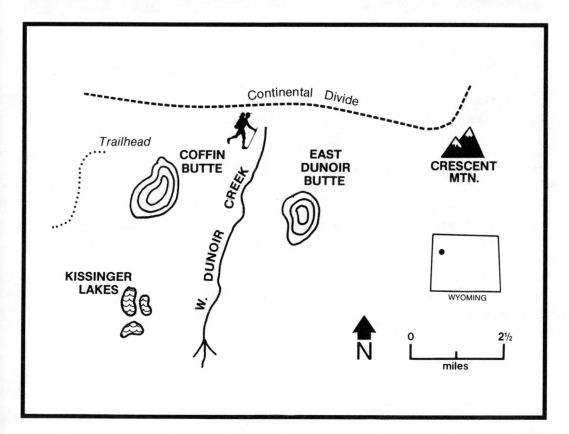

Continental Divide

Trailhead

COFFIN
BUTTE

EAST
DUNOIR
BUTTE

CRESCENT
MTN.

W. DUNOIR CREEK

KISSINGER
LAKES

WYOMING

N

0   2½
miles

🚶 MT. McKINLEY TREK

Traverse an exquisite wilderness at the foot of Mt. McKinley, the mountain the natives call Denali, "the great one." This is a delicate world of tundra, snow and ice, 37 species of mammals (including grizzly bear, fox and wolf), 130 types of birds, and rushing rivers and quiescent lakes. Ever-present looms the 20,000-foot Denali which dominates the Alaskan skyline for hundreds of miles. We'll meet in Anchorage, train to Denali National Park and then fly to its remote western edge where we set up our first camp. For the next 10 days, we hike through the most solitary and splendid portion of America's most spectacular mountain park. The hiking is rugged and involves fording icy streams. Expect to carry your personal gear and a portion of the trip food for approximately eight miles each day over rough, trailless terrain. On the final day of the hike we reach Wonder Lake and the only road in this region, upon which we are driven to Camp Denali, a private lodge where we enjoy hot showers and a sumptuous feast. The next day is a bus ride along the length of the Park to McKinley Village, and then a train ride back to Anchorage in comfort and style. A gala farewell dinner and victory celebration closes the spectacular expedition through Denali National Park.

LENGTH OF TRIP: 12 days

DEPARTURE DATES: Aug. 10, 24

TOTAL COST: $1,170

TYPE OF PAYMENT ACCEPTED: Check, Visa, MC

RESERVATIONS/DEPOSIT: $300 deposit 90 days prior to trip

CANCELLATION POLICY: Graduated cancellation schedule; no-shows get no refund

DEPARTURE LOCATION: Denali National Park **NEAREST AIRPORT:** Anchorage, AK

TRANSPORTATION INFORMATION: Arrangements included

HEALTH, FITNESS OR AGE REQUIREMENTS: Good physical condition; 18-65 years old

TYPE OF WEATHER TO EXPECT: 40-70° F; rain and snow possible

BEST TYPE OF CLOTHING AND FOOTWEAR: Equipment list available

PERSONAL GEAR REQUIRED: Equipment list available

WHAT NOT TO BRING: Excess

PHOTO POSSIBILITIES: Fantastic

FISHING POSSIBILITIES: Fantastic

LICENSE REQUIREMENT: Subject to U.S. National Park policy

BEST TYPE OF FISHING TACKLE: Lightweight fly

REPRESENTATIVE MENU—BREAKFAST: Dried eggs, coffee

LUNCH: Dried fruit, beverage, sandwich

DINNER: Trout, berries, dried vegetables, meats, dessert

CHORES/DUTIES GUESTS ARE EXPECTED TO HELP WITH: Carry food, prepare camp

ADDITIONAL SPECIAL INFORMATION: This is a rugged and remote trip. Not for the dilettante traveler, nor one who is used to servants

NAME OF OUTFITTER: SOBEK Expeditions

ADDRESS: P.O. Box 7007

CONTACT: Beth Lonergan

CITY: Angels Camp

TITLE: Travel agent

STATE: California   **ZIP:** 95222

TELEPHONE: (209) 736-4524

NUMBER OF YEARS IN BUSINESS: 11

NUMBER OF STAFF: 12

SPECIALIZING IN: Exotic whitewater river trips, culture contact, wilderness encounters on seven continents

Photo: Bart Henderson

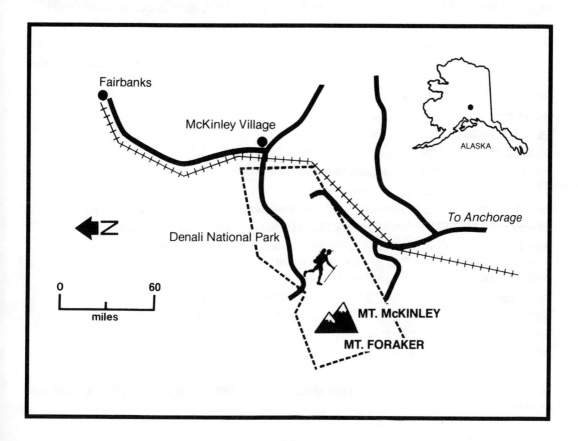

Fairbanks

McKinley Village

ALASKA

To Anchorage

Denali National Park

N

0   60

miles

MT. McKINLEY

MT. FORAKER

37

BACKPACKING BARRANCA DEL COBRE

This is an opportunity to go back in time. Barranca del Cobre, or Copper Canyon, of Mexico's Sierra Madre Occidental is carved by the Rio Urque to a depth of approximately 6,000 feet, deeper than the Grand Canyon of Arizona. It is accessible from the Chihuahua-al-Pacifica railroad by primitive, unmarked trails known only to the Indian inhabitants of the region. The highlands of the Sierra Madre are pine-forested with elevations of 7,000-9,000 feet. Descending into the canyons, thickets of oak, pine and juniper along the upper slopes give way to a thorny aridness typical of the lower Chihuahuan Desert. Sheltered side canyons are moist and semitropical with occasional hot springs, thriving groves of citrus and bananas, and rare flocks of large-billed parrots. Though shy and retiring, Tarahumara Indians are frequently seen tending their farms, herding their flocks of goats across precipitous heights, or traveling with burros to and from trading centers situated along the railway. Backpacking or exploratory trips with pack animals into the canyons of the Sierra Madre, or visits to the 1,010-foot falls at Basaseachic can be arranged as trips of nine days or longer. These trips encourage personal growth through wilderness experience.

LENGTH OF TRIP: 9 days   **DEPARTURE DATES:** Oct.-April

TOTAL COST: $495   **TYPE OF PAYMENT ACCEPTED:** Any

RESERVATIONS/DEPOSIT: $100 deposit 30 days in advance

CANCELLATION POLICY: Forfeit deposit, refund balance of fee

DEPARTURE LOCATION: Chihuahua City, MX   **NEAREST AIRPORT:** Chihuahua City, MX

TRANSPORTATION INFORMATION: Taxi or city bus

HEALTH, FITNESS OR AGE REQUIREMENTS: Ability to carry 50-60 lb. pack over rough terrain

TYPE OF WEATHER TO EXPECT: Hot to moderately cold, occasional rain

BEST TYPE OF CLOTHING AND FOOTWEAR: Loose-fitting jeans, poly underwear, GI jungle boots

PERSONAL GEAR REQUIRED: Personal duffle, tourist card, passport or birth certificate or voter registration

SPECIAL GEAR/EQUIPMENT REQUIRED: None

WHAT NOT TO BRING: Firearms, radios, pets, drugs

PHOTO POSSIBILITIES: Fantastic

FISHING POSSIBILITIES: Poor

REPRESENTATIVE MENU—BREAKFAST: Hot cereal, Tang

LUNCH: Salami, cheese, crackers, gorp

DINNER: Mountain House freeze-dried, instant cheesecake, coffee

CHORES/DUTIES GUESTS ARE EXPECTED TO HELP WITH: Camp set-up, meals

ADDITIONAL SPECIAL INFORMATION: Participants are expected to respect Indian property and customs, and to conduct themselves with discretion

NAME OF OUTFITTER: Outback Expeditions, Inc.

ADDRESS: P.O. Box 44   **CONTACT:** Larry G. Humphreys

CITY: Terlingua   **TITLE:** Senior guide

STATE: Texas   **ZIP:** 79852   **TELEPHONE:** (915) 371-2490

NUMBER OF YEARS IN BUSINESS: 14   **NUMBER OF STAFF:** 5-6

SPECIALIZING IN: Backpacking, mountaineering, rafting, canoeing

SPECIAL PHILOSOPHY, CREDO, GOALS BEHIND BUSINESS: Personal growth through wilderness experience

Photo: Outback Expeditions

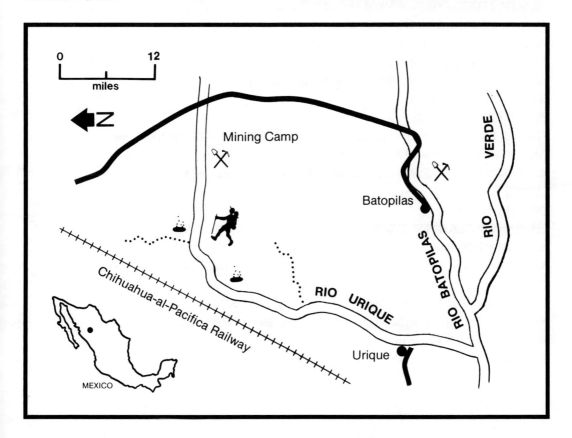

0   12

miles

N

Mining Camp

⛏

RIO VERDE

⛏

Batopilas

RIO BATOPILAS

RIO

Chihuahua-al-Pacifica Railway

RIO URIQUE

Urique

MEXICO

39

ISLE ROYALE FOOT TRAILS

As the early morning mist covers the bay, you wait to board the ferry for an exciting three-hour, 22-mile trip to the "Island." As you travel past the last point of land, the captain points out the Witches Tree. He also slows the boat down to allow you to glimpse the overturned wreck of the steamer "America," which sunk in the early 1900s. The ferry then chugs around the island to your drop-off point at McCargoe Cove where you can find prehistoric copper mines. The trail takes you through the forests until you reach Chikenbone Lake, an ideal spot for pike fishing. When you reach the Greenstone Trail, you follow it until you climb over Mt. Siskiwit, Ishpeming Point and Mount Desor which peaks at 1,300 feet. Continuing to Sugar Mountain, you make camp at Senter Point, located on Siskiwit Bay amid the homeland of moose. One walks through your camp that night. After a good breakfast the next morning, hike over Feldtmann Ridge and talk to the ranger manning the lookout tower. Set up camp at Feldtmann Lake and hike to Rainbow Cove to watch the sun set over Lake Superior, a glorious sight. On the last day of your trek, walk to the Windigo Inn and ranger station and continue to Grand Portago and the ferry that waits to take you home.

LENGTH OF TRIP: 7 days

DEPARTURE DATES: May-October

TOTAL COST: $237.86 incl. tax

TYPE OF PAYMENT ACCEPTED: Check, Visa, MC

RESERVATIONS/DEPOSIT: $25 deposit per person 2 weeks prior to trip

CANCELLATION POLICY: No refund

DEPARTURE LOCATION: Grand Portage, MN

NEAREST AIRPORT: Duluth, MN; Thunder Bay, Ontario

TRANSPORTATION INFORMATION: Car rental from Duluth or bus from Thunder Bay

HEALTH, FITNESS OR AGE REQUIREMENTS: Good health, feet in shape

TYPE OF WEATHER TO EXPECT: 45-80° F, sun and rain

BEST TYPE OF CLOTHING AND FOOTWEAR: Good hiking shoes

PERSONAL GEAR REQUIRED: Personal duffle

SPECIAL GEAR/EQUIPMENT REQUIRED: Rain suit

WHAT NOT TO BRING: Dog

PHOTO POSSIBILITIES: Fantastic

FISHING POSSIBILITIES: Excellent

LICENSE REQUIREMENT: None

BEST TYPE OF FISHING TACKLE: Packrod and lures

REPRESENTATIVE MENU—BREAKFAST: Freeze-dried dehydrated foods

LUNCH: Same

DINNER: Same

CHORES/DUTIES GUESTS ARE EXPECTED TO HELP WITH: Self-guided

NAME OF OUTFITTER: Bear Track Outfitting Co.

ADDRESS: Box 51

CONTACT: David and Cathi Williams

CITY: Grand Marais

TITLE: Owners

STATE: Minnesota **ZIP:** 55604

TELEPHONE: (218) 387-1162

NUMBER OF YEARS IN BUSINESS: 12

NUMBER OF STAFF: 3

SPECIALIZING IN: Canoe trips, backpacking, solo-canoeing, cross-country skiing and winter camping

SPECIAL PHILOSOPHY, CREDO, GOALS BEHIND BUSINESS: Introduce and educate people to the wilderness with appreciation to preserve it.

Photo: Cliff Reynolds

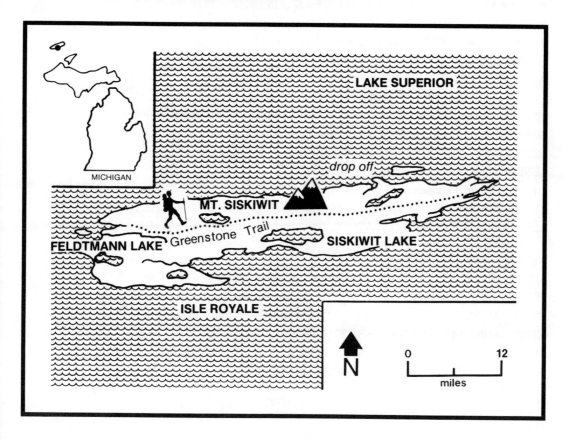

KENAI MOUNTAINS/HARDING ICEFIELD

A boat full of people and packs plows across the grey waters of Tustumena Lake. Two hours later the backpackers are zigzagging up a little-used (except by bears, wolves and moose) trail to Lake Emma where the expert fishermen in the group hopefully will catch a supper of Dolly Varden trout. The next morning finds the group attacking a stiff climb up and over 3,000-foot Nikanorka Mountain. Wolf tracks on the trail lead the party into the alpine world of the Kenai Mountains. From here braided glacial rivers, snowfields, high green meadows and talus slopes dominate the scenery. Dall sheep watch the intruders trudge by and an eagle sails along the cliffs seeking an unwary marmot. Dwarfed by the immensity of the Harding Icefield, the group slowly undulates along the snow-covered ice. The lush, boulder-strewn expanse of the Killey River Valley welcomes them, and a small black bear plays hide and seek with an upright species he has never encountered before. Killey River bounces down 200 feet of misty gorge. The group continues out of the valley to Sunshine Pass and the headwaters of the Funny River. They continue across the alpine tundra fragrant with heather in search of the trail that leads back to Tustumena Lake and civilization.

LENGTH OF TRIP: 9 days   **DEPARTURE DATES:** June 23, July 7

TOTAL COST: $545   **TYPE OF PAYMENT ACCEPTED:** Check

RESERVATIONS/DEPOSIT: $200 deposit 30 days in advance

CANCELLATION POLICY: Forfeit all monies paid

DEPARTURE LOCATION: Soldotna, AK   **NEAREST AIRPORT:** Kenai, AK

TRANSPORTATION INFORMATION: Will be picked up by outfitter

HEALTH, FITNESS OR AGE REQUIREMENTS: Good physical condition; 16 years old minimum

TYPE OF WEATHER TO EXPECT: Below freezing to 75° F

BEST TYPE OF CLOTHING AND FOOTWEAR: Equipment list available

PERSONAL GEAR REQUIRED: Equipment list available

SPECIAL GEAR/EQUIPMENT REQUIRED: 2-pc. rain suit

WHAT NOT TO BRING: Firearms, radio

PHOTO POSSIBILITIES: Fantastic

FISHING POSSIBILITIES: Good   **LICENSE REQUIREMENT:** 1 or 10-day, $5-15

BEST TYPE OF FISHING TACKLE: Lightweight packrod spinning outfit

REPRESENTATIVE MENU—BREAKFAST: Granola, fruit, eggs

LUNCH: Cheese, sausage, crackers

DINNER: Soup, freeze-dried main course, pilot bread, dessert

CHORES/DUTIES GUESTS ARE EXPECTED TO HELP WITH: Clean up and latrine

ADDITIONAL SPECIAL INFORMATION: Good physical condition and no walking impairment are more important than experience

NAME OF OUTFITTER: Kenai Guide Service

ADDRESS: Box 40   **CONTACT:** George R. Pollard

CITY: Kasilof   **TITLE:** Owner

STATE: Alaska   **ZIP:** 99610   **TELEPHONE:** (907) 262-5496

NUMBER OF YEARS IN BUSINESS: 30   **NUMBER OF STAFF:** 2-4

SPECIALIZING IN: Wilderness backpacking in Alaska's finest areas for this purpose

SPECIAL PHILOSOPHY, CREDO, GOALS BEHIND BUSINESS: To preserve the quality of life found only in the wilderness

Photo: Kenai Guide Service

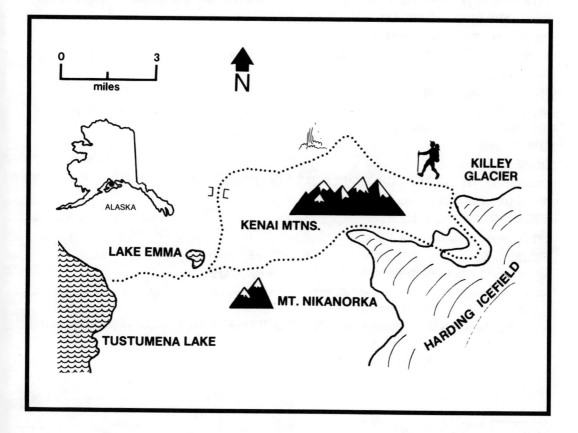

🥾 THE OTHER HAWAII

During our sojourn in the "other" Hawaii, we will hike, camp, and explore the exotic natural beauty of the Hawaii of old as it still exists on the outer islands. With 10 days on the "big island" of Hawaii, we will hike the Waipio Valley, a six-mile-long gorge bounded by 2,000-foot-high walls, swim under a beautiful waterfall and camp at Keokea. We will also swim and snorkel in the warm waters of Hapuna Beach, and then make a summit hike on Mauna Kea (13,796 feet), the highest peak in the Pacific. Driving down the beautiful Kona Coast, we stop at Hawaii Volcanoes National Park to hike across the still steaming Kilauea Caldera to explore Mauna Ulu, a recently active volcano. When we hop over to Maui, the next five days will include a memorable sunrise from the summit of 10,023-foot Haleakala Volcano and then camp at Hosmer Grove, a beautiful hardwood forest at 8,000 feet. A two-day hike with 30-lb. backpacks trips across the moonscape of craters which form the seven-mile-long crater floor. We will walk on Sliding Sands Trail in a landscape of colorful cinder cones and rare silversword plants. Our accommodations will be in beach camps and state park cabins, with our last night spent at an inn in the picturesque whaling port of Lahaina.

LENGTH OF TRIP: 15 days   **DEPARTURE DATES:** April 7, Oct. 6, Dec. 19

TOTAL COST: $890 plus airfare   **TYPE OF PAYMENT ACCEPTED:** Check, AMEX

RESERVATIONS/DEPOSIT: $200 to confirm space

CANCELLATION POLICY: Forfeit payment

DEPARTURE LOCATION: Hilo, Hawaii   **NEAREST AIRPORT:** Hilo, Hawaii

TRANSPORTATION INFORMATION: Mountain Travel leader picks up group at airport

HEALTH, FITNESS OR AGE REQUIREMENTS: Active, healthy people who like to walk

TYPE OF WEATHER TO EXPECT: Generally fair, showers possible

BEST TYPE OF CLOTHING AND FOOTWEAR: Hiking clothes

PERSONAL GEAR REQUIRED: Personal items

SPECIAL GEAR/EQUIPMENT REQUIRED: Good hiking boots

PHOTO POSSIBILITIES: Fantastic

FISHING POSSIBILITIES: None

REPRESENTATIVE MENU—BREAKFAST: All meals consist of fresh fruit, vegetables and seafood prepared in gourmet dishes by trip leaders

LUNCH: Same

DINNER: Same

CHORES/DUTIES GUESTS ARE EXPECTED TO HELP WITH: Pitch tents

NAME OF OUTFITTER: Mountain Travel

ADDRESS: 1398 Solano Ave.

CITY: Albany

STATE: California   **ZIP:** 94706   **TELEPHONE:** (415) 527-8100

NUMBER OF YEARS IN BUSINESS: 17   **NUMBER OF STAFF:** 18

SPECIALIZING IN: Expeditions and outings to wilderness regions on five continents (treks, climbs, raft trips, camel trips, game safaris).

SPECIAL PHILOSOPHY, CREDO, GOALS BEHIND BUSINESS: We specialize in hiking expeditions for small groups (15 or less) with expert guides.

Photo: Jean Tiura

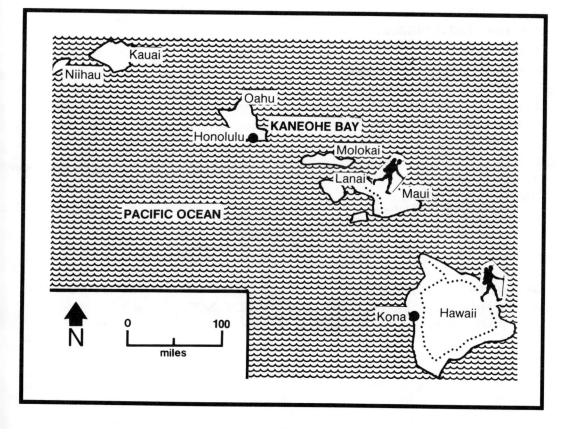

MEXICO VOLCANOES CLIMB

This trip must be looked upon as a way to experience a foreign mountain climb as well as a foreign way of life. We go out of our way to make both the mountains and Mexico a special adventure and experience. South of the border, a great mountain vacation awaits. High volcanoes reaching 17,400, 17,700 and 18,800 feet in elevation are matched by the warm climate and warm hearts of a great people. We will stay with a Mexican climber's family, allowing us many inside treats of experiencing the way of life within a Mexican home. Special feasts and our own fiesta will accompany our visit with our new friends. Open markets, fresh fruit, handmade baskets, brooms and blankets will greet us in small villages en route to the volcanoes. At the base of Popo, the smallest of the three mentioned, lies a beautiful climber's lodge equipped with beds, showers and a cafe, and it houses climbers from around the world. This will be our lodging while climbing Popo and Ixta, the two nearby giants. We will climb two volcanoes on the nine-day trips and three volcanoes (Orizaba) on the 11-day trips. One must be in good shape to tackle three volcanoes in one trip.

LENGTH OF TRIP: 9-11 days, incl. travel   **DEPARTURE DATES:** November–January

TOTAL COST: $750 plus $330 airfare   **TYPE OF PAYMENT ACCEPTED:** Check, money order

RESERVATIONS/DEPOSIT: $250 deposit by closing date for trip

CANCELLATION POLICY: Partial or total refund based on reason and our costs

DEPARTURE LOCATION: Mexico City   **NEAREST AIRPORT:** Mexico City, Mexico

TRANSPORTATION INFORMATION: Hire taxi from airport to hotel, $8/car

HEALTH, FITNESS OR AGE REQUIREMENTS: Good physical condition; mid-teens and older

TYPE OF WEATHER TO EXPECT: Hot days, cold nights

BEST TYPE OF CLOTHING AND FOOTWEAR: Casual clothing, adequate hiking shoes

PERSONAL GEAR REQUIRED: Personal duffle

SPECIAL GEAR/EQUIPMENT REQUIRED: Equipment list available

WHAT NOT TO BRING: Excess baggage

PHOTO POSSIBILITIES: Fantastic

FISHING POSSIBILITIES: None

REPRESENTATIVE MENU—BREAKFAST: Local foods

LUNCH: Same

DINNER: Same

CHORES/DUTIES GUESTS ARE EXPECTED TO HELP WITH: Whatever needs doing

NAME OF OUTFITTER: Colorado Mountain School

ADDRESS: P.O. Box 2015A   **CONTACT:** Mike Donahue

CITY: Estes Park   **TITLE:** Director

STATE: Colorado   **ZIP:** 80517   **TELEPHONE:** (303) 586-5758

NUMBER OF YEARS IN BUSINESS: 10   **NUMBER OF STAFF:** 9-12

SPECIALIZING IN: Mountain climbing and backcountry adventures

SPECIAL PHILOSOPHY, CREDO, GOALS BEHIND BUSINESS: We believe that it is the experience that counts most and gear all of our outings to a completely individualized experience.

Photo: Colorado Mountain School

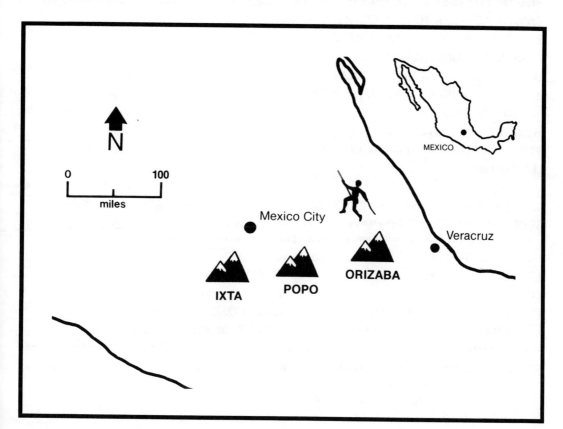

GLACIER CLIMBING EXPEDITION

The seven largest glaciers in the Rocky Mountain States and the highest peak in Wyoming are located in the Wind River Range. Twenty miles of scenic high country and the Continental Divide separate the glaciers from the nearest trail head. Traversing this remote high country will be the focus of the 14-day glacier climbing expedition. After two days of technical rock climbing instruction and preparation at our high altitude mountain base camp, we'll head for the glacier fields. Camping on, exploring and climbing the mighty snow and ice fields provide a unique outdoor experience. Intensive instruction in all phases of ice climbing, including use of crampons, ice axes and ropes, will precede a glacial ascent of a major peak. If conditions are right, the goal will be 13,875-foot Gannett Peak, the highest mountain in Wyoming. This expedition is demanding but well within the capabilities of the well conditioned individual seeking the serious challenges of the outdoors. No prior technical or glacier climbing is necessary, and all climbing equipment is furnished. This program is designed for adults and teenagers with prior outdoor experience. You will be required to cook and set up camps, but we feed our participants well. Trust us.

LENGTH OF TRIP: 14 days

TOTAL COST: $635

RESERVATIONS/DEPOSIT: 25% by June 15

CANCELLATION POLICY: No refunds after May 1

DEPARTURE LOCATION: Wyoming base camp   **NEAREST AIRPORT:** Rock Springs, WY

DEPARTURE DATES: July 18

TYPE OF PAYMENT ACCEPTED: Check, cash

TRANSPORTATION INFORMATION: Will pick up at Rock Springs; also special transportation arranged to and from Denver, Colorado—$85 round trip.

HEALTH, FITNESS OR AGE REQUIREMENTS: Good physical condition; 14 years old minimum

TYPE OF WEATHER TO EXPECT: Mountain weather

BEST TYPE OF CLOTHING AND FOOTWEAR: Wool; hiking boots

PERSONAL GEAR REQUIRED: Equipment list available

SPECIAL GEAR/EQUIPMENT REQUIRED: All climbing gear, tents and packs provided

WHAT NOT TO BRING: Anything not on list

PHOTO POSSIBILITIES: Fantastic

FISHING POSSIBILITIES: None

REPRESENTATIVE MENU—BREAKFAST: "We feed our participants very well—trust us."

LUNCH: Ditto

DINNER: Ditto

CHORES/DUTIES GUESTS ARE EXPECTED TO HELP WITH: Cooking, pitching/striking camp

ADDITIONAL SPECIAL INFORMATION: This is a very demanding trip from a physical standpoint. You must be in good physical condition with some prior backpacking experience.

NAME OF OUTFITTER: Wind River Mountain Guides

ADDRESS: 6678 S. Arapahoe Dr.   **CONTACT:** Roland L. Ryan

CITY: Littleton   **TITLE:** Director/owner

STATE: Colorado   **ZIP:** 80120   **TELEPHONE:** (303) 794-9518

NUMBER OF YEARS IN BUSINESS: 22   **NUMBER OF STAFF:** 8-10

SPECIALIZING IN: Backpacking, technical rock and glacier climbing, kayaking, rafting and bike touring

SPECIAL PHILOSOPHY, CREDO, GOALS BEHIND BUSINESS: To provide challenging and maturing experiences in the great outdoors.

Photo: Kachemak Alpine Guides

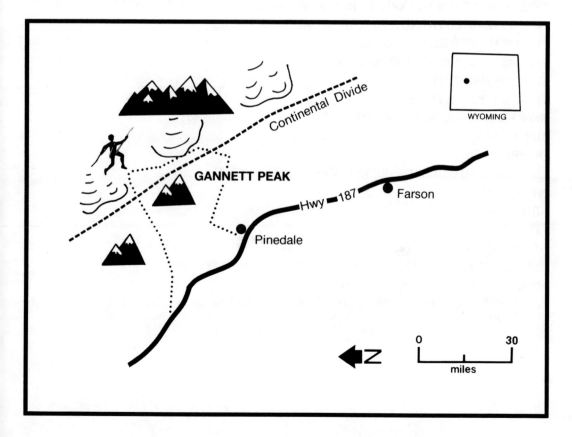

Continental Divide

WYOMING

GANNETT PEAK

Hwy 187   Farson

Pinedale

N

0   30
miles

CLIMB OF THE GRAND TETON

The adventure begins with a day at Basic School, followed by a day at Intermediate School. Upon completion of these programs, the next step is a climb of the Grand Teton, a grandiose monolith that rises 13,766 feet above sea level. The first day of the two-day climb begins at 10 a.m. This is a hard day of hiking up a steep trail that is eight miles long and one mile up. Base camp is on the Lower Daddle at 11,500 feet. The second day begins at the pre-dawn hour of 3 a.m. After a hasty breakfast and a cup of tea, we begin the approach in the dark. Daylight finds us at the base of the climb. Four hours later we have reached the summit and the view is spectacular. We can see the mountains around Sun Valley to the west, the Wind River to the east, Yellowstone and the Bear Tooths to the north and the Wyoming Range to the south. Our view is only limited by the curvature of the earth. We descend the Owen Route via one overhanging rappel and we reach base camp by 1 p.m. By 6 p.m. we have returned to the parking lot, tired but impressed with ourselves for having climbed one of America's greatest peaks. These two days have installed a self respect in the clients for themselves, as well as for the mountains and their strength.

LENGTH OF TRIP: 2 days   **DEPARTURE DATES:** Daily, mid-July through August

TOTAL COST: $140   **TYPE OF PAYMENT ACCEPTED:** MC

RESERVATIONS/DEPOSIT: $60 deposit 2 weeks prior to trip

CANCELLATION POLICY: Money refunded if advance notice given

DEPARTURE LOCATION: Jenny Lake, WY   **NEAREST AIRPORT:** Jackson, WY

TRANSPORTATION INFORMATION: Taxi

HEALTH, FITNESS OR AGE REQUIREMENTS: Good physical condition

TYPE OF WEATHER TO EXPECT: Rain, snow, sunshine

BEST TYPE OF CLOTHING AND FOOTWEAR: Winter clothing

PERSONAL GEAR REQUIRED: Personal duffle and food

SPECIAL GEAR/EQUIPMENT REQUIRED: None

PHOTO POSSIBILITIES: Fantastic

FISHING POSSIBILITIES: None

REPRESENTATIVE MENU—BREAKFAST: Clients provide own food

LUNCH: Same

DINNER: Same

CHORES/DUTIES GUESTS ARE EXPECTED TO HELP WITH: None

NAME OF OUTFITTER: Exum Mountain Guides

ADDRESS: Box 580

CITY: Wilson

STATE: Wyoming   **ZIP:** 83041   **TELEPHONE:** (303) 733-2297

NUMBER OF YEARS IN BUSINESS: 55   **NUMBER OF STAFF:** 15

SPECIALIZING IN: Climbing schools and guided climbs

SPECIAL PHILOSOPHY, CREDO, GOALS BEHIND BUSINESS: To give the clients a terrific day in the mountains.

Photo: Exum Mountain Guides

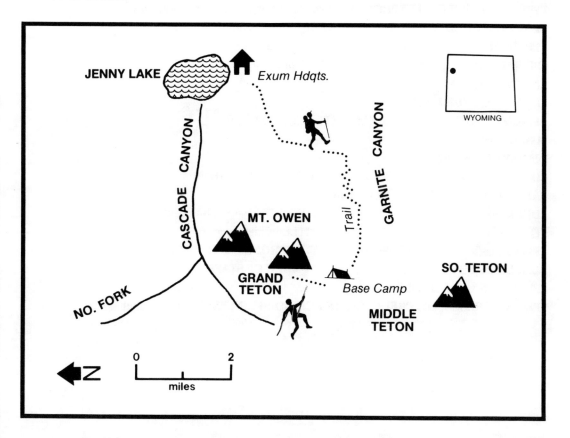

WEST BUTTRESS MT. McKINLEY TREK

Climbing to the summit of Mt. McKinley, the top of North America, demands a certain kind of attitude and physical conditioning. If you have "it," sign up for this 17-21 day expedition in Alaska's mountains. The trek begins in the rustic town of Talkeetna, 125 miles north of Anchorage. Participants board ski-equipped bushplanes for the flight into base camp on the Kahiltna glacier. From there the trekkers are surrounded by ice and snow-covered peaks of the Alaska range. The group skis or snowshoes over the next 10 days to the 14,000-foot level of Mt. McKinley where Camp III is established and serves as the serious starting point for the climb to the summit. A long climb to camps IV and V in the thin air tops out at 17,200 feet. The group rests at Camp V and ensures that all is in order for Mt. McKinley. The climate will most likely have been reduced to arctic conditions with subzero temperatures, proving why excellent physical conditioning and a strong desire to reach the summit is imperative in participants. The descent will be a heady mixture of accomplishment and a sense of self-confidence from completing this difficult and challenging trek.

LENGTH OF TRIP: 17-21 days

DEPARTURE DATES: Throughout May, June

TOTAL COST: $1,700

TYPE OF PAYMENT ACCEPTED: Check, cash

RESERVATIONS/DEPOSIT: $425 deposit 25 days prior to departure

CANCELLATION POLICY: Funds are applied to future trip

DEPARTURE LOCATION: Talkeetna, AK   **NEAREST AIRPORT:** Anchorage, AK

TRANSPORTATION INFORMATION: Taxi, train, or rental car ($30+)

HEALTH, FITNESS OR AGE REQUIREMENTS: High level of physical fitness

TYPE OF WEATHER TO EXPECT: Arctic conditions with subzero temperatures

BEST TYPE OF CLOTHING AND FOOTWEAR: Equipment list available

PERSONAL GEAR REQUIRED: Equipment list available

SPECIAL GEAR/EQUIPMENT REQUIRED: Equipment list available

PHOTO POSSIBILITIES: Fantastic

FISHING POSSIBILITIES: None

REPRESENTATIVE MENU—BREAKFAST: Dehydrated foods

LUNCH: Dehydrated foods

DINNER: Dehydrated foods

CHORES/DUTIES GUESTS ARE EXPECTED TO HELP WITH: None

NAME OF OUTFITTER: Genet Expeditions

ADDRESS: Talkeetna

CONTACT: Harry Johnson, III

CITY: Talkeetna

TITLE: Chief guide

STATE: Alaska   **ZIP:** 99676

TELEPHONE: (907) 376-5120

NUMBER OF YEARS IN BUSINESS: 16

NUMBER OF STAFF: 5-10

SPECIALIZING IN: Mountaineering

SPECIAL PHILOSOPHY, CREDO, GOALS BEHIND BUSINESS: "To the summit"

Photo: Genet Expeditions

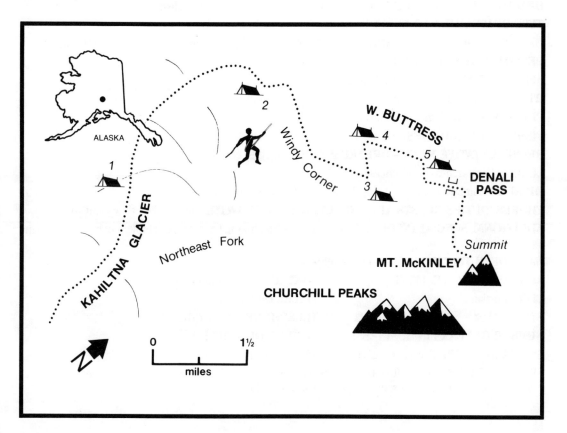

ALASKA

KAHILTNA GLACIER

Northeast Fork

Windy Corner

1

2

3

4

W. BUTTRESS

5

DENALI PASS

Summit

MT. McKINLEY

CHURCHILL PEAKS

0   1½

miles

MT. HOOD WITH DOG SUPPORT

Man's best friend lives up to the expression on this wilderness trek in Oregon's Mount Hood National Forest. Alaskan Malamutes have been bred specifically for use as freight animals, a task at which they excel, to help man experience the great outdoors in the most ecologically and environmentally sound way. This seven-day, 50-mile hike with light packs on the participants and the dogs begins at the spectacular Columbia River Gorge and follows Eagle Creek past plunging waterfalls, high bridges and a tunnel that actually passes behind a waterfall. The second day's hike leads through a deep forest to Wahtum Lake and a well-deserved lunch. Camp that night at Indian Springs offers dramatic vistas of Mt. Adams, Mt. Hood and Mt. St. Helens. The next day's hike takes trekkers closer to Mt. Hood to a rustic log cabin for the night to rest up before ascending the mountain. By early afternoon, the timberline is reached and the view is breathtaking. The last few days are spent soaking up the scenery and then spending a night at the magnificent Timberline Lodge to enjoy its sauna, heated pool, bar, showers and other "luxuries" after a week in the wilderness. Participants are encouraged to help work, feed and groom the dogs to add to this rewarding experience.

LENGTH OF TRIP: 7 days   **DEPARTURE DATES:** July 16 and 30, 1984

TOTAL COST: $545   **TYPE OF PAYMENT ACCEPTED:** Any

RESERVATIONS/DEPOSIT: $125 ASAP

CANCELLATION POLICY: Non-refundable deposit; balance refunded if spot is filled

DEPARTURE LOCATION: Portland, OR   **NEAREST AIRPORT:** Portland, OR

TRANSPORTATION INFORMATION: All transportation is provided

HEALTH, FITNESS OR AGE REQUIREMENTS: Ability to walk long distance

TYPE OF WEATHER TO EXPECT: Generally clear and warm; rain possible

BEST TYPE OF CLOTHING AND FOOTWEAR: Lightweight hiking boots, synthetic clothing

PERSONAL GEAR REQUIRED: Personal duffle

SPECIAL GEAR/EQUIPMENT REQUIRED: None

WHAT NOT TO BRING: Dogs, heavy clothing, heavy boots

PHOTO POSSIBILITIES: Fantastic

FISHING POSSIBILITIES: Poor

REPRESENTATIVE MENU—BREAKFAST: Bacon, eggs, cereal

LUNCH: Sandwiches, meat, cheese

DINNER: Hamburgers, pizza, tacos, little or no freeze-dried food

CHORES/DUTIES GUESTS ARE EXPECTED TO HELP WITH: None unless they want to

ADDITIONAL SPECIAL INFORMATION: Be sure that hiking boots are well broken in before trip; bring plenty of film

NAME OF OUTFITTER: Wilderness Freighters

ADDRESS: 2166 S.E. 142nd   **CONTACT:** John Simonson

CITY: Portland   **TITLE:** Owner/operator

STATE: Oregon   **ZIP:** 97233   **TELEPHONE:** (503) 761-7428

NUMBER OF YEARS IN BUSINESS: 6   **NUMBER OF STAFF:** 4

SPECIALIZING IN: Backpacking, cross-country skiing, snowshoeing, dogsledding, dogpacking

SPECIAL PHILOSOPHY, CREDO, GOALS BEHIND BUSINESS: We enjoy showing people what we like to do. It enables us to spend more time with our dogs.

Photo: Wilderness Freighters

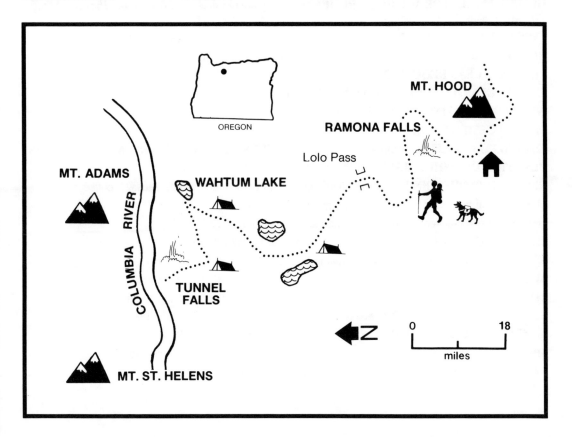

🦙🚶 HOME RANCH LLAMA TREKS

Take a hike and leave the luggage to the llamas. The Home Ranch Llama Treks are low-key, easy expeditions to the wilderness areas outside of Steamboat Springs, Colorado. The five-day, four-night trip begins with a big breakfast at the Home Ranch main lodge. The morning air is cool and scented with evergreen as the llama trekkers are introduced to their animals. After the llamas' panniers are packed, the group heads up the trail to North Lake where we base camp for the trip. The lake is situated at 10,300 feet in the heart of the Mt. Zirkel wilderness. Brook trout rise almost continuously as the group tries to decide what to do the next day. The choices are to hike to the summit of 12,000-foot Lost Ranger Peak, or hike over to Wolverine Basin where Ptarmigan Lake lies and fish. The decision is made while eating a steak dinner with baked potatoes. We arise the next morning, check our fishing gear and pack lunches for the hike to Ptarmigan Lake. It isn't long before we have several nice cut-throats in the creel and we return to base camp and cook the fresh fish over the open fire. The next few days are passed hiking the Continental Divide, meteor gazing at night and observing elk and eagles before returning to the Home Ranch.

LENGTH OF TRIP: 4, 5 days   **DEPARTURE DATES:** Varies

TOTAL COST: $75/person/day plus 3.6% tax   **TYPE OF PAYMENT ACCEPTED:** Check, cash, money order

RESERVATIONS/DEPOSIT: $100 deposit

CANCELLATION POLICY: No refund if cancelled within one month of trip

DEPARTURE LOCATION: The Home Ranch   **NEAREST AIRPORT:** Steamboat Springs, CO

TRANSPORTATION INFORMATION: Free pickup at airport

HEALTH, FITNESS OR AGE REQUIREMENTS: Adequate physical condition; under 16 years old must be accompanied by guardian

TYPE OF WEATHER TO EXPECT: Sunny, warm days, cool nights, occasional showers

BEST TYPE OF CLOTHING AND FOOTWEAR: Equipment list available

PERSONAL GEAR REQUIRED: Personal duffle

SPECIAL GEAR/EQUIPMENT REQUIRED: None

WHAT NOT TO BRING: Guests limited to 25 lbs. duffle

PHOTO POSSIBILITIES: Fantastic

FISHING POSSIBILITIES: Fantastic   **LICENSE REQUIREMENTS:** Non-resident $7-18

BEST TYPE OF FISHING TACKLE: Fly rod, spinning gear

REPRESENTATIVE MENU—BREAKFAST: Orange juice, scrambled eggs, sausage, coffee

LUNCH: Trail mix, ham and swiss on rye, pretzels, fruit, juice

DINNER: Fried chicken, salad, potatoes and gravy, vegetable, dessert

CHORES/DUTIES GUESTS ARE EXPECTED TO HELP WITH: None

NAME OF OUTFITTER: Home Ranch Llama Trekking

ADDRESS: Box 822K   **CONTACT:** Peter Nichols

CITY: Clark   **TITLE:** Owner, guide, outfitter

STATE: Colorado   **ZIP:** 80428   **TELEPHONE:** (303) 879-1780

NUMBER OF YEARS IN BUSINESS: 4   **NUMBER OF STAFF:** 2

SPECIALIZING IN: Hiking pack trips with llamas to carry camping gear, food, clothing, etc.

SPECIAL PHILOSOPHY, CREDO, GOALS BEHIND BUSINESS: "Take a hike and leave the luggage to the llamas." Trips are easy going and low-key

Photo: Peter Nichols

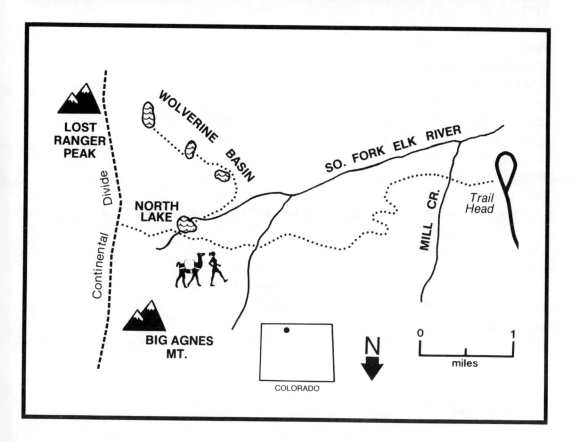

🦙🦙🚶 DIAMOND PEAK LLAMA TREK

Members of the "Lost Wagon Train" of 1853 passed south of Diamond Peak in their desperate struggle to reach the Willamette Valley before being trapped by winter snows. It was the end of October before they made it to safety, cutting rough roads ahead of them as they went. This wilderness remains as primitive today as it was then, inhabited by wildlife and barely trespassed by meandering trails which we follow during our two excursions into the heart of its beauty and solitude. And to assist us in walking softly and leaving no trace of our passage are gentle, strong llamas who carry our gear. For four days and three nights we and our llamas visit this peaceful area after walking four and a half miles from Shelter Cove Resort into the base camp at Yoran Lake, gaining 1,200 feet in elevation. There is plenty of time to explore and hike the mountainous surroundings and fish for brook and rainbow trout in the lake. Meals will include biscuits, eggs and sausage for breakfast, pita sandwiches for lunch and sherried game hens, Dutch oven caraway bread and peach cobbler for dinner, accompanied by select wines. Participants are expected to lead their llamas and assist in camp care and clean-up.

LENGTH OF TRIP: 4 days   **DEPARTURE DATES:** Aug. Sept.

TOTAL COST: $270   **TYPE OF PAYMENT ACCEPTED:** Any

RESERVATIONS/DEPOSIT: $50 deposit 30 days before departure

CANCELLATION POLICY: No refund if cancel within 30 days of trip

DEPARTURE LOCATION: Shelter Cove Resort   **NEAREST AIRPORT:** Eugene, OR

TRANSPORTATION INFORMATION: Will arrange for charter flight service or car rental

HEALTH, FITNESS OR AGE REQUIREMENTS: Normal health; adults only

TYPE OF WEATHER TO EXPECT: Warm to hot, occasional showers

BEST TYPE OF CLOTHING AND FOOTWEAR: Layers, sturdy footwear

PERSONAL GEAR REQUIRED: Equipment list available

SPECIAL GEAR/EQUIPMENT REQUIRED: Fishing gear

WHAT NOT TO BRING: Radio, tape deck

PHOTO POSSIBILITIES: Fantastic

FISHING POSSIBILITIES: Good   **LICENSE REQUIREMENTS:** OR

BEST TYPE OF FISHING TACKLE: Light spinning tackle and fly fishing

REPRESENTATIVE MENU—BREAKFAST: Sausage, eggs, hashbrowns, biscuits

LUNCH: Pocket bread sandwiches

DINNER: Sherried game hens, Dutch oven caraway bread, salad, wine, cobbler

CHORES/DUTIES GUESTS ARE EXPECTED TO HELP WITH: Lead llamas, camp care

NAME OF OUTFITTER: G. Jelinek's Oregon Wilderness Llama Tours

ADDRESS: P.O. Box 7515   **CONTACT:** Gary Jelinek

CITY: Eugene   **TITLE:** Outfitter

STATE: Oregon   **ZIP:** 97401   **TELEPHONE:** (503) 995-6208

NUMBER OF YEARS IN BUSINESS: 3   **NUMBER OF STAFF:** 2

SPECIALIZING IN: Llama treks

SPECIAL PHILOSOPHY, CREDO, GOALS BEHIND BUSINESS: Walking softly in the wilderness, no-trace camping

Photo: G. Jelinek

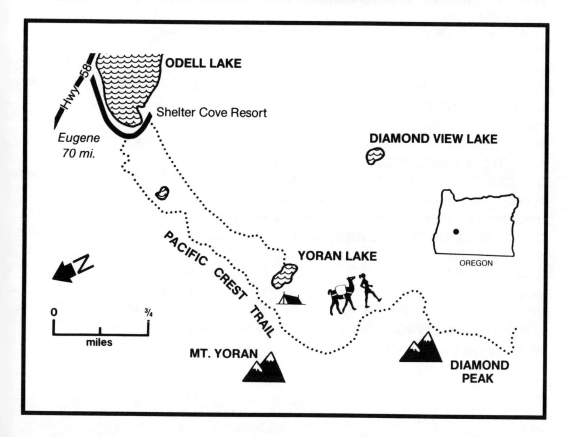

ʞ RAWAH WILDERNESS LLAMA PACK TRIP

Our backcountry adventure starts high in the Colorado mountains of the Rawah Wilderness Area. After introductions to llama companions and stowing our gear in their packs, we set out. Climbing gradually through stands of whispering aspen and following the tumbling Laramie River, we befriend our silent and surefooted llamas. After six rather steep but tranquil miles, we make camp in a lush alpine meadow. The brilliant wildflowers carpeting the landscape and the craggy peaks looming overhead leave us speechless. After a savory dinner, we blissfully slip into slumber under a sky silvery with stars. The smell of fresh-brewed coffee awakes us in the clean morning air and the omelette and homemade rolls fuel us for the short, slow hike up the tundra pass. Our view is spectacular because it extends east to the plains and the distant towns, and hints of a valley in the other direction. We continue hiking and are rewarded by four shimmering lakes below, one marked with rings of rising trout. We choose this lake for our next campsite. After lunching on pita sandwiches and brownies, we take our fishing rods to the water's edge. After two more days of relaxing and exploring this 11,000-foot high valley and its lakes, we depart.

LENGTH OF TRIP: 4 days

DEPARTURE DATES: To be determined

TOTAL COST: $280

TYPE OF PAYMENT ACCEPTED: Check, cash

RESERVATIONS/DEPOSIT: 50% deposit when booking

CANCELLATION POLICY: Forfeit deposit unless exceptional circumstances

DEPARTURE LOCATION: Fort Collins, CO

NEAREST AIRPORT: Fort Collins, CO

TRANSPORTATION INFORMATION: We could pick up, but we suggest checking into a local motel the day before the departure.

HEALTH, FITNESS OR AGE REQUIREMENTS: Good physical condition, ability to do strenuous hiking at high elevations.

TYPE OF WEATHER TO EXPECT: Generally sunny, cool, possible shower

BEST TYPE OF CLOTHING AND FOOTWEAR: Equipment list available

PERSONAL GEAR REQUIRED: Equipment list available

SPECIAL GEAR/EQUIPMENT REQUIRED: Tent and sleeping bag

WHAT NOT TO BRING: Heavy bag and tent

PHOTO POSSIBILITIES: Fantastic

FISHING POSSIBILITIES: Fantastic

LICENSE REQUIREMENT: CO

BEST TYPE OF FISHING TACKLE: Fly fishing, spin gear

REPRESENTATIVE MENU—BREAKFAST: Omelette, hashbrowns, coffee

LUNCH: Pita sandwiches, homemade brownie

DINNER: Teriyaki chicken, vegetables, salad, dessert, soda, wine

CHORES/DUTIES GUESTS ARE EXPECTED TO HELP WITH: None

NAME OF OUTFITTER: Rocky Mountain Llama Treks

ADDRESS: Sugarloaf Star Route

CONTACT: Steve Eandi

CITY: Boulder

TITLE: Owner, guide

STATE: Colorado   **ZIP:** 80302

TELEPHONE: (303) 449-9941

NUMBER OF YEARS IN BUSINESS: 4

NUMBER OF STAFF: 2

SPECIALIZING IN: Llama wilderness pack trips

SPECIAL PHILOSOPHY, CREDO, GOALS BEHIND BUSINESS: Low impact camping

Photo: Rocky Mountain Llama Treks

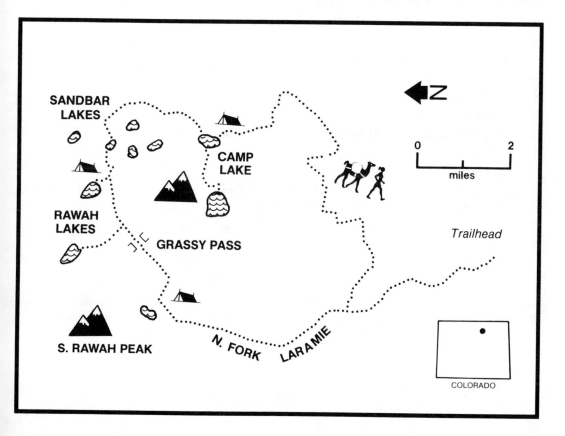

PACKHORSES TO MT. EDZIZA PARK

Iskut Trail and River Adventures introduces you to the other-worldly beauty of the Edziza plateau, one of the most interesting volcanic areas in North America. Dominated by ice-coated Mt. Edziza, a dormant volcano 9,143 feet high, the plateau's outstanding scenic charm never fails to please the few visitors who venture here. Our pack horses will carry all gear and camping equipment, allowing participants to only carry light daypacks. A floatplane transports us to the Edziza area and we hike from Buckley Lake on the northern boundary of Mt. Edziza Provincial Park up through rugged forests to the lunar-like plateau. We spend five days exploring the vast ash, cinder and sand fields, through strange lava formations and past perfectly symmetrical cinder cones. Time permitting, we may venture to the Tahweh hot springs for a rejuvenating soak. The isolation, topography and vegetation make this region a prime habitat for large populations of caribou, mountain goat and stone sheep. The Tahltan guide will show us the trails, lookouts, camps and graves of his ancestors. Numerous ancient Tahltan implements, carved in obsidian, have been discovered on the Edziza plateau.

LENGTH OF TRIP: 7 days

DEPARTURE DATES: August 12 and 18

TOTAL COST: $725

TYPE OF PAYMENT ACCEPTED: Check only

RESERVATIONS/DEPOSIT: 25% with reservation

CANCELLATION POLICY: Money forfeited

DEPARTURE LOCATION: Iskut, B.C.,   **NEAREST AIRPORT:** Iskut, B.C.

TRANSPORTATION INFORMATION: Free bus transportation included

HEALTH, FITNESS OR AGE REQUIREMENTS: Good physical condition; 14 years old minimum

TYPE OF WEATHER TO EXPECT: Rain, sunshine, cold, hot

BEST TYPE OF CLOTHING AND FOOTWEAR: Good hiking boots

PERSONAL GEAR REQUIRED: Sleeping bag, day pack, rain gear

SPECIAL GEAR/EQUIPMENT REQUIRED: Equipment list available

WHAT NOT TO BRING: 25 bls. duffle limit

PHOTO POSSIBILITIES: Fantastic

FISHING POSSIBILITIES: None

REPRESENTATIVE MENU—BREAKFAST: Pancakes with maple syrup

LUNCH: Sandwiches

DINNER: Chicken curry, rice, salad, fruit

CHORES/DUTIES GUESTS ARE EXPECTED TO HELP WITH: Setting up tent, washing own dishes

NAME OF OUTFITTER: Iskut Trail and River Adventures

ADDRESS: 1103-207 W. Hastings St.   **CONTACT:** Hedi Kottner

CITY: Vancouver   **TITLE:** Promoting agent

STATE: B.C., Canada   **ZIP:** V6B 1H7   **TELEPHONE:** (604) 669-5175

NUMBER OF YEARS IN BUSINESS: 3   **NUMBER OF STAFF:** 7-9

SPECIALIZING IN: Trailriding, rafting, hiking

SPECIAL PHILOSOPHY, CREDO, GOALS BEHIND BUSINESS: To protect wilderness from destruction (dams, mining). The more people who see this area, the better the chance of protection

Photo: Hedi Kottner

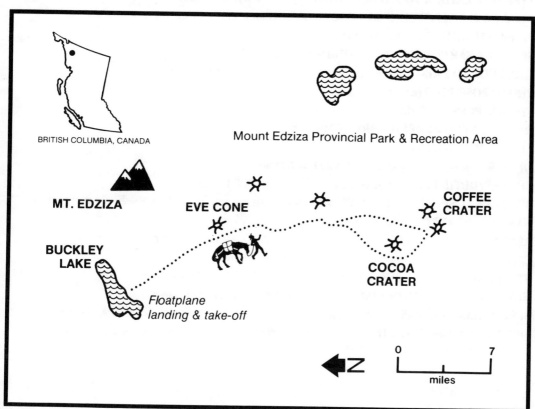

BRITISH COLUMBIA, CANADA

Mount Edziza Provincial Park & Recreation Area

MT. EDZIZA

EVE CONE

COFFEE CRATER

BUCKLEY LAKE

COCOA CRATER

Floatplane landing & take-off

N

0   7
miles

63

HAVASUPAI HIKING/HORSE CAMPING

We walk or ride horseback the seven and a half miles from Hilltop, enjoying the wonderland home of the Supai Indians. We pass through redrock cliffs, crystalline rivers, pass Indian gardens and green trees. The warmth of the village is left behind, however, as we move down the canyon about two miles until we reach our camp based near the 115-foot high Havasu Falls. Camp is made and punctuated with good food and comfort next to the lovely pools formed by travertine in the water. Over the next few days, we will appreciate five striking waterfalls ranging from 50-200 feet high, hike to view points and antiquities, swim everywhere along the river and sometimes just loaf next to a favorite waterfall. Supai ideally suits those who want to lay back and commune with nature, swim and hike. Evenings are spiced with canyon tales, lore and legends and walks in the night-time beauty of the canyon and river. Campers can join in camp cooking and clean up, visit the Supais and fellow campers, or enjoy solitude. The guide has over 30 years experience and will take hikers on treks suited to their abilities. The trip back out to Hilltop is a sad culture shock because you have just visited Shangri-la.

LENGTH OF TRIP: 5 days   **DEPARTURE DATES:** Summer

TOTAL COST: $450   **TYPE OF PAYMENT ACCEPTED:** Check, cash

RESERVATIONS/DEPOSIT: 50% with reservation

CANCELLATION POLICY: No refund unless space is filled

DEPARTURE LOCATION: Hilltop, AZ   **NEAREST AIRPORT:** Phoenix, AZ

TRANSPORTATION INFORMATION: Suggest weekly car rental

HEALTH, FITNESS OR AGE REQUIREMENTS: Must be capable of walking 3 miles

TYPE OF WEATHER TO EXPECT: Warm to hot, comfortable nights

BEST TYPE OF CLOTHING AND FOOTWEAR: Hiking shoes, swimming gear

PERSONAL GEAR REQUIRED: Swimming shoes

SPECIAL GEAR/EQUIPMENT REQUIRED: Lightweight tent

WHAT NOT TO BRING: Heavy hiking boots, booze, cold weather clothes

PHOTO POSSIBILITIES: Fantastic

FISHING POSSIBILITIES: Fair

REPRESENTATIVE MENU—BREAKFAST: Eggs, bacon, sourdough

LUNCH: Pack own from variety

DINNER: Steak, Dutch oven baking, salad, vegetables

CHORES/DUTIES GUESTS ARE EXPECTED TO HELP WITH: None

ADDITIONAL SPECIAL INFORMATION: Those with extreme fear of heights should avoid Supai

NAME OF OUTFITTER: Adventure Trails, Inc.

ADDRESS: P.O. Box 1494   **CONTACT:** Dana W. Burden

CITY: Wickenburg   **TITLE:** President/guide

STATE: Arizona   **ZIP:** 85358   **TELEPHONE:** (602) 684-3106

NUMBER OF YEARS IN BUSINESS: 4   **NUMBER OF STAFF:** Varies

SPECIALIZING IN: Trail rides by horse or mule, camping, hiking in Havasupai, Grand Canyon

SPECIAL PHILOSOPHY, CREDO, GOALS BEHIND BUSINESS: Provide opportunity for people to visit exotic destinations by horse, preferably their own

Photo: Joseph Daniel

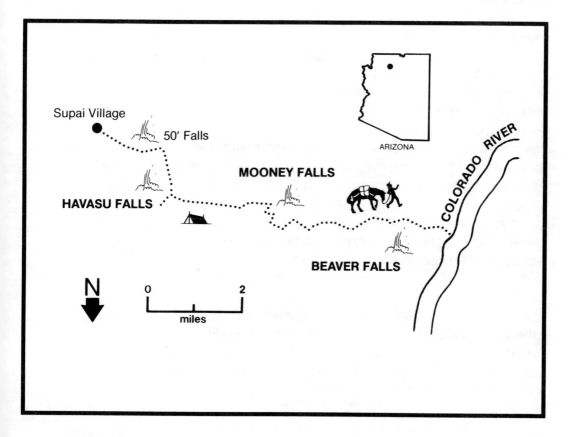

Supai Village
50' Falls
MOONEY FALLS
HAVASU FALLS
BEAVER FALLS
COLORADO RIVER
ARIZONA
N
0   2
miles

HORSEPACKING TO ERICKSON BASIN

We arrive in base camp in Hoyt Canyon, curious about this horsepacking trip into the lakes country of Utah's high Uintas. Horsepacking has the reputation of being cadillac camping, so we figure we'll fare okay, no matter what lies over the next mountain. The first camp is on a pretty lake just a couple of hours out of base camp, enough time in the saddle to get acquainted with our four-legged friends and work up a brisk appetite for a Dutch oven dinner with Bannock bread, fresh squash and a garden salad. Bedrolls are already spread in tents with floors and screened doors. By 10 the next morning, breakfast is a good feeling inside, tents are struck, bedrolls rolled and pack animals loaded. Soon there is a call to cinch up and mount up and we move onto a spike camp at Yellow Pine Lakes. It is midafternoon when we descend from the ridge and reach these two sky-blue lakes. The next day we lay over, exploring on foot, riding out to a fishing hole for Brookies and relaxing. The third day we move again, this time reaching our destination of Erickson Basin where you feel you might be the first white man to tread. By day 10, we are fast friends with our horses, camping is routine, appetites are astounding, time is no longer a concern and we hate to see it end.

LENGTH OF TRIP: 10 days   **DEPARTURE DATES:** Autumn/special arrangement

TOTAL COST: $900   **TYPE OF PAYMENT ACCEPTED:** Check, cash, t.c.

RESERVATIONS/DEPOSIT: $100 deposit 10 days after booking

CANCELLATION POLICY: Deposit refunded on 30 days' notice

DEPARTURE LOCATION: Kamas, UT   **NEAREST AIRPORT:** Salt Lake City, UT

TRANSPORTATION INFORMATION: Limo; Park City Transportation Inc., $12.50 each way with party of four or more

HEALTH, FITNESS OR AGE REQUIREMENTS: Normal physical condition

TYPE OF WEATHER TO EXPECT: Warm days, cool nights

BEST TYPE OF CLOTHING AND FOOTWEAR: Jeans, long-sleeve shirt, hiking or cowboy boots

PERSONAL GEAR REQUIRED: Personal duffle

SPECIAL GEAR/EQUIPMENT REQUIRED: None

WHAT NOT TO BRING: Junk food

PHOTO POSSIBILITIES: Fantastic

FISHING POSSIBILITIES: Good   **LICENSE REQUIREMENTS:** 2, 5 or 15-day, under $1

BEST TYPE OF FISHING TACKLE: Collapsible spin rod and reel with mepps, flat fish, finn lures

REPRESENTATIVE MENU—BREAKFAST: Hot cereal, meat, eggs, pancakes, coffee

LUNCH: Sandwiches, carrot sticks, cookies, fruit

DINNER: Chicken, beef, steak

CHORES/DUTIES GUESTS ARE EXPECTED TO HELP WITH: Pitch tent

NAME OF OUTFITTER: Piute Creek Outfitters Inc.

ADDRESS: Rt. 1A   **CONTACT:** Arch and Barbara Arnold

CITY: Kamas   **TITLE:** Owners, operators

STATE: Utah   **ZIP:** 84036   **TELEPHONE:** (801) 783-4317; 486-2607

NUMBER OF YEARS IN BUSINESS: 10   **NUMBER OF STAFF:** 4

SPECIALIZING IN: Horsepacking in the wilderness of the Wasatch National Forest

SPECIAL PHILOSOPHY, CREDO, GOALS BEHIND BUSINESS: Low-impact camping, self-sufficiency, guest participation where inclination and ability indicate

Photo: Piute Creek Outfitters

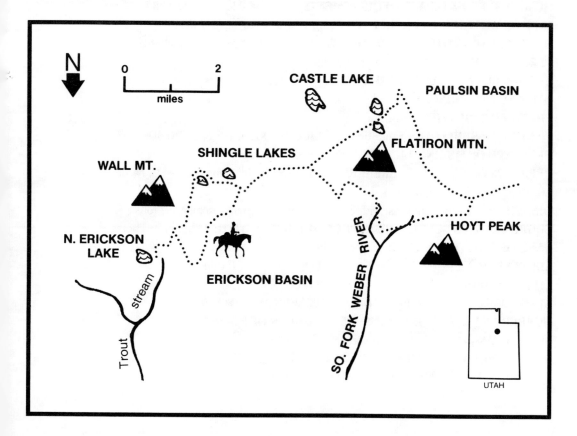

N

0   2
miles

CASTLE LAKE

PAULSIN BASIN

FLATIRON MTN.

SHINGLE LAKES

WALL MT.

HOYT PEAK

N. ERICKSON LAKE

stream

ERICKSON BASIN

SO. FORK WEBER RIVER

Trout

UTAH

SAWTOOTH WILDERNESS PACK TRIP

After meeting our guests the night before in Stanley, Idaho, we move out the next morning to our starting point, Pettit Lake. Here we will join the rest of the crew and the trusty steeds. Bring carrots and sugar cubes; horses like to be bribed! After packing the horses, we head up the canyon to Toxaway Lake, riding past waterfalls and other small no-name ponds. We break for lunch before riding over Sand Mountain Pass and onto our base camp at Edun Lake. The next three days are spent riding the open country to new lakes, fishing for trout, admiring the wildflowers, glissading the snowfields, hiking to hidden meadows, taking a swim and enjoying the sunshine. Your guide can take you to Glenns Peak, which is easily conquered, even by little old ladies. The view from the top is worth every terrifying minute as you look 360 degrees to count the numerous lakes. Time always goes too fast in the high country. The last day travelling to Pettit Lake, we cross over Sand Mountain Pass again, then travel back up Snowyside Peak Pass, around Snowyside Peak. This is your last chance to see a mountain goat before dropping into the glacial canyon that holds Twin and Alice lakes. Arriving back at Pettit Lake, it's time to kiss your horse goodbye and trade addresses with your new friends.

LENGTH OF TRIP: 5 days

DEPARTURE DATES: Sept. 10-Oct. 10

TOTAL COST: $475

TYPE OF PAYMENT ACCEPTED: Any

RESERVATIONS/DEPOSIT: 25% deposit 30 days prior to departure

CANCELLATION POLICY: After 30 days, forfeit deposit

DEPARTURE LOCATION: Stanley, ID   **NEAREST AIRPORT:** Boise, ID

TRANSPORTATION INFORMATION: National Car Rental in Boise has drop-off in Stanley

HEALTH, FITNESS OR AGE REQUIREMENTS: Must be able to ride and hike

TYPE OF WEATHER TO EXPECT: Cool sunny days, occasional showers

BEST TYPE OF CLOTHING AND FOOTWEAR: Hard-soled boots, warm clothes

PERSONAL GEAR REQUIRED: Personal duffle, sleeping bag

SPECIAL GEAR/EQUIPMENT REQUIRED: Rain gear, sunglasses

WHAT NOT TO BRING: Tape decks, pets, radios

PHOTO POSSIBILITIES: Fantastic

FISHING POSSIBILITIES: Fantastic   **LICENSE REQUIREMENTS:** ID

BEST TYPE OF FISHING TACKLE: Fly fishing or spin cast

REPRESENTATIVE MENU—BREAKFAST: Homemade cinnamon rolls, eggs, bacon, coffee

LUNCH: Sandwiches, chips, fruit, cookies

DINNER: Stuffed chicken breast with cheese sausage, rice, salad, homemade rolls

CHORES/DUTIES GUESTS ARE EXPECTED TO HELP WITH: Community chores

NAME OF OUTFITTER: Mystic Saddle Ranch

ADDRESS: P.O. Box 165-AA   **CONTACT:** Jeff Bitton

CITY: Mtn. Home   **TITLE:** Owner

STATE: Idaho   **ZIP:** 83647   **TELEPHONE:** (208) 587-5937

NUMBER OF YEARS IN BUSINESS: 15   **NUMBER OF STAFF:** 6-8

SPECIALIZING IN: Packtrips by horsepack

SPECIAL PHILOSOPHY, CREDO, GOALS BEHIND BUSINESS: Our goal is showing our guests "our" wilderness while expanding their understanding of their surroundings

Photo: Mystic Saddle Ranch

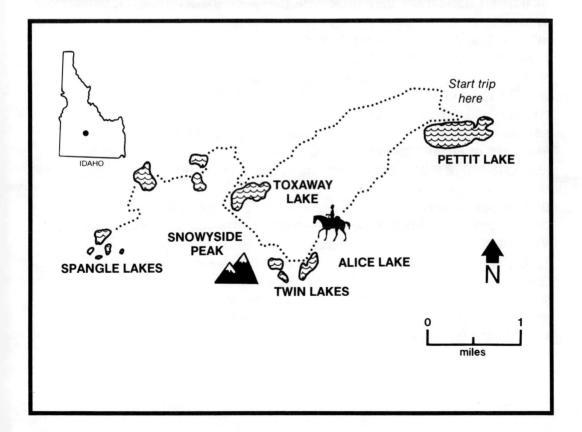

Start trip here

PETTIT LAKE

IDAHO

TOXAWAY LAKE

SNOWYSIDE PEAK

SPANGLE LAKES

ALICE LAKE

TWIN LAKES

N

0   1
miles

 THREE PARK SPECTACULAR

Few experiences compare with a 230-mile horsepack adventure. For 10 days you will be guided through a wilderness that includes hidden bedrock canyons near Utah's Zion National Park and the painted limestone spires of Bryce. This country has changed little since it was first experienced by explorers centuries earlier. During the first week you will make camp at the edge of a lush mountain meadow and follow the trail through dark-fringed forests and quaking aspen stands. Along the way, old homesteads and remnants of ancient Indian settlements are intriguing reminders of a frontier past. The scenery makes a dramatic change when we reach the high desert grasslands and a horse-drawn chuckwagon joins the trek. Hawks, wild turkeys and pronghorn antelope are often seen during the last days. And don't be surprised if the stories around the campfire are interrupted by the occasional howl of a coyote. On the final morning, pause to reflect on this sweeping expanse of land as the sun rises and glints across the walls of Toroweap. The Grand Canyon makes a fitting conclusion to your introduction to the old ways of the older West. The main difference in your modern experience of it will be the warm sleeping bag and gourmet meals of steak, Dutch oven potatoes and fresh fruit.

LENGTH OF TRIP: 10 days **DEPARTURE DATES:** May 20, Aug. 19, Sept. 24

TOTAL COST: $660 **TYPE OF PAYMENT ACCEPTED:** Check, cash, t.c.

RESERVATIONS/DEPOSIT: 1/3 deposit 60 days prior to departure

CANCELLATION POLICY: No refund

DEPARTURE LOCATION: Kanab, UT **NEAREST AIRPORT:** St. George, UT

TRANSPORTATION INFORMATION: Free pickup or rent car

HEALTH, FITNESS OR AGE REQUIREMENTS: Good health; 9 years old minimum

TYPE OF WEATHER TO EXPECT: Dry, warm days, cool nights

BEST TYPE OF CLOTHING AND FOOTWEAR: Western wear, riding boots, head gear

PERSONAL GEAR REQUIRED: Personal duffle, rain gear

SPECIAL GEAR/EQUIPMENT REQUIRED: Camping gear, tent

WHAT NOT TO BRING: 30 lbs. baggage limit

PHOTO POSSIBILITIES: Fantastic

FISHING POSSIBILITIES: Aug. trip only **LICENSE REQUIREMENTS:** Utah

BEST TYPE OF FISHING TACKLE: Pack rod

REPRESENTATIVE MENU—BREAKFAST: Bacon, eggs, hot cakes, coffee

LUNCH: Sandwiches, fruit

DINNER: Steak, Dutch oven potatoes, vegetable, cobbler, coffee, lemonade

CHORES/DUTIES GUESTS ARE EXPECTED TO HELP WITH: Care for own horse, tent set-up

NAME OF OUTFITTER: Honeymoon Trail Co.

ADDRESS: P.O. Box A **CONTACT:** Mel Heaton

CITY: Moccasin **TITLE:** Owner/operator

STATE: Arizona **ZIP:** 86022 **TELEPHONE:** (602) 634-7292

NUMBER OF YEARS IN BUSINESS: 11 **NUMBER OF STAFF:** 5-40

SPECIALIZING IN: Covered wagon treks and horsepack trips

Photo: Honeymoon Trail Co.

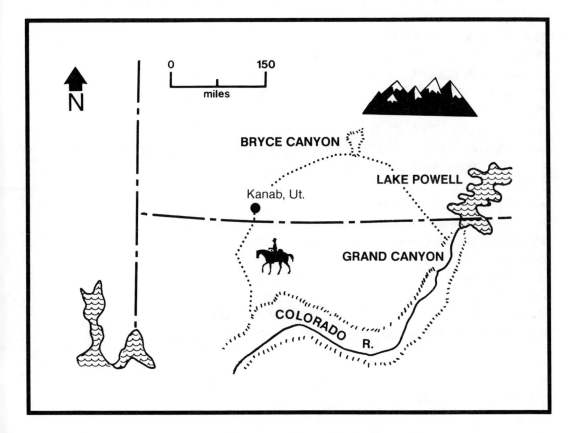

HUMMINGBIRD BASIN HORSEPACKING

The city dust will have barely settled on your shoulders when you hit the trail in this horsepacking adventure in the Absaroka/Beartooth Wilderness. The Absaroka Mountains tower above us, seemingly blocking our forward trail. Your sturdy mount capably finds sure footing as we maneuver the switchback trails seeking the 11,000-foot pass of Mt. Wallace. As you reach down and give him a pat on the neck, a new friendship will blossom and grow with each day of this week-long trip. Upon reaching your goal, you will be well rewarded with a 360-degree view of the majestic wilderness you are just beginning to explore. Days will be spent riding through the heart of the Absaroka/Beartooth Wilderness. From the lush forested floors of the river canyons to the alpine tundra and snow-covered slopes above timberline, you will experience a beauty and solitude so rare today. As you lie back next to the glowing campfire after a hearty meal, it will be hard to recall just what those pressing problems of days past were. The star-filled heavens, the lonesome melody of a coyote, and the comradeship of fellow adventurers are all that make up your world this night. You will emerge from this wilderness with an improved outlook on life.

LENGTH OF TRIP: 7 days   **DEPARTURE DATES:** August 12-18; August 20-26

TOTAL COST: $595   **TYPE OF PAYMENT ACCEPTED:** Cash, check

RESERVATIONS/DEPOSIT: $200 deposit. Balance due two weeks before trip.

CANCELLATION POLICY: Refunds for cancellation or no-show if trip is filled.

DEPARTURE LOCATION: Livingston, MT   **NEAREST AIRPORT:** Bozeman

TRANSPORTATION INFORMATION: Local motel provides pickup from airport for $20/carload

HEALTH, FITNESS OR AGE REQUIREMENTS: Able to ride 2-4 hours minimum daily. Under 14 years old must have prior approval

TYPE OF WEATHER TO EXPECT: Warm days, cool to cold nights, possible rain

BEST TYPE OF CLOTHING AND FOOTWEAR: Comfortable, durable. Hiking and riding boots

PERSONAL GEAR REQUIRED: Sleeping bag, personal duffle (sugg. list provided)

SPECIAL GEAR/EQUIPMENT REQUIRED: Fishing gear and license

WHAT NOT TO BRING: Limited to two duffle bags, unless prearranged

PHOTO POSSIBILITIES: Limitless

FISHING POSSIBILITIES: Fantastic   **LICENSE REQUIREMENTS:** Weekly $20

BEST TYPE OF FISHING TACKLE: Spinning or fly, breakdown poles, hard cases

REPRESENTATIVE MENU—BREAKFAST: Eggs, potatoes, bacon

LUNCH: Sandwich, fruit, candy

DINNER: Meat, vegetable, potato, dessert

CHORES/DUTIES GUESTS ARE EXPECTED TO HELP WITH: None, but welcome to help

NAME OF OUTFITTER: Absaroka Outfitters and Guide Service

ADDRESS: Box AM   **CONTACT:** Allen Russell

CITY: Clyde Park   **TITLE:** Owner/operator

STATE: Montana   **ZIP:** 59018   **TELEPHONE:** (406) 686-4732; (415) 924-4391

NUMBER OF YEARS IN BUSINESS: 6   **NUMBER OF STAFF:** 10

SPECIALIZING IN: Wilderness horsepack adventures, photography, fishing

SPECIAL PHILOSOPHY, CREDO, GOALS BEHIND BUSINESS: A journey into the Absaroka-Beartooth Wilderness is a step back in time, where man himself is a visitor who does not remain. This extraordinary country's magic is revealed only to those who seek. After you have touched it, and it you, its spirit will remain with you

Photo: Absaroka Outfitters

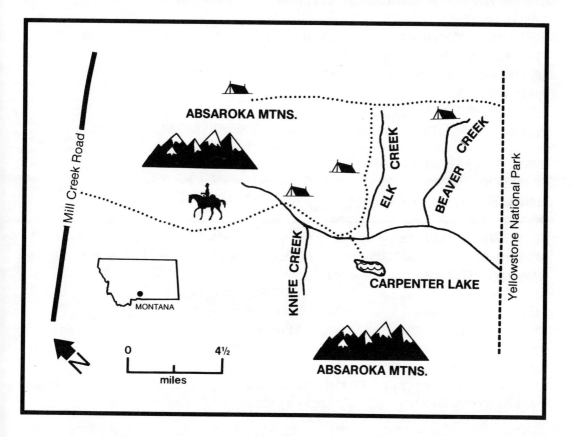

MT. ZIRKLE WILDERNESS AREA

Most of our summer horsepack trips are in the Mt. Zirkel Wilderness Area, 114 square miles of streams and lakes for fantastic trout fishing in the Rocky Mountains. The crew is experienced and I have been hunting, guiding and packing horses for over 30 years. Trips can be custom-designed, but on any trip lasting three to five days, you can expect to pack into an area which would have good fishing for Brookies, German Browns, Native Cutthroats and Rainbow trout. We would also take advantage of riding trails to Mt. Snow Glaciers and down into valleys carpeted with wildflowers. The days are sunny and warm and the evenings are refreshingly cool. Pollution, smog and the bustling of the busy world are left behind as you spend the afternoon fishing, hiking and observing deer, elk, and an abundance of all animals which inhabit the area. From the beautiful region in northwestern Colorado, you will witness spectacular scenery that extends into Wyoming, Utah and Colorado. We provide horses for riding and packing equipment, as well as food, cooking and eating utensils, tents, etc., but you will be responsible for your own sleeping bag. Please write or call us, telling us about your group and what you want, and we will try to arrange a trip to fit your particular wishes.

LENGTH OF TRIP: 3-7 days

TOTAL COST: $55/day per person

RESERVATIONS/DEPOSIT: 50% ASAP

CANCELLATION POLICY: Total refund if space is filled

DEPARTURE LOCATION: Triangle 3 Ranch

TRANSPORTATION INFORMATION: Will pick up

HEALTH, FITNESS OR AGE REQUIREMENTS: Must be physically able to ride horses

TYPE OF WEATHER TO EXPECT: Warm days, cool nights

BEST TYPE OF CLOTHING AND FOOTWEAR: Long-sleeved shirts, warm coats, heels on boots

PERSONAL GEAR REQUIRED: Sleeping bag, fishing gear

SPECIAL GEAR/EQUIPMENT REQUIRED: None

WHAT NOT TO BRING: Keep luggage at 40 lbs.

PHOTO POSSIBILITIES: Fantastic

FISHING POSSIBILITIES: Fantastic

BEST TYPE OF FISHING TACKLE: Casting, fly rods for trout

REPRESENTATIVE MENU—BREAKFAST: Bacon, eggs, pancakes, french toast

LUNCH: Sandwiches, munchies

DINNER: Steak, baked potatoes, vegetables

CHORES/DUTIES GUESTS ARE EXPECTED TO HELP WITH: Relaxing and enjoying themselves

ADDITIONAL SPECIAL INFORMATION: We have excellent guides and well broke mountain horses

NAME OF OUTFITTER: Triangle 3 Ranch

ADDRESS: Box 14

CITY: Steamboat Springs

STATE: Colorado   **ZIP:** 80477

NUMBER OF YEARS IN BUSINESS: 21

DEPARTURE DATES: Client's choice

TYPE OF PAYMENT ACCEPTED: Any

NEAREST AIRPORT: Steamboat Springs, CO

LICENSE REQUIREMENT: CO resident or non-resident, $3-35

CONTACT: Delby Heid

TITLE: Owner

TELEPHONE: (303) 879-1257

NUMBER OF STAFF: 4

SPECIALIZING IN: Horsepack trips in the Mt. Zirkle Wilderness Area

SPECIAL PHILOSOPHY, CREDO, GOALS BEHIND BUSINESS: Taking small groups and giving them lots of personal attention

Photo: Del Heid

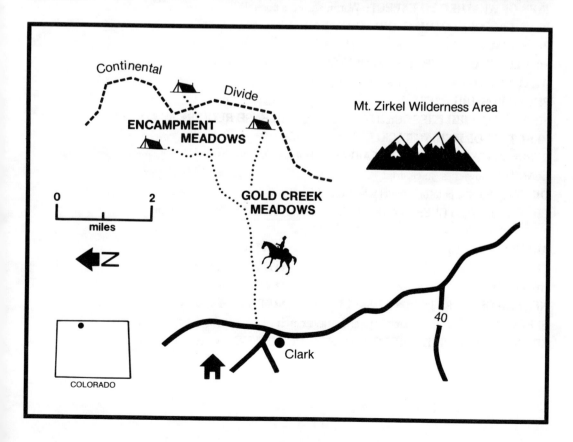

Continental

Divide

ENCAMPMENT MEADOWS

Mt. Zirkel Wilderness Area

0   2
miles

GOLD CREEK MEADOWS

N

COLORADO

Clark

40

HELLS CANYON ON HORSEBACK

This adventure begins immediately because Red's Horse Ranch in the Eagle Cap Wilderness Area is inaccessible by road! After flying or packing into the ranch, you prepare for Hells Canyon on horseback. The ride starts in the Imnoha Canyon, which was part of the noble Nez Perce Indians' homeland. We climb on horseback up the steep walls to the summit between Amineha Canyon and Hells Canyon, and then enjoy the breathtaking experience of looking down into the deepest canyon of North America. We descend into the depths of Hells Canyon and as we work our way down to the Snake River, we may glimpse deer, elk and bear. Wildflowers burst into color around us and deep side canyons wind away, inviting exploration amid the fantastic scenery. The horses lead us along 80 miles of the canyon, passing beneath sheer cliffs that extend up and out of sight. We set up camp each night and try to catch fish that we can cook over the open fire to eat for dinner. If nothing bites, there's always steak and potatoes. Other meals include hot cakes, eggs, bacon, sandwiches and fruits to satisfy the huge appetites we develop on horseback as we journey through some of Oregon's most impressive wilderness.

LENGTH OF TRIP: 7-10 days

DEPARTURE DATES: May 16-26

TOTAL COST: $546-780

TYPE OF PAYMENT ACCEPTED: Check, cr. cards

RESERVATIONS/DEPOSIT: 40% deposit at least 30 days before trip

CANCELLATION POLICY: Forfeit deposit if less than 30 days before trip

DEPARTURE LOCATION: Enterprise, OR

NEAREST AIRPORT: Pendleton, OR

TRANSPORTATION INFORMATION: $45 fee for transportation from Pendleton

HEALTH, FITNESS OR AGE REQUIREMENTS: None

TYPE OF WEATHER TO EXPECT: Warm, showers possible

BEST TYPE OF CLOTHING AND FOOTWEAR: Jeans, riding boots

PERSONAL GEAR REQUIRED: Sleeping bag, personal gear, sunglasses

SPECIAL GEAR/EQUIPMENT REQUIRED: Rain coat, warm jacket

WHAT NOT TO BRING: 70 lbs. limit per person

PHOTO POSSIBILITIES: Great

FISHING POSSIBILITIES: Great

LICENSE REQUIREMENTS: 10 day

BEST TYPE OF FISHING TACKLE: Spinner outfit

REPRESENTATIVE MENU—BREAKFAST: Hot cakes, eggs, bacon

LUNCH: Sandwiches, juice, fruit

DINNER: Steaks, potatoes, vegetable, fruit, dessert

CHORES/DUTIES GUESTS ARE EXPECTED TO HELP WITH: Pitch tents

NAME OF OUTFITTER: High Country Outfitters, Inc.

ADDRESS: Box 26

CONTACT: Cal Henry

CITY: Joseph

TITLE: President

STATE: Oregon **ZIP:** 97846

TELEPHONE: (503) 432-9171

NUMBER OF YEARS IN BUSINESS: 21

NUMBER OF STAFF: 4-10

SPECIALIZING IN: Horseback trips and guest ranch

SPECIAL PHILOSOPHY, CREDO, GOALS BEHIND BUSINESS: To help people see the great outdoors

Photo: Cal Henry

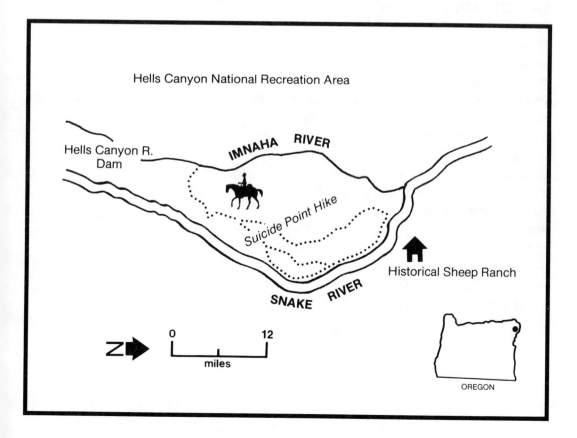

Hells Canyon National Recreation Area

Hells Canyon R. Dam

IMNAHA RIVER

Suicide Point Hike

Historical Sheep Ranch

SNAKE RIVER

N

0   12
miles

OREGON

🐎 6-DAY FULL CIRCLE RIDE

Whether you are an accomplished rider or a novice, experienced guides and packers will ensure you have an authentic western outdoors pack trip. Banff National Park, the gateway to remote wilderness areas, has been the base of Warner and MacKenzie Guiding and Outfitting for 22 years. On the first day, riders meet at the Outfitting office to be transported by van to the trailhead corral at Mt. Norquay. There they are met by their guides and mount up for the 11-mile ride over Elk Lake Summit between Brewster Mountain and Cascade Mountain, to Stony Creek Camp. The next morning a ride heads upstream to the origin of Stony Creek and returns to camp for the night. On the third day, the riders roll up their duffels and mount their trusty steeds for the 10-mile ride to Flints Park camp. Riders have a choice on the fourth day to travel to either Block Mountain or Cuthead Viewpoint, both popular spots for the photographer and fisherman. Mystic Camp is the destination on day five and the last night of camping of the Full Circle ride. The final day of riding is a scenic nine-mile trip back to Mt. Norquay and the trailhead corral. The circle has been completed on this horseback riding wilderness adventure amid splendid mountain scenery.

LENGTH OF TRIP: 6 days

DEPARTURE DATES: Saturdays, Wednesdays

TOTAL COST: $477 Canadian

TYPE OF PAYMENT ACCEPTED: Any

RESERVATIONS/DEPOSIT: $100 when booking

CANCELLATION POLICY: Nonrefundable

DEPARTURE LOCATION: Banff, Alberta   **NEAREST AIRPORT:** Calbary, Alberta

TRANSPORTATION INFORMATION: Bus

HEALTH, FITNESS OR AGE REQUIREMENTS: None

TYPE OF WEATHER TO EXPECT: Warm days, cool nights

BEST TYPE OF CLOTHING AND FOOTWEAR: Casual, warm clothing; riding boots; rain gear

PERSONAL GEAR REQUIRED: Sleeping bag, air mattress

SPECIAL GEAR/EQUIPMENT REQUIRED: None

PHOTO POSSIBILITIES: Fantastic

FISHING POSSIBILITIES: Fantastic   **LICENSE REQUIREMENTS:** Canada National Park $4

BEST TYPE OF FISHING TACKLE: Fly fishing

REPRESENTATIVE MENU—BREAKFAST: Full course

LUNCH: Picnic style

DINNER: Full course

CHORES/DUTIES GUESTS ARE EXPECTED TO HELP WITH: None

NAME OF OUTFITTER: Holiday on Horseback

ADDRESS: Box 2280   **CONTACT:** Ron Warner

CITY: Banff   **TITLE:** President

STATE: Alberta, Canada **ZIP:** T0L 0C0   **TELEPHONE:** (403) 762-4551

NUMBER OF YEARS IN BUSINESS: 22   **NUMBER OF STAFF:** 50

SPECIALIZING IN: Horseback riding, wilderness adventure

Photo: Bruno Engler

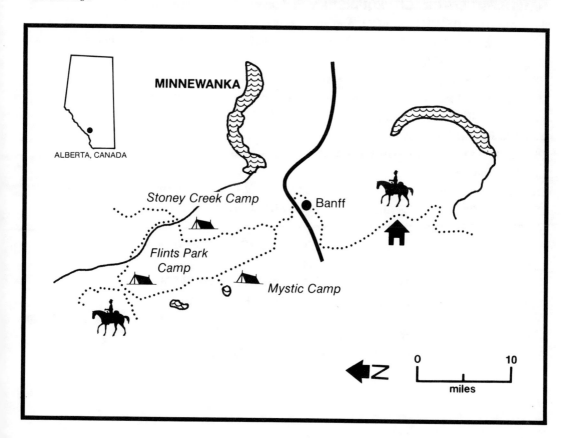

MINNEWANKA

ALBERTA, CANADA

Stoney Creek Camp

Banff

Flints Park
Camp

Mystic Camp

N

0   10
miles

TETON PRAIRIE SCHOONER HOLIDAY

Like "sails on a sea of grass" is the description of covered wagons that inspired the name prairie schooners. A nation moved west through hardships and trials, gaining a strength which still survives today. Venture into the past and relive the experiences of early pioneers who expanded our nation's frontiers. Modern-day pioneers are met in Jackson, Wyoming and transported to the wagon train. At the call "roll the wagons," the prairie schooners line out for the trek along the backroad of the Targhee National Forest. Gentle riding horses are available for those who would like to ride in rotation with other guests. The wagons travel to a new camp each day. Those who like to ride horseback can enjoy daily rides from camp into the beautiful surrounding countryside. Two evenings are spent on the shores of high mountain lakes. Once camp is reached, you will have time to hike, swim, ride or just relax. Tasty meals for hearty appetites are rustled up in Dutch ovens over the open fire. Indians and mountain men are passing visitors. Your evenings will be passed singing around the campfire, listening to yarns about the Old West and enjoying good old-fashioned hoe-down square dancing. Then sleep under the open sky or in the covered wagons.

LENGTH OF TRIP: 4 days

DEPARTURE DATES: June 18-August 27

TOTAL COST: $325 adults; 10% discount children 4-14 years old

TYPE OF PAYMENT ACCEPTED: Any

RESERVATIONS/DEPOSIT: $100 deposit 10 days after reservation

CANCELLATION POLICY: After 30 days, deposit is forfeited

DEPARTURE LOCATION: Jackson, WY

NEAREST AIRPORT: Jackson, WY

TRANSPORTATION INFORMATION: Free minibus

HEALTH, FITNESS OR AGE REQUIREMENTS: None

TYPE OF WEATHER TO EXPECT: Warm days, cool nights, some showers

BEST TYPE OF CLOTHING AND FOOTWEAR: Comfortable shoes, 2 pairs jeans, 2 long-sleeved shirts

PERSONAL GEAR REQUIRED: Personal duffle, flashlight, camera, film, towel, soap, etc.

SPECIAL GEAR/EQUIPMENT REQUIRED: All furnished

WHAT NOT TO BRING: No suitcases—duffle bags only

PHOTO POSSIBILITIES: Fantastic

FISHING POSSIBILITIES: Poor

REPRESENTATIVE MENU—BREAKFAST: Hot cakes, bacon, hashbrowns

LUNCH: Sloppy joes

DINNER: Barbequed chicken, baked beans, fruit salad, vegetable, coffee, punch

CHORES/DUTIES GUESTS ARE EXPECTED TO HELP WITH: As many or few as desired

NAME OF OUTFITTER: Bar-T-Five, Inc.

ADDRESS: Box 2140

CONTACT: Bill or Joyce Thomas

CITY: Jackson

TITLE: Owners

STATE: Wyoming   **ZIP:** 83001

TELEPHONE: (307) 733-5386

NUMBER OF YEARS IN BUSINESS: 11

NUMBER OF STAFF: 20

SPECIALIZING IN: Teton Prairie Schooner Holiday, Jackson Hole Horseback Holiday, Covered Wagon Cookout and Wild West Show

SPECIAL PHILOSOPHY, CREDO, GOALS BEHIND BUSINESS: Rough it in comfort

Photo: Bar-T-Five Outfitters

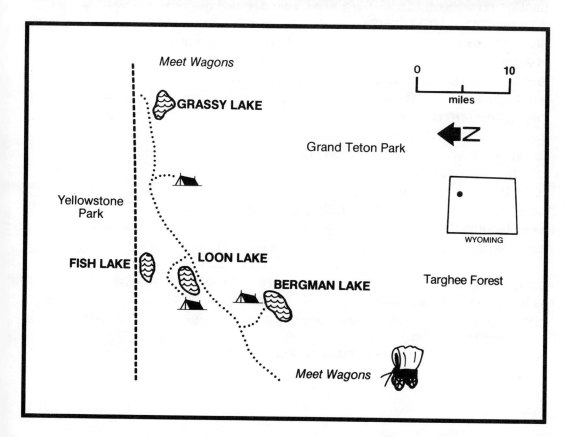

Meet Wagons

GRASSY LAKE

Grand Teton Park

0   10
miles

N

WYOMING

Yellowstone
Park

FISH LAKE

LOON LAKE

BERGMAN LAKE

Targhee Forest

Meet Wagons

81

YELLOWSTONE HOTPOT ADVENTURE

After a quick equipment check in preparation for the next week's journey, a farewell gourmet dinner is presented to the skiers at Lone Mountain Ranch. For the next seven days there will be no more tables, chairs, tablecloths or even choice of dinner. The following morning we head out via bus for West Yellowstone and then take the over-the-snow coach to Old Faithful and the snow-blanketed interior of Yellowstone National Park. Leaving the din of snowmobiles behind we climb into our cross-country skis and hoist our 55 pound packs. The first night's camp is quickly reached along the Firehole River. The guides efficiently set up camp and soon we are sipping hot tea and stirring the pot of hot shrimp curry. For the next two days we cross and recross the Continental Divide and are rewarded by Rocky Mountain vistas, buffalo grazing in the snow and thrilling downhill runs. We end our third day at Yellowstone's nirvana, Three River Junction. Here we spend two days wearing swimsuits and indulging in the sport of hotpotting. At the confluence of two very cold rivers and one very hot river lies a shallow pool perfectly heated to soothe tired muscles. Rejuvenated, we continue our skiing trek around the big game animals and thermal springs, returning tired but content at week's end to the ranch.

LENGTH OF TRIP: 6-7 days   **DEPARTURE DATES:** April

TOTAL COST: $95/person/day   **TYPE OF PAYMENT ACCEPTED:** Check, Visa, MC, AMEX

RESERVATIONS/DEPOSIT: 25% with reservation

CANCELLATION POLICY: Forfeit deposit

DEPARTURE LOCATION: Lone Mountain Ranch   **NEAREST AIRPORT:** Bozeman, Montana

TRANSPORTATION INFORMATION: Free pickup at airport

HEALTH, FITNESS OR AGE REQUIREMENTS: Good physical condition—strenuous trip

TYPE OF WEATHER TO EXPECT: 0-45° F

BEST TYPE OF CLOTHING AND FOOTWEAR: Layered cross-country ski clothes

PERSONAL GEAR REQUIRED: Sleeping bag, pad, personal duffle

SPECIAL GEAR/EQUIPMENT REQUIRED: Skis, boots, poles

WHAT NOT TO BRING: Heavy alpine skis converted for cross country

PHOTO POSSIBILITIES: Fantastic

FISHING POSSIBILITIES: None

REPRESENTATIVE MENU—BREAKFAST: Coffee, juice, omelette

LUNCH: Hot tea, juice, cheese

DINNER: Shrimp curry, rice, juice, tea, cheesecake

CHORES/DUTIES GUESTS ARE EXPECTED TO HELP WITH: None

NAME OF OUTFITTER: Lone Mountain Ranch

ADDRESS: Box 145   **CONTACT:** Steve Shimek

CITY: Big Sky   **TITLE:** Assistant Manager

STATE: Montana   **ZIP:** 59716   **TELEPHONE:** (406) 995-4644

NUMBER OF YEARS IN BUSINESS: 11   **NUMBER OF STAFF:** 40

SPECIALIZING IN: Cross-country skiing, wilderness skiing, helicopter nordic skiing, horseback riding, wilderness horsepacking

SPECIAL PHILOSOPHY, CREDO, GOALS BEHIND BUSINESS: Sensitivity and appreciation of wilderness

Photo: Lone Mountain Ranch

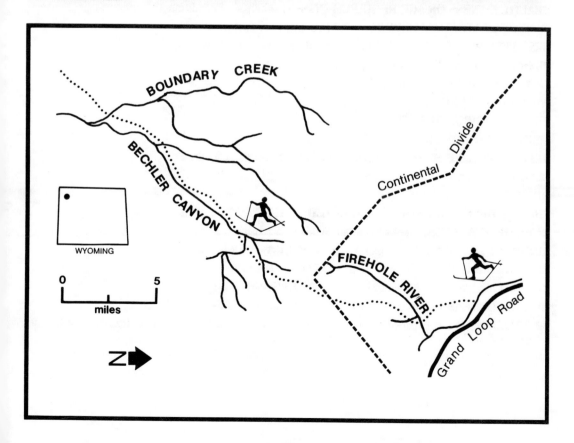

🎿 YELLOWSTONE SKI TOUR/SNOWSHOE

Rough it this New Year's Eve in Yellowstone National Park. This seven-day ski tour and snowshoe trip will be an adventure but still feature the pleasures of hot meals and warm beds. During the winter months Yellowstone reveals a different personality as one of nature's most precious sanctuaries. We tour along silent forest trails, past elk and bison wintering next to the warmth of the thermal springs. Geysers erupt as we glide past the spectacular display. We witness snow-sculptured geyser basins, dramatic frozen waterfalls and high alpine lakes in this whitewashed paradise. This tour is for beginners, and experienced instructors will guide the novice winter adventurers on wilderness treks into the backcountry. Plenty of time for practice is ensured before setting out into the fields. Ski and snowshoe rentals are available at Snow Lodge where we spend our nights and eat breakfast and dinner. Lunch is of the sack variety eaten on the trail. Evenings are spent around the Lodge's fireplace for story telling, singing and good conversation while sipping wine or warm drinks. Then guests retire to their dormitory-style rooms with shared bathroom facilities, and rest up for another day of exploring and fresh air in this wild area of northwest Wyoming.

LENGTH OF TRIP: 7 days **DEPARTURE DATES:** December

TOTAL COST: $445 **TYPE OF PAYMENT ACCEPTED:** Check

RESERVATIONS/DEPOSIT: $100 deposit 10 days prior to departure

CANCELLATION POLICY: Forfeit all monies paid

DEPARTURE LOCATION: Jackson, WY **NEAREST AIRPORT:** Jackson, WY

TRANSPORTATION INFORMATION: Airport limo $5

HEALTH, FITNESS OR AGE REQUIREMENTS: Good physical condition

TYPE OF WEATHER TO EXPECT: 0-32° F, sunny to snowstorms

BEST TYPE OF CLOTHING AND FOOTWEAR: Equipment list available

PERSONAL GEAR REQUIRED: Equipment list available

SPECIAL GEAR/EQUIPMENT REQUIRED: Cross-country skis, poles, boots

WHAT NOT TO BRING: Drugs, radio, gun, dog

PHOTO POSSIBILITIES: Fantastic

FISHING POSSIBILITIES: None

REPRESENTATIVE MENU—BREAKFAST: Varies at Lodge Restaurant

LUNCH: Sack lunch

DINNER: Varies at Lodge Restaurant

CHORES/DUTIES GUESTS ARE EXPECTED TO HELP WITH: None

NAME OF OUTFITTER: Rocky Mountain Wilderness Experience, Inc.

ADDRESS: Station #27, P.O. Box 63 **CONTACT:** Dick Rosenow

CITY: Lakewood **TITLE:** President

STATE: Colorado **ZIP:** 80215 **TELEPHONE:** (303) 232-0371

NUMBER OF YEARS IN BUSINESS: 15 **NUMBER OF STAFF:** 8

SPECIALIZING IN: Backpacking, mountain climbing school and trips, cross-country skiing and snowshoeing

SPECIAL PHILOSOPHY, CREDO, GOALS BEHIND BUSINESS: To provide an educational, instructional, quality wilderness experience for the beginner and experienced adventurer

Photo: Rocky Mountain Wilderness Experience

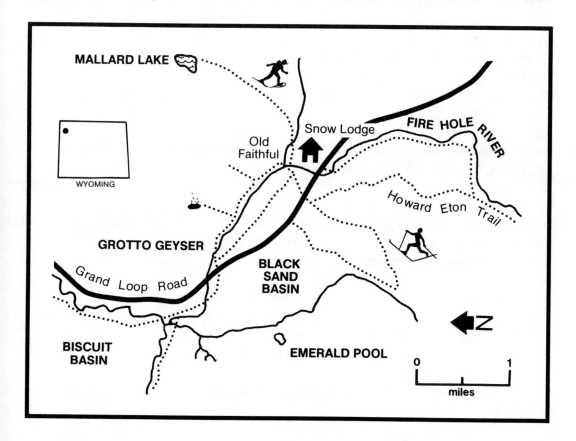

MALLARD LAKE

Snow Lodge

FIRE HOLE RIVER

Old
Faithful

WYOMING

Howard   Eton   Trail

GROTTO GEYSER

Grand   Loop   Road

BLACK
SAND
BASIN

N

BISCUIT
BASIN

EMERALD POOL

0   1
miles

GUNFLINT TRAIL SKI-THRU PROGRAM

Skiing all day in tracked trails, up hill and down, along ridgetops and through low-shaded spruce swamps, we began our Ski-Thru tour at one of the southernmost lodges on the Gunflint Trail. We returned to the lodge at dusk to warm up by our own woodstove with cups of hot spiced wine. All our meals were prepared for us and this night we had a delicious Lake Superior trout supper. The next day we skied again, and returned to the lodge to warm up in the sauna. On the third day, as we finished breakfast coffee, we watched a dog team race by the window. The sled dogs were our ride to Youngs' cabin. We stayed in a beautiful little room in their home and the dogs occasionally howled during the night. On the fourth day of the tour we trekked along the Banadad Trail, skiing 15 miles to one of the northern lodges. Ravens called overhead and chickadees and whiskey jacks followed us. We saw the deep punch-holes in the snow left by moose and the delicate tracks of mice and moles. When we arrived at the lodge, our car was waiting outside of our cabin. The next day we strapped snowshoes to our feet and climbed to the top of a palisade to gaze across white lakes and the green pine-covered hills of Canada. The next morning, we reluctantly left for home.

LENGTH OF TRIP: 5 days　　　　**DEPARTURE DATES:** Mid-December to early April

TOTAL COST: $198 per person　　　**TYPE OF PAYMENT ACCEPTED:** Check, Visa, MC

RESERVATIONS/DEPOSIT: $40 deposit within 7 days of reservation

CANCELLATION POLICY: Deposit is forfeited

DEPARTURE LOCATION: Any of 4 lodges on **NEAREST AIRPORT:** Duluth, MN
Gunflint Trail

TRANSPORTATION INFORMATION: Bus, rental car

HEALTH, FITNESS OR AGE REQUIREMENTS: Healthy, mid-teens and older

TYPE OF WEATHER TO EXPECT: Mild to cold winter weather, snow

BEST TYPE OF CLOTHING AND FOOTWEAR: Ski gear

PERSONAL GEAR REQUIRED: Personal duffle

SPECIAL GEAR/EQUIPMENT REQUIRED: Ski equipment (can be rented from outfitter)

WHAT NOT TO BRING: Pets

PHOTO POSSIBILITIES: Good

FISHING POSSIBILITIES: Ice Fishing　　　**LICENSE REQUIREMENTS:** MN $7.50-22.50

BEST TYPE OF FISHING TACKLE: Spoons, minnows

REPRESENTATIVE MENU—BREAKFAST: Eggs, bacon, rolls, drink

LUNCH: Sandwiches, fruit, chips, drink

DINNER: Steaks, salad, vegetable, homemade bread, dessert

CHORES/DUTIES GUESTS ARE EXPECTED TO HELP WITH: None

ADDITIONAL SPECIAL INFORMATION: Make sure car is in good condition

NAME OF OUTFITTER: Cross-country Ski-Thru Program

ADDRESS: GT 10　　　　**CONTACT:** Dave and Barb Tuttle

CITY: Grand Marais　　　**TITLE:** Owners, Bearskin Lodge Ski Touring Center

STATE: Minnesota　　**ZIP:** 55064　　**TELEPHONE:** (800) 328-3325

NUMBER OF YEARS IN BUSINESS: 11　**NUMBER OF STAFF:** 7

SPECIALIZING IN: Cross-country skiing

SPECIAL PHILOSOPHY, CREDO, GOALS BEHIND BUSINESS: To offer a comfortable wilderness experience

Photo: Bearskin Lodge

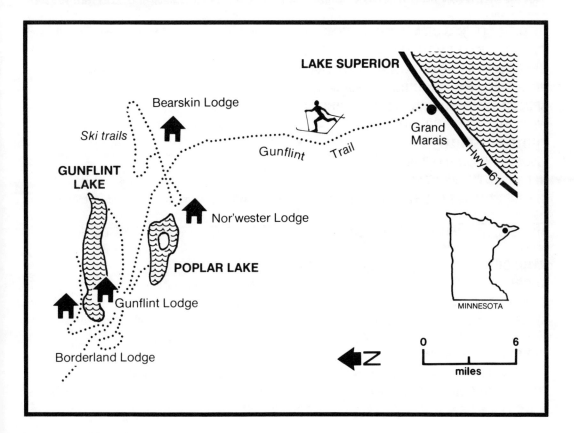

LAKE SUPERIOR

Bearskin Lodge

Ski trails

Gunflint Trail

Grand Marais

Hwy 61

GUNFLINT LAKE

Nor'wester Lodge

POPLAR LAKE

Gunflint Lodge

MINNESOTA

Borderland Lodge

N

0   6
miles

AROUND THE RIM SKI TOUR

A ski tour around the rim of Crater Lake is a 36-mile winter adventure for the hardy skier, and an outstanding experience totally beyond what the summer tourist finds. Vistas of the lake and Cascade mountain range change constantly as the tour swings close to the rim and meanders away again. At our departure from the Visitor Center in Rim Village, Mt. Shasta, Mt. McLoughlin and Union Peak may appear, setting the mood for entering the wilderness. The day-skiing areas are soon left behind as we traverse the steep slopes and cliff faces behind the highest peaks on the rim. The second morning we ski through forests of hemlock and red fir, highlighted by colorful rocks from the cataclysmic eruption of the ancient volcano Mt. Mazama, which created America's deepest lake. Our camp that night is near Mt. Scott, a distinctive twin-peaked mountain that is the highest peak in the park at 9,000 feet. We reach Kerr Notch the third morning, and depending on the avalanche hazard, we will ski under the Dutton Cliffs or detour along the canyon of San Creek. Views of Klamath Lakes, Crater Peak and, if we're lucky, the Phantom Ship from Sun Notch, ease the return to "the real world" that afternoon. We are secure in our knowledge that we saw the true face of the rim.

LENGTH OF TRIP: 3 days

DEPARTURE DATES: Varies

TOTAL COST: $45 per person, guide service only.

TYPE OF PAYMENT ACCEPTED: Check, cash

RESERVATIONS/DEPOSIT: $9 deposit (20%)

CANCELLATION POLICY: Deposit forfeited; if group is too small, trip will be cancelled

DEPARTURE LOCATION: Visitor Center, Rim Village

NEAREST AIRPORT: Klamath Falls

TRANSPORTATION INFORMATION: Your car must have traction tires and/or devices with you for snowy roads

HEALTH, FITNESS OR AGE REQUIREMENTS: Must be able to ski 12-15 miles carrying 40+ lb. pack

TYPE OF WEATHER TO EXPECT: 15-55° F, sun or snow

BEST TYPE OF CLOTHING AND FOOTWEAR: Equipment list available

PERSONAL GEAR REQUIRED: Equipment list available

SPECIAL GEAR/EQUIPMENT REQUIRED: Equipment list available

WHAT NOT TO BRING: Pets

PHOTO POSSIBILITIES: Fantastic

FISHING POSSIBILITIES: None

REPRESENTATIVE MENU: Supply your own

CHORES/DUTIES GUESTS ARE EXPECTED TO HELP WITH: Carry own pack, set up tent, prepare own meals, etc.

ADDITIONAL SPECIAL INFORMATION: We reserve the right to cancel or postpone trip due to hazardous weather

NAME OF OUTFITTER: Crater Lake Ski Service

ADDRESS: Crater Lake National Park

CONTACT: Sara Shapiro

CITY: Crater Lake

TITLE: Partner

STATE: Oregon   **ZIP:** 97604

TELEPHONE: Winter (503) 594-2361

NUMBER OF YEARS IN BUSINESS: 6

NUMBER OF STAFF: 2-4

SPECIALIZING IN: Cross-country skiing, guided ski tours at Crater Lake National Park

SPECIAL PHILOSOPHY, CREDO, GOALS BEHIND BUSINESS: We love Crater Lake and we love to help people see and enjoy its unique winter beauty on skis

Photo: Greg Wiedle

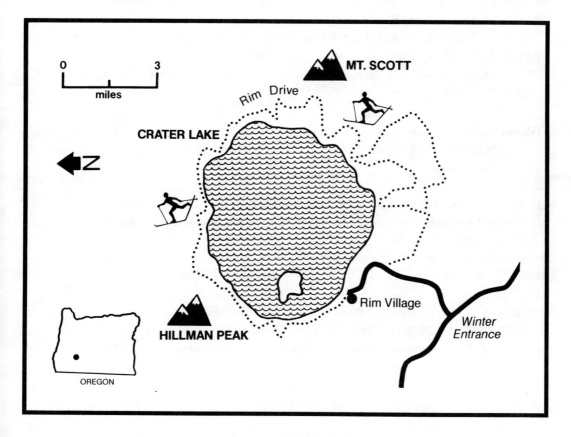

0   3
miles

MT. SCOTT

Rim   Drive

CRATER LAKE

N

HILLMAN PEAK

Rim Village

Winter
Entrance

OREGON

TENTH MOUNTAIN SYSTEM

Imagine yourself on the tail of a telemark turn, knee-deep in powder, descending a wide open slope of crystal delight. Skiing the Tenth Mountain Trail and Hut System isn't all telemarks, as it does have its uphill moments. But the pack on your back reminds you that you are skiing the backcountry of Vail. The huts provide a comfortable and cozy setting at the end of the day with the warm fire and dormitory-style sleeping quarters. Meals are a culinary delight that enhance this skiing experience with unusual and delectable variations. And the comradery of the group is what makes it all seem perfect as everyone reflects on the day's events or anticipates tomorrow's surprises. Early morning tempts us out on a sunrise tour and we ski silently out to Rocky Fork Bowl. The sky lights up with the first rays of dawn and the distant peaks are brushed with color. The experience is one of simplicity and reverence. After a hearty breakfast of eggs and sausage wrapped in tortillas back at the cabin, we ski eight miles down to the Diamond J Ranch, a rustic log lodge. The next day we move on to the Crooked Creek Hut for another authentic backcountry experience in a pristine setting of open parks and alpine peaks. We spend the night on the deck watching the earth go round.

LENGTH OF TRIP: 5-6 days

DEPARTURE DATES: Vary

TOTAL COST: $340-390

TYPE OF PAYMENT ACCEPTED: Check, cash

RESERVATIONS/DEPOSIT: 40% deposit with reservation

CANCELLATION POLICY: Forfeit deposit

DEPARTURE LOCATION: Aspen and Eagle trail   **NEAREST AIRPORT:** Aspen, Avon, Colorado

TRANSPORTATION INFORMATION: Free transportation from lodging or airport

HEALTH, FITNESS OR AGE REQUIREMENTS: Good physical condition, intermediate ski ability

TYPE OF WEATHER TO EXPECT: Sun and snow

BEST TYPE OF CLOTHING AND FOOTWEAR: Equipment list available

PERSONAL GEAR REQUIRED: Equipment list available

SPECIAL GEAR/EQUIPMENT REQUIRED: Metal-edged skis, backcountry touring boots, skis, boots

WHAT NOT TO BRING: Dogs

PHOTO POSSIBILITIES: Fantastic

FISHING POSSIBILITIES: None

REPRESENTATIVE MENU—BREAKFAST: Eggs, sausage in tortillas

LUNCH: Fruits, cheeses

DINNER: Shrimp, vegetable, bouillabaisse, noodle stew, rolls, dessert

CHORES/DUTIES GUESTS ARE EXPECTED TO HELP WITH: Carrying some food

ADDITIONAL SPECIAL INFORMATION: Out-of-state participants must acclimatize themselves in the area for 3-4 days prior to trip.

NAME OF OUTFITTER: Crooked Creek Ski Touring

ADDRESS: Box 3142

CONTACT: Buck Elliott

CITY: Vail

TITLE: Director

STATE: Colorado   **ZIP:** 81658

TELEPHONE: (303) 949-5682

NUMBER OF YEARS IN BUSINESS: 6

NUMBER OF STAFF: 3

SPECIALIZING IN: Winter ski touring adventures, specifically guided tours on the Tenth Mountain Trail and Hut System.

Photo: Ken Redding

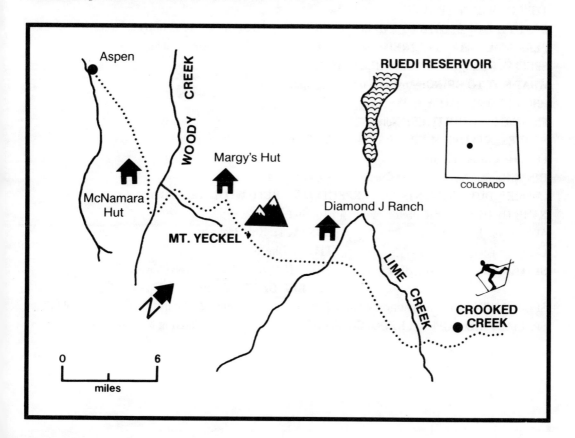

Aspen

WOODY CREEK

RUEDI RESERVOIR

Margy's Hut

McNamara Hut

MT. YECKEL

Diamond J Ranch

COLORADO

LIME CREEK

CROOKED CREEK

N

0   6
miles

YURT-TO-YURT BACKCOUNTRY TOUR

"Backcountry touring is unmatched as a complete skiing experience. The backcountry holds so many wonders for the tourer—untracked snow, limitless terrain, and a chance to feel the unique and changing mood of the winter mountains. It's the solitude and remoteness which make backcountry skiing a special thing when shared with companions," said Teton Mountain Tour's Director Kirk Bachman. This special sport is facilitated by the TMT's hut system of three years which service an 18-mile route through the Big Hole Mountains, adjacent to the Tetons. A yurt is a round tent-like structure used commonly by Asian herdsmen as a home. Supported by a substantial wood frame, the yurt is able to withstand the rigors of winter. The three wood-heated shelters provide access to superb powder bowls and magnificent vistas of the Teton range. Experienced ski mountaineers guide participants through the white expanse and teach the grace of the telemark turn, making downhill skiing on cross-country skis fun instead of a lesson in survival. Combine a good skiing experience with a delicious warm meal, cozy surroundings and friendly skiing companions and you have all the makings of an unforgettable ski vacation.

LENGTH OF TRIP: 2-5 days   **DEPARTURE DATES:** Season begins November 15

TOTAL COST: Varies   **TYPE OF PAYMENT ACCEPTED:** Check, cash, Visa, MC

RESERVATIONS/DEPOSIT: 50% with booking

CANCELLATION POLICY: Deposit credited towards future tour

DEPARTURE LOCATION: Driggs, ID   **NEAREST AIRPORT:** Jackson Hole, WY

TRANSPORTATION INFORMATION: Bus, shuttle, rental car

HEALTH, FITNESS OR AGE REQUIREMENTS: Good physical condition

TYPE OF WEATHER TO EXPECT: Snow

BEST TYPE OF CLOTHING AND FOOTWEAR: Layered clothing, backcountry ski touring equipment

PERSONAL GEAR REQUIRED: Skis, boots, poles, backpack, personal duffle

SPECIAL GEAR/EQUIPMENT REQUIRED: None

WHAT NOT TO BRING: Anything not on equipment list

PHOTO POSSIBILITIES: Fantastic

FISHING POSSIBILITIES: None

REPRESENTATIVE MENU—BREAKFAST: Fruit dumplings

LUNCH: Cheese, bread, wine

DINNER: Quiche, soup, hors d'oeuvres, ice cream

CHORES/DUTIES GUESTS ARE EXPECTED TO HELP WITH: Depends on tour

NAME OF OUTFITTER: Teton Mountain Touring, Inc.

ADDRESS: Box 514   **CONTACT:** Kirk Bachman

CITY: Driggs   **TITLE:** Director

STATE: Idaho   **ZIP:** 83422   **TELEPHONE:** (208) 354-2768 (Nov.-April)

NUMBER OF STAFF: 10

SPECIALIZING IN: Backcountry ski tour, hut-to-hut skiing, touring school at Grand Targhee Ski Resort

SPECIAL PHILOSOPHY, CREDO, GOALS BEHIND BUSINESS: Catering to all levels of skiing

Photo: Bill Ross

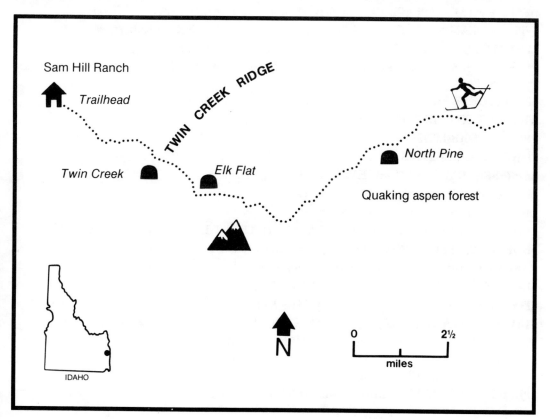

Sam Hill Ranch

Trailhead

TWIN CREEK RIDGE

North Pine

Twin Creek

Elk Flat

Quaking aspen forest

N

0   2½

miles

IDAHO

THE HUT-TO-HUT REGULAR WEEK TOUR

Indulge in premier cross-country skiing in New York's Central Adirondack Mountains, a six-million-acre park. Within these ridges lies the Siamese Ponds Wilderness. Throughout six days you will ski to a different cabin or inn as you traverse Kunjamuck Valley and numerous mountains, ponds, beaver meadows and brooks in the wilderness area. The Kunjamuck trail is skiable and diverse, from winding hiking trails to broad old logging roads. There is some climbing and we may be breaking trail in new snow occasionally. Each tour has two experienced guides to accommodate different levels of skiing ability. We average nine miles daily, or four to six hours of skiing, interspersed with periodic rest or photo breaks and a trail lunch which may consist of sandwiches, gorp and fruit. The experience is best suited to intermediate skiers, although advanced novices in good physical condition will appreciate it as well. The outfitter provides transport of luggage, lodging, three meals daily, experienced guides and on-trail ski instruction. You just need to carry a light day pack with your lunch, sunglasses, extra mittens, hat and wool sweater. Nights will be spent in warm comfortable surroundings, either a modern chalet on a mountain or two rustic cabins at the edge of a secluded pond. All are winterized.

LENGTH OF TRIP: 6 days

DEPARTURE DATES: January-March

TOTAL COST: $285

TYPE OF PAYMENT ACCEPTED: Check

RESERVATIONS/DEPOSIT: $50 with reservation

CANCELLATION POLICY: All but deposit refunded; deposit with 21 days notice

DEPARTURE LOCATION: Indian Lake, NY   **NEAREST AIRPORT:** Albany, NY

TRANSPORTATION INFORMATION: We will pick up passengers on shared cost basis

HEALTH, FITNESS OR AGE REQUIREMENTS: Intermediate skier in good condition

TYPE OF WEATHER TO EXPECT: Temperatures ranging from sub-zero to 30s; snow

BEST TYPE OF CLOTHING AND FOOTWEAR: Cross-country skiing clothing, layers

PERSONAL GEAR REQUIRED: Light sleeping bag, down jacket, small flashlight, sunglasses, ski waxes, spare ski tip

SPECIAL GEAR/EQUIPMENT REQUIRED: Equipment list available

WHAT NOT TO BRING: Excess anything

PHOTO POSSIBILITIES: Good

FISHING POSSIBILITIES: None

REPRESENTATIVE MENU—BREAKFAST: Ham, eggs, pancakes

LUNCH: Sandwiches, fruit, gorp, juice, cookies

DINNER: Chicken, potatoes, vegetables, cake

CHORES/DUTIES GUESTS ARE EXPECTED TO HELP WITH: One or two meals prepared by group

ADDITIONAL SPECIAL INFORMATION: Vegetarian cooking upon request

NAME OF OUTFITTER: Adirondack Hut to Hut Tours

ADDRESS: Rd. 1, Box 85   **CONTACT:** John Borel, Walter Blank

CITY: Ghent   **TITLE:** Partners

STATE: New York   **ZIP:** 12075   **TELEPHONE:** (518) 449-5098; 828-7007

NUMBER OF YEARS IN BUSINESS: 5   **NUMBER OF STAFF:** 4 per tour

SPECIALIZING IN: Guided wilderness ski tours cabin to cabin; high country telemark tours, weekend telemark camps, pre-wilderness instruction

SPECIAL PHILOSOPHY, CREDO, GOALS BEHIND BUSINESS: We had an idea of the kind of skiing we found most exciting and rewarding, and we want to share it with others.

Photo: J. Borel

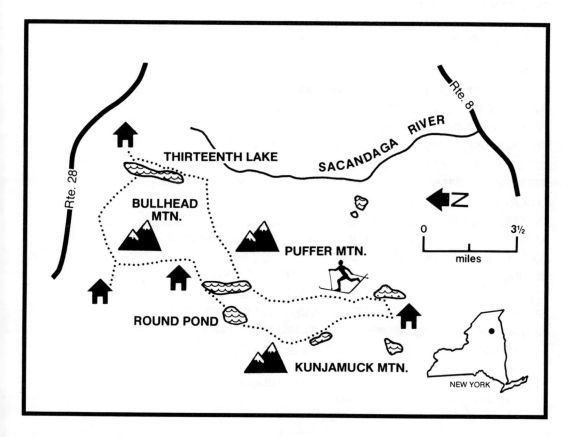

BUTTERMILK SPRING SKI RENDEZVOUS

When the sun starts baking the bowls of the Eastern Sierra, you can ski the finest corn snow to be found anywhere in the world. The warm spring days complemented by the crisp high country nights produce the silken corn runs of the High Sierra. Whether on cross country, mountaineering or alpine ski gear, come join us this and every Memorial Day weekend to ski the Bishop Skyline. The majestic 13,000-foot peaks of Mt. Tom, Basin and Humphreys offer exhilarating 4,000-5,000-foot ski descents by creatively connecting incredible canyons, gullies and bowls all filled with fantastic corn snow. Each morning we rise at first light to a hearty breakfast and begin our climb through the desert-hued spring wildflowers. Topping out on our ski fantasia by mid-morning, we ensure skiing the spring corn at its perfection. Wide arcing telemarks, figure eights and elevens and extreme laughter highlight the skiing. Each afternoon we return to the Buttermilk country, the warm craggy hills beneath the peaks, to indulge in apres-ski sunbathing, bouldering and barbeques. Soaking in hot springs nightly is "de rigeur." Our spring rendezvous is comfortably stocked, guaranteeing the ultimate in food and spirits.

LENGTH OF TRIP: 4 days

DEPARTURE DATES: Memorial Day weekend

TOTAL COST: $320

TYPE OF PAYMENT ACCEPTED: Check, cash

RESERVATIONS/DEPOSIT: $100 deposit within 30 days of booking

CANCELLATION POLICY: Deposit less $50 prior to 30 days; nonrefundable after

DEPARTURE LOCATION: Bishop, CA

NEAREST AIRPORT: Los Angeles; Reno, NV

TRANSPORTATION INFORMATION: Bus, car rental flight charters

HEALTH, FITNESS OR AGE REQUIREMENTS: Good health

TYPE OF WEATHER TO EXPECT: Cool mornings, hot afternoons

BEST TYPE OF CLOTHING AND FOOTWEAR: Shorts, windproof jacket and pants, visor, sunglasses, medium weight hiking boot, gaitors, light gloves

PERSONAL GEAR REQUIRED: Sleeping bag, metal-edge skis, running shoes, sun lotion, water bottle, day pack, lip balm

SPECIAL GEAR/EQUIPMENT REQUIRED: Climbing skins, avalanche beacons

WHAT NOT TO BRING: Anything you won't share with the group

PHOTO POSSIBILITIES: Fantastic

FISHING POSSIBILITIES: Good

LICENSE REQUIREMENTS: CA

BEST TYPE OF FISHING TACKLE: Lures for trout

REPRESENTATIVE MENU—BREAKFAST: Hot cakes, cereal, yogurt, fruit

LUNCH: Bagels, cream cheese, fruit

DINNER: Salad, ribs, wine, cobbler, lemons

ADDITIONAL SPECIAL INFORMATION: Please advise to medications, disabilities, etc.

NAME OF OUTFITTER: Alpine Expeditions

ADDRESS: Box 1751

CONTACT: Chris Cox

CITY: Bishop

TITLE: Alpine Guide

STATE: California   **ZIP:** 93514

TELEPHONE: (619) 873-5617

NUMBER OF YEARS IN BUSINESS: 25   **NUMBER OF STAFF:** 4

SPECIALIZING IN: Alpine adventures in the medium of rock, ice or snow. Sharing together the freedom, the challenge and the wonders of the mountains world wide.

SPECIAL PHILOSOPHY, CREDO, GOALS BEHIND BUSINESS: Natural ability to relate our knowledge in a warm, friendly and imaginative way.

Photo: Allan Bard

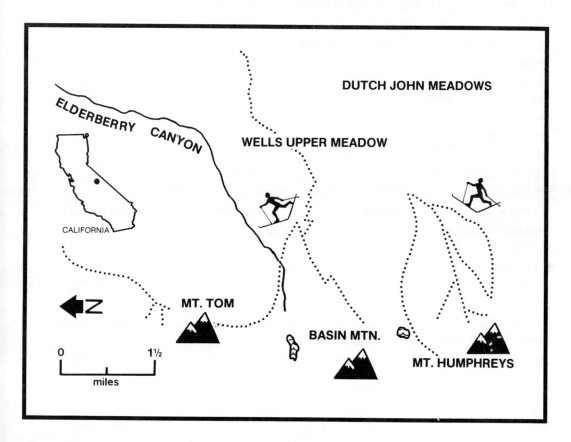

MT. SANFORD TELEMARK DESCENT

This expedition begins in true Alaskan fashion—in a tiny bush plane laden with packs and skis, bouncing to a halt on a rough dirt landing strip. Next comes a two-day tundra ramble to the Sheep Glacier. In season, the tundra is lush with new greenery and flowers, nesting birds, grazing caribou, foxes and other wildlife. They are as curious about you as you are about them. The Wrangell Mountains' massive ice-covered volcanoes rise abruptly above the gentle tundra sweep. On the glacier, a long and strenuous (but nontechnical) climb begins up its immense slopes. Travel days alternate with storm days. Views extend across the roof of North America. On a clear day from the summit, views span over 400 miles and include five mountain ranges and three of North America's highest peaks. The classic ski descent from the summit's perpetual winter and thin, 16,000-foot atmosphere is one of the longest runs in the world. It can be easily handled by strong skiers on nordic mountaineering gear. Snow can range from wind-crust to slush to midsummer powder. Skiers leave the glacier rubber-legged, grinning and sunburned and reenter summer's fresh green world as they descend to the airstrip to be picked up.

LENGTH OF TRIP: 14 days

DEPARTURE DATES: May-July

TOTAL COST: $500 and up

TYPE OF PAYMENT ACCEPTED: Check, cash

RESERVATIONS/DEPOSIT: $200 deposit at least two months in advance

CANCELLATION POLICY: No refunds if cancelled less than 30 days before trip

DEPARTURE LOCATION: Gulkana/Chis- **NEAREST AIRPORT:** Anchorage, AK
tochina strips

TRANSPORTATION INFORMATION: Rental car or carpool

HEALTH, FITNESS OR AGE REQUIREMENTS: Strong, intermediate ability

TYPE OF WEATHER TO EXPECT: Cold to hot; be prepared

BEST TYPE OF CLOTHING AND FOOTWEAR: Equipment list available

PERSONAL GEAR REQUIRED: Equipment list available

SPECIAL GEAR/EQUIPMENT REQUIRED: Equipment list available

WHAT NOT TO BRING: More than you can carry!

PHOTO POSSIBILITIES: Fantastic

FISHING POSSIBILITIES: None

REPRESENTATIVE MENU—BREAKFAST: Porridge, whole milk, drinks

LUNCH: Energy balls, dried fruit, chocolate, crackers, kippers

DINNER: Parmesan, browned butter and herb spaghetti, soup, cheesecake

CHORES/DUTIES GUESTS ARE EXPECTED TO HELP WITH: All; our trips are participatory

ADDITIONAL SPECIAL INFORMATION: Brochure available

NAME OF OUTFITTER: PRISM Ski Touring

ADDRESS: Box 136

CONTACT: Bill Glude

CITY: Girdwood

TITLE: Proprietor

STATE: Alaska   **ZIP:** 99587

TELEPHONE: (907) 783-2945

NUMBER OF YEARS IN BUSINESS: 8   **NUMBER OF STAFF:** 1

SPECIALIZING IN: Alaskan backcountry skiing; custom trips

SPECIAL PHILOSOPHY, CREDO, GOALS BEHIND BUSINESS: We hope PRISM will provide a positive prototype for responsible development of winter tourism in Alaska.

Photo: Bill Glude

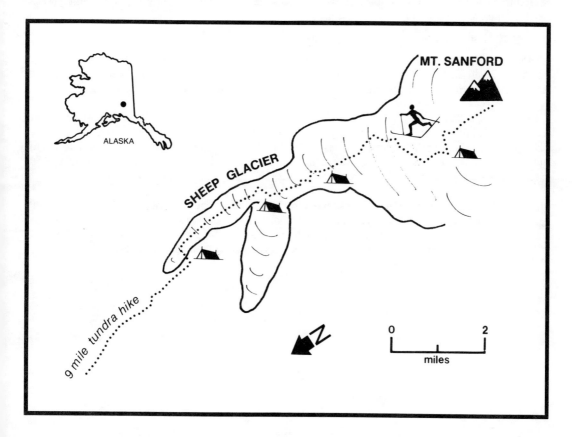

ALASKA

MT. SANFORD

SHEEP GLACIER

9 mile tundra hike

0   2

miles

 # HELICOPTER SKIING

Imagine this: awakening in a remote but plush mountain lodge deep in the Canadian Rockies. You assemble with the rest of your group of eight to 10 fellow travellers for a hearty mountaineer's breakfast, then lift off in a modern jet-powered helicopter for an experience that will live for all time in your memory. You settle gently on the very summits of the most awe-inspiring mountain peaks in North America. You disembark on virgin terrain that no road will ever conquer, in air so fresh and pure it almost seems to cleanse the spirit, so clear you can see forever. Accompanied by an experienced mountain guide, you ski mountains that were known only to a few prospectors, loggers and mountaineers. The only sounds are those of nature—the mountain breeze keening through crags, perhaps the clatter of a herd of mountain goats, or the piercing cry of an eagle. You leave your mark as a pattern of curving tracks on expansive white snowfields. The skiing conditions are far removed from the tracked slopes of typical ski resorts, and the sense of complete freedom frees the spirit. Whether you choose the Bugaboos, Cariboos, or Bobbie Burns, you will spend days "coptering" the incredible, unspoiled mountain wilderness with its soaring peaks and fabled glaciers.

CANADIAN MOUNTAIN HOLIDAYS (CMH)
P.O. Box 1660, Banff, Alberta, Canada T0L 0C0
Mark Kingsbury, General manager
(403) 762-4531

Valemount is the site of 5-day heli-skiing packages. Guests are based in the Alpine Motel in Valemount, B.C. and have access to 40,000 meters of skiing during this trip. Prices range from $1,270 for a single in the low season to $1,460 in the high. Double occupancy ranges from $1,190 to $1,370. From Valemount, you can ski both the Cariboo and Monashee Mountains.

Revelstoke, B.C. is 413 km west of Calgary, Alberta. Skiers stay at a Regent Motor Inn for seven days and ski the Monashee and Selkirk mountains. The package includes round trip bus from Calgary, box lunch in-bound, seven full days at the Inn, meals, use of all facilities, guide service, 30,500 meters helicopter lift and local taxes. Single: $1,805-$2,135. Double: $1,705-$2,035, depending on season.

Cariboos are spectacular mountains in British Columbia, Canada. The CMH Cariboo Lodge, 500 km west of Edmonton, is home to skiers participating in this seven-day excursion. Less demanding, more relaxed skiing is also available in this package. The package includes round trip bus trip from Edmonton to staging area and helicopter to Lodge, box lunch en route, seven full days at the Lodge, meals, guide service, 30,500 meters helicopter lift and local taxes. Prices from $1,235-$2,635, depending on room and season.

Bugaboos Mountains are more than you can possibly ski in one trip. The CMH Bugaboo Lodge, B.C., is 300 km from Calgary and houses skiers in twin or double rooms with a variety of options available (i.e. fireplace, massage room, drying room, sauna, etc.). Package includes round trip bus from Calgary to staging area, helicopter lift and local taxes. Prices from $1,235-$2,635, depending on room and season.

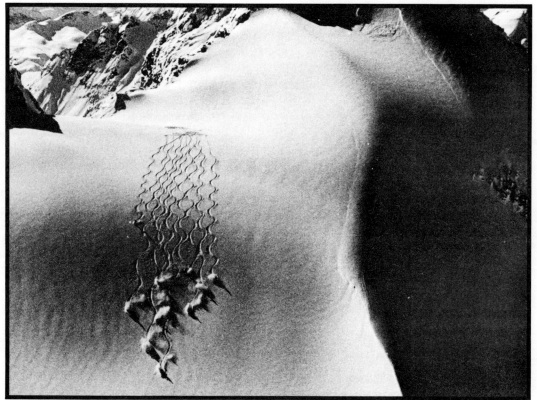

Photo: Prism Ski Touring

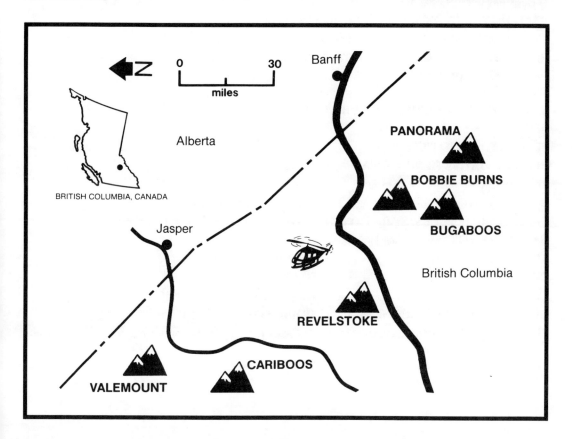

RUTH GLACIER SKI-JORING

Alaska Mountain Treks will introduce you to dogsledding and the Great White North during its short summer season. The base camp is set into the southern flanks of Mt. McKinley, also known as Denali, and trekkers will set out on dog sled and ski touring expeditions over an eight-day period to explore the Ruth Glacier. Guide Steve Hackett has degrees in geophysics and geology and has lived in Alaska since 1971. He will conduct a glaciology workshop to help trekkers better understand the delicate habitat of this area. In addition, participants will be introduced to the remote mountains, rivers and waterways of this Alaskan wilderness. Expeditions are designed to suit the interests and experience of the participants, as they combine adventure trips with learning wilderness skills and environmental education. The dog sleds provide support for skiing and mountaineering activities as well as ski-joring, where the skiers are pulled along by the dogsled team, a fun snow sport. Learned wilderness skills will include crevasse rescue, avalanche awareness, snow camping and ascending/descending skiing techniques, including the telemark turn, in the spectacular Ruth Gorge area.

LENGTH OF TRIP: 1 hour to 8 days

DEPARTURE DATES: May 1–June 15

TOTAL COST: $25/person per hour to $1065/person for 8 days

TYPE OF PAYMENT ACCEPTED: Cashier's check, cash

RESERVATIONS/DEPOSIT: Reservations not required

CANCELLATION POLICY: Payment refundable up to 10 days before trip

DEPARTURE LOCATION: Talkeetna, AK   **NEAREST AIRPORT:** Talkeetna, AK

TRANSPORTATION INFORMATION: Train, taxi, rental car, limo or charter plane from Anchorage or Fairbanks International Airports to Talkeetna

HEALTH, FITNESS OR AGE REQUIREMENTS: Good health

TYPE OF WEATHER TO EXPECT: 10°F-80°F; sunny to blowing snow

BEST TYPE OF CLOTHING AND FOOTWEAR: Winter mountain gear

PERSONAL GEAR REQUIRED: Good winter gear, warm boots, skiing gear and basic mountaineering gear for seminars

SPECIAL GEAR/EQUIPMENT REQUIRED: Skis and warm boots

PHOTO POSSIBILITIES: Fantastic

FISHING POSSIBILITIES: None

REPRESENTATIVE MENU—BREAKFAST: Sourdough hot cakes

LUNCH: Cheese, bread, meats or fish

DINNER: Sweet and sour dinner, vegetables, juice and blueberry cheesecake

CHORES/DUTIES GUESTS ARE EXPECTED TO HELP WITH: Minor daily cleanup

NAME OF OUTFITTER: Alaska Mountain Treks

ADDRESS: P.O. Box 600   **CONTACT:** Steve Hackett

CITY: Moose Pass   **TITLE:** Guide

STATE: Alaska   **ZIP:** 99631   **TELEPHONE:** (907) 288-3610

NUMBER OF YEARS IN BUSINESS: 4   **NUMBER OF STAFF:** 2-3

SPECIALIZING IN: Outfitting custom trips into Alaska's national parks/preserves/monuments, wildlife refuges and wild, scenic river systems

SPECIAL PHILOSOPHY, CREDO, GOALS BEHIND BUSINESS: Personalized wilderness trips into seldom visited remote mountains, rivers and waterways in Alaska

Photo: Steve Hackett

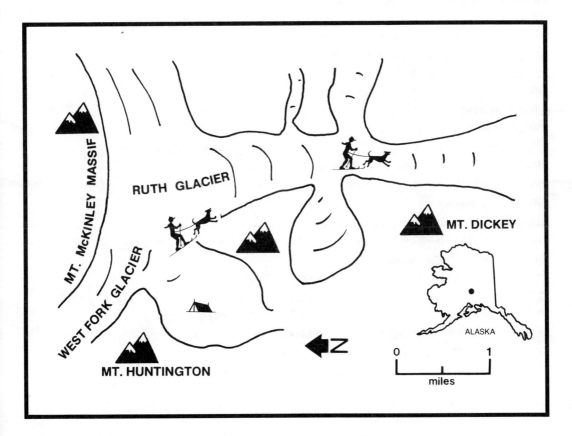

GATES-OF-THE-ARCTIC EXPEDITION

The Brooks Mountain Range is silent under its blanket of ice and snow. Deserted valleys, windswept snow sculptures, moonlit snowscapes and Northern Lights in the evening, tracks in the snow. The wilderness residents are watching you—moose, caribou, wolves, Canadian jays and ravens. Sourdough offers a unique opportunity for experiencing this wonderful wilderness area at a seldom-visited time of year by dogsled, the old and honorable means of visiting the winter arctic. Bettles is the staging area for the expedition. The dogs will be raring to go so hold onto your knit hat as you take off. Your destination is the Gates-of-the-Arctic area on the North Fork of the Koyukuk River. The Nunamiut Eskimos are at home here and still travel from their village of Anaktuvuk Pass to hunt and trap fur bearers. Routed primarily along an old trail, you camp at some of the same sites which Robert Marshall and Ernie Johnson used while exploring this "blank spot on a map" nearly five decades ago. Your camps are cabins and heated tents. The trip will terminate within view of the Gates-of-the-Arctic near the northern limits of the treeline. A ski plane will return you to Bettles, allowing a scenic overview of the immense expanse of the land that has been your home for over seven days.

LENGTH OF TRIP: 10 days

DEPARTURE DATES: Feb.-April

TOTAL COST: $1,200

TYPE OF PAYMENT ACCEPTED: Cash, t.c. cashiers

RESERVATIONS/DEPOSIT: $200 deposit when booking

CANCELLATION POLICY: Loss of deposit

DEPARTURE LOCATION: Bettles, AK   **NEAREST AIRPORT:** Bettles, AK

TRANSPORTATION INFORMATION: N/A

HEALTH, FITNESS OR AGE REQUIREMENTS: Good physical condition

TYPE OF WEATHER TO EXPECT: -30° - +30° F

BEST TYPE OF CLOTHING AND FOOTWEAR: Winter expedition gear

PERSONAL GEAR REQUIRED: Personal duffle, sleeping bag

SPECIAL GEAR/EQUIPMENT REQUIRED: List provided

WHAT NOT TO BRING: Alcohol during the winter

PHOTO POSSIBILITIES: Fantastic

FISHING POSSIBILITIES: Fantastic   **LICENSE REQUIREMENTS:** 10 days $15

BEST TYPE OF FISHING TACKLE: Provided for ice fishing

REPRESENTATIVE MENU—BREAKFAST: Bacon, eggs, toast

LUNCH: Trail lunch

DINNER: Steaks, potatoes, vegetables, dessert

CHORES/DUTIES GUESTS ARE EXPECTED TO HELP WITH: Fetch water, firewood, pitch camp

NAME OF OUTFITTER: Sourdough Outfitters

ADDRESS: General Delivery   **CONTACT:** David Ketscher

CITY: Bettles   **TITLE:** President

STATE: Alaska   **ZIP:** 99726   **TELEPHONE:** (907) 692-5252

NUMBER OF YEARS IN BUSINESS: 10   **NUMBER OF STAFF:** 4-8

SPECIALIZING IN: Wilderness trips in Alaska's Brook Range

SPECIAL PHILOSOPHY, CREDO, GOALS BEHIND BUSINESS: We are Christians and run our business in such a way to bring glory to God.

Photo: John David Ketshcer

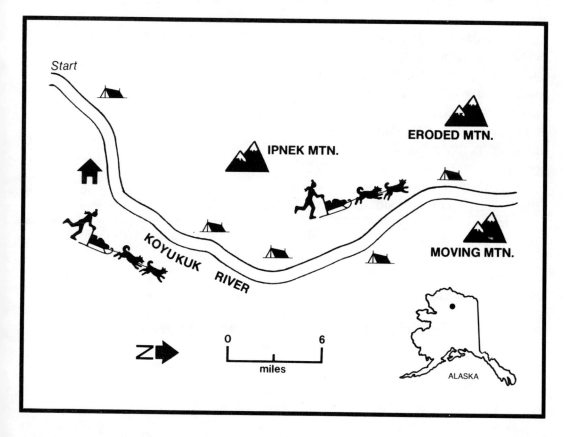

105

TOKRAT RIVER TRIP

Sliding along on frosted runners, one may experience the predominant face of Alaska—winter! You will assist the guide and dog driver handle a large freighting team, braking to lessen the careening sled speed and then leaning hard to one side on icy curves. The Stampede trail covers variable terrain and while the participant mostly rides, there will be hills and mountain passes to walk or jog up. Much of the trail follows rivers where overflow water, glare ice, and open holes must be negotiated. Caribou, moose, sheep and small game are usually viewed from the comfort of the runners. Cozy, warm nights are spent in Park Services patrol cabins of Denali National Park while low temperatures outside may be putting frosting on the dogs and sled gear. With luck, you will hear a wolf howl and see the loping track of the lonely wolverine. Mountain scenery is spectacular with Mt. Denali (called Mt. McKinley by white man) presiding over the rose-tinted alpine glow. Denali is the highest peak in North America, and its silent presence will emphasize the primitive yet beautiful surroundings. Even though you will be out amid these wilds for six days you will be well fed with meat, rice, eggs and bacon. However, the guide warns that this trek is not for the "faint-hearted."

LENGTH OF TRIP: 5-6 days

DEPARTURE DATES: Nov.-March

TOTAL COST: $600 per person

TYPE OF PAYMENT ACCEPTED: Check, cash

RESERVATIONS/DEPOSIT: 20% deposit

CANCELLATION POLICY: Refund up until 10 days prior to trip date

DEPARTURE LOCATION: Lignite Stampede Trail   **NEAREST AIRPORT:** Fairbanks, AK

TRANSPORTATION INFORMATION: Rent a car or take Sunday only train from Fairbanks.

HEALTH, FITNESS OR AGE REQUIREMENTS: "Vigorous" fitness

TYPE OF WEATHER TO EXPECT: Cool, possibly cold.

BEST TYPE OF CLOTHING AND FOOTWEAR: Heavy-duty Arctic gear, vapor barrier boots

PERSONAL GEAR REQUIRED: Personal duffle, sleeping bag, insulated pants

SPECIAL GEAR/EQUIPMENT REQUIRED: Vapor barrier boots

WHAT NOT TO BRING: Excess luggage

PHOTO POSSIBILITIES: Good, but winterize camera

FISHING POSSIBILITIES: None

REPRESENTATIVE MENU—BREAKFAST: Eggs, bacon, rolls, sausage

LUNCH: Cheese, salami, crackers

DINNER: Meat, rice, frozen vegetables, bread, dessert

CHORES/DUTIES GUESTS ARE EXPECTED TO HELP WITH: Cooking, care of dogs

ADDITIONAL SPECIAL INFORMATION: These trips can be rigorous, depending on the weather. They are not for the faint-hearted.

NAME OF OUTFITTER: Denali Dog Tours and Wilderness Freighters

ADDRESS: Box 1

CONTACT: Dennis Kogl

CITY: McKinley Park

TITLE: Operator/guide

STATE: Alaska   **ZIP:** 99755

TELEPHONE: (907) 683-2314

NUMBER OF YEARS IN BUSINESS: 10

NUMBER OF STAFF: 3

SPECIALIZING IN: Dogteam trips and ski tour support

SPECIAL PHILOSOPHY, CREDO, GOALS BEHIND BUSINESS: To see the park during the less travelled, quiet and uncrowded time.

Photo: Dennis Kogl

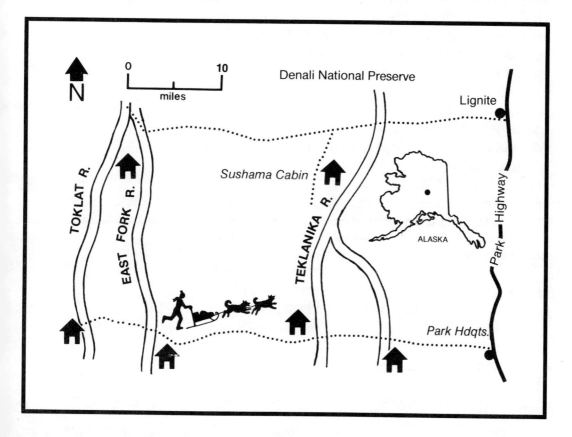

GRAND TETON SNOWMOBILE TOUR

Civilization is pretty scarce out here anyway, but you will find what little there is at the cozy, timbered Turpin Meadow Ranch, 40 miles from the nearest town of Jackson Hole, Wyoming. This is the beginning of an eight-day, seven-night expedition in the winter wilds. In the evening, spirits and stories about the day will complement the hearty fare and big log fire. After a good night's rest, we are up and at 'em again as we head off into the open snowfields on snowmobiles. While roaming for three days in this wilderness we stop for lunch at another remote snowbound ranch, the Goosewing Ranch. After seeing the rugged beauty and vastness of the West, we will spend two days in Yellowstone Park and see Old Faithful, Yellowstone Falls and what the summer tourists want to see but often miss—big game animals who winter near the warmth of the thermal springs. To prepare you for re-entry into civilization, we spend the last two nights in the rompin', stompin' western town of Jackson! You stay at the small friendly Western Hotel, located a short stroll from the bright lights of the town square and the world famous Million Dollar Cowboy Bar, where you can tell everybody of the wonders you just witnessed during your trek in the Grand Tetons.

LENGTH OF TRIP: 8 days

DEPARTURE DATES: January-October

TOTAL COST: $985 double occupancy

TYPE OF PAYMENT ACCEPTED: Check, credit card

RESERVATIONS/DEPOSIT: $200 with confirmation

CANCELLATION POLICY: Forfeit deposits plus cost of space non-resaleable

DEPARTURE LOCATION: Jackson Hole, WY   **NEAREST AIRPORT:** Jackson Hole, WY

TRANSPORTATION INFORMATION: Included

HEALTH, FITNESS OR AGE REQUIREMENTS: Normal good health; 7 years old minimum

TYPE OF WEATHER TO EXPECT: Cold clear days, possible snow

BEST TYPE OF CLOTHING AND FOOTWEAR: Provided

PERSONAL GEAR REQUIRED: Personal duffle

SPECIAL GEAR/EQUIPMENT REQUIRED: None

WHAT NOT TO BRING: Excess luggage

PHOTO POSSIBILITIES: Fantastic

FISHING POSSIBILITIES: None

REPRESENTATIVE MENU—BREAKFAST: Ham, eggs, toast, coffee

LUNCH: Sandwiches, soup

DINNER: Meat or fish, vegetables, beverage, dessert

CHORES/DUTIES GUESTS ARE EXPECTED TO HELP WITH: None

ADDITIONAL SPECIAL INFORMATION: This vacation is for young and old and offers a unique picture of Yellowstone and Grand Teton national parks during the winter.

NAME OF OUTFITTER: Old West Tours

ADDRESS: P.O. Box 3322

CONTACT: Jim Wallace

CITY: Jackson Hole

TITLE: President

STATE: Wyoming   **ZIP:** 83001

TELEPHONE: (307) 733-7131

NUMBER OF STAFF: 5

SPECIALIZING IN: Adventure travel

SPECIAL PHILOSOPHY, CREDO, GOALS BEHIND BUSINESS: The client is our only concern.

Photo: Wyoming Travel Commission

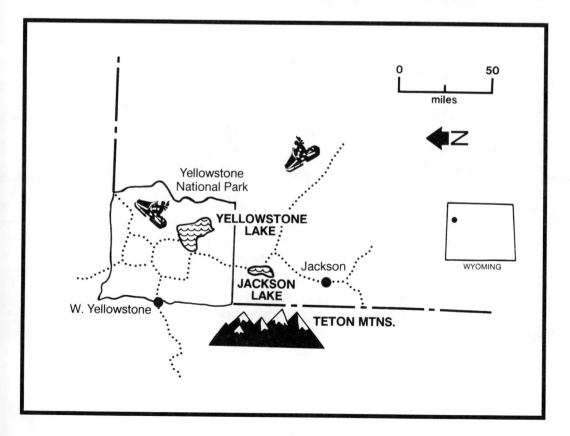

🚴 TUPPER FARM WANDERER

The Tupper Farm Wanderer is a five-day bicycle tour that roams through the magnificent, unspoiled heartland of Vermont near Rochester. Following broad valleys along six different rivers and crossing panoramic wooded ridges, participants cycle in a pastoral wonderland. Tennis and invigorating lake or river swimming are everyday options, as well as the tour's Finnish sauna on two nights. Scenic vistas from behind handlebars include stately Killington Peak, sunsets over the lush Green Mountains, six historic covered bridges and the exquisite, jewel-like villages of Sharon, Windsor, Randolph, South Royalton and Brookfield. Antiques are sold from colonial buildings, craft galleries feature local artisans and painters, and shaded village greens are perfect settings for partaking of refreshments sold at the friendly general store. Daily mileage varies but every night brings hearty homecooked dinners and warm, comfortable beds at country inns. Breakfast and lunch are also provided. Bicyclists need to bring appropriate clothing but can rent bikes and helmets from the organizers. Tours depart from Rochester from mid-May through September, allowing cycling through New England's lilac-perfumed spring or crisp, colorful autumn.

LENGTH OF TRIP: 5 days

DEPARTURE DATES: Mid-May thru Sept.

TOTAL COST: Write for details

TYPE OF PAYMENT ACCEPTED: Check, money order

RESERVATIONS/DEPOSIT: Need deposit 2-3 weeks prior to trip

CANCELLATION POLICY: Deposit forfeited

DEPARTURE LOCATION: Rochester, VT   **NEAREST AIRPORT:** Rutland, VT

TRANSPORTATION INFORMATION: Taxi

HEALTH, FITNESS OR AGE REQUIREMENTS: None

TYPE OF WEATHER TO EXPECT: Sunny

BEST TYPE OF CLOTHING AND FOOTWEAR: Equipment list available

PERSONAL GEAR REQUIRED: Personal duffle

SPECIAL GEAR/EQUIPMENT REQUIRED: Bicycle (yours or rent one of ours)

WHAT NOT TO BRING: Pets

PHOTO POSSIBILITIES: Fantastic

FISHING POSSIBILITIES: Fantastic   **LICENSE REQUIREMENT:** State

BEST TYPE OF FISHING TACKLE: Fly fishing

REPRESENTATIVE MENU—BREAKFAST: Hearty country breakfasts

LUNCH: Gourmet picnics

DINNER: Sumptuous homecooked dinners

CHORES/DUTIES GUESTS ARE EXPECTED TO HELP WITH: None

NAME OF OUTFITTER: Vermont Bicycle Touring

ADDRESS: Box 711-FW   **CONTACT:** Bruce Burgess

CITY: Bristol   **TITLE:** Associate Director

STATE: Vermont   **ZIP:** 05443   **TELEPHONE:** (802) 453-4811

NUMBER OF YEARS IN BUSINESS: 13   **NUMBER OF STAFF:** 30

SPECIALIZING IN: Country inn bicycling vacations

Photo: Bruce Burgess

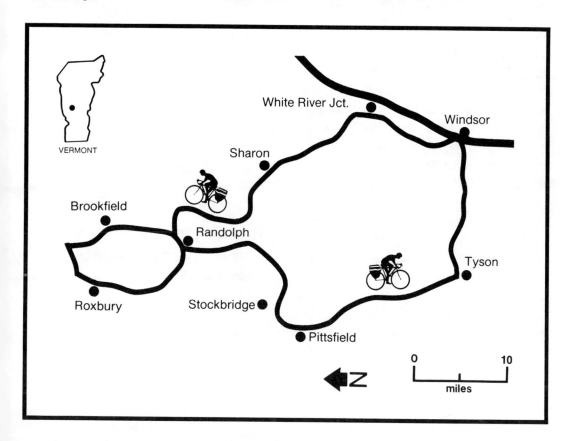

HIGH SIERRA ADVANCED BICYCLE TOUR

This is not a bicycle tour for the meek, timid or out of shape. Tourers must be seasoned cyclists who are experienced with 100-mile rides. And for those who can hack it, they will be open-mouthed at the beauty that awaits them, beginning just nine miles into the trip as they crest Brockway Summit at 7,000 feet. The crystalline waters of Lake Tahoe lie 1,000 feet below, framed by snow-capped peaks. More panoramas lie ahead in this nine-day, 739-mile tour through the heart of the High Sierras, including Carson Valley, Mono Lake Basin and the beautiful meadows of Yosemite's high country. But breathtaking views are just one of the many rewards for the advanced cyclist who will complete over 50,000 feet of total climbing before the trek ends. Upon arrival at camp each evening, hors d'oeuvres will be spread and a hearty delicious dinner will follow. At the end of the three toughest days that total 99, 114 and 115 miles each will be a long soak in natural hot springs. A well-deserved rest day is taken at Devil's Postpile National Monument, where pentagon-shaped basaltic columns rise 60 feet to form an unusual wall. The adventurous can hike the two miles to the 140-foot plunge of Rainbow Falls on the San Joaquin River. And another reward? . . . the thrilling descents to those 50,000 feet of climbing!

LENGTH OF TRIP: 9 days

DEPARTURE DATES: July 21

TOTAL COST: $360; $306 with 30-day advance payment; $270 group of 4 or more

TYPE OF PAYMENT ACCEPTED: Check only

RESERVATIONS/DEPOSIT: 35% 30 days advance

CANCELLATION POLICY: No refund unless someone fills spot

DEPARTURE LOCATION: Truckee, CA   **NEAREST AIRPORT:** Reno, NV

TRANSPORTATION INFORMATION: Bus, or we provide shuttle service evening prior to tour

HEALTH, FITNESS OR AGE REQUIREMENTS: Able to ride 100 miles/daily; 18 years old minimum

TYPE OF WEATHER TO EXPECT: Beautiful, possible shower

BEST TYPE OF CLOTHING AND FOOTWEAR: Cycling clothes, shoes, gloves, helmet

PERSONAL GEAR REQUIRED: Camping gear, low-geared bicycle

SPECIAL GEAR/EQUIPMENT REQUIRED: Small pannier recommended

WHAT NOT TO BRING: Bring medium-sized bag or pack only; no eating/cooking gear

PHOTO POSSIBILITIES: Fantastic

FISHING POSSIBILITIES: None

REPRESENTATIVE MENU—BREAKFAST: Hotcakes, eggs, granola

LUNCH: Sandwiches, salad, soda

DINNER: Soup, salad, BBQ chicken, corn, rice, dessert, wine

CHORES/DUTIES GUESTS ARE EXPECTED TO HELP WITH: None

NAME OF OUTFITTER: Sierra Bicycle Touring Company (Sierra Bicycle Promotions, Inc.)

ADDRESS: P.O. Box 5453   **CONTACT:** Larry Glickfeld

CITY: Incline Village   **TITLE:** Tour Director

STATE: Nevada   **ZIP:** 89450   **TELEPHONE:** (702) 831-3576

NUMBER OF YEARS IN BUSINESS: 2   **NUMBER OF STAFF:** 4

SPECIALIZING IN: Bicycle tours: leisure, intermediate and advanced level. Mostly in Sierras, also coast and Baja.

SPECIAL PHILOSOPHY, CREDO, GOALS BEHIND BUSINESS: To have lots of fun in conjunction with bicycle touring.

Photo: L. Glickfield

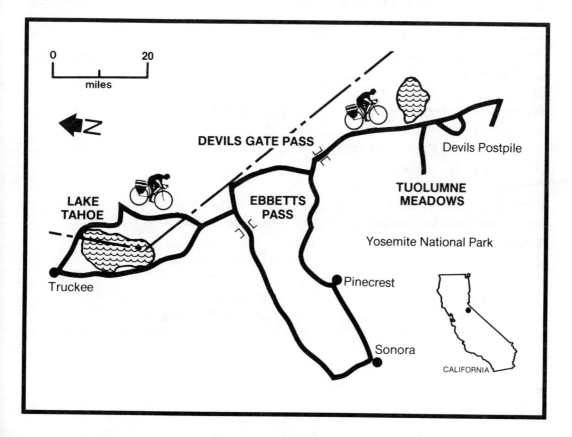

CENTRAL COLORADO BICYCLE TOUR

With our luggage loaded in the support van and final bicycle and equipment checks completed, we pedal north on our bike trek that will circle the Elk and Sawatch mountain ranges in central Colorado. After a visit to the historic mining town that is now the ski resort of Crested Butte, we ride a bus over a rough gravel road to Paonia Reservoir to resume our cycling adventure. Next we cycle through the beautiful Crystal River Valley where we visit the abandoned marble quarry and mill before spending the night in the elegant Redstone Inn. By following winding back roads and a bike path, we arrive in Aspen the next day. Our itinerary includes an extra day in this exciting cosmopolitan mountain town with plenty of optional activities such as browsing the boutiques, soaking in the jacuzzi at our inn, or cycling to the base of the picturesque Maroon Bells peaks. Rested and well fed, we are now ready to tackle the alpine world of Independence Pass on day five. At the summit we are rewarded with incredible views and a long coast to the Arkansas River Valley. The next afternoon finds us at the Monarch Lodge enjoying the outdoor hot tub, health club and racquetball courts before our final dinner together and then pedal back to Gunnison.

LENGTH OF TRIP: 7 days   **DEPARTURE DATES:** June-August

TOTAL COST: $539   **TYPE OF PAYMENT ACCEPTED:** Check, cash, t.c.

RESERVATIONS/DEPOSIT: $125 deposit 3 weeks in advance

CANCELLATION POLICY: Deposit forfeited unless notified 3 weeks prior

DEPARTURE LOCATION: Gunnison, CO   **NEAREST AIRPORT:** Gunnison, CO

HEALTH, FITNESS OR AGE REQUIREMENTS: Good physical condition, 18 years old minimum.

TYPE OF WEATHER TO EXPECT: Hot and dry

BEST TYPE OF CLOTHING AND FOOTWEAR: T-shirt, windbreaker, bike shorts, running or biking shoes

PERSONAL GEAR REQUIRED: Suggested list available

SPECIAL GEAR/EQUIPMENT REQUIRED: Helmets, 10-speed bike (can be rented from outfitter)

WHAT NOT TO BRING: Large suitcases

PHOTO POSSIBILITIES: Fantastic

FISHING POSSIBILITIES: Good   **LICENSE REQUIREMENT:** Colorado

BEST TYPE OF FISHING TACKLE: small spinners, fly fishing

REPRESENTATIVE MENU—BREAKFAST: Omelettes, biscuits

LUNCH: Fruit, yogurt, cheese, juice

DINNER: Prime rib, salad bar, dessert

CHORES/DUTIES GUESTS ARE EXPECTED TO HELP WITH: None

ADDITIONAL SPECIAL INFORMATION: Brochure available

NAME OF OUTFITTER: Colorado Bicycle Tours

ADDRESS: P.O. Box 45   **CONTACT:** Roger and Kathy Cox

CITY: Pitkin   **TITLE:** Directors

STATE: Colorado   **ZIP:** 81241   **TELEPHONE:** (303) 641-4240

NUMBER OF YEARS IN BUSINESS: 4   **NUMBER OF STAFF:** 2 per trip

SPECIALIZING IN: Deluxe inn-to-inn, van supported bicycle tours in Colorado. Conventional paved road touring and mountain bike tours.

SPECIAL PHILOSOPHY, CREDO, GOALS BEHIND BUSINESS: Our program provides the encouragement and support to make bicycle touring in Colorado as much fun as possible.

Photo: Colorado Bicycle Tours

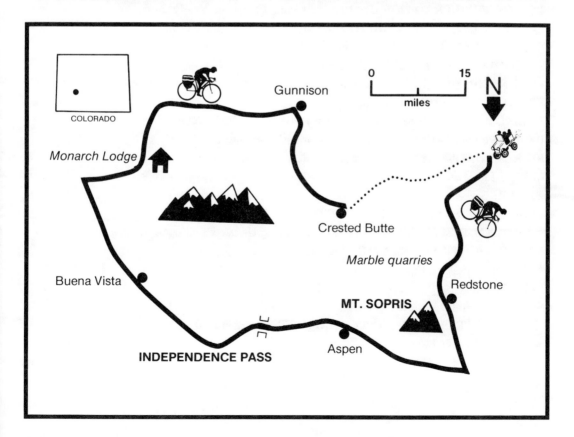

COLORADO

Gunnison

0   15
miles

N

Monarch Lodge

Crested Butte

Marble quarries

Buena Vista

Redstone

MT. SOPRIS

INDEPENDENCE PASS

Aspen

🚴 CAPE COD VACATION

Miles of cycling trails make Cape Cod and Martha's Vineyard extraordinary places for a week on two wheels. We begin by pedaling east from Falmouth along quiet country roads bordering the south shore. Continuing east, we ride on the Cape Cod Rail Trail through woodlands of red oak and pitch pine and past salt water ponds. From Nauset Beach on the Cape Cod National Seashore we ride into the crafts-filled village of Wellfleet. The next two days give us the opportunity to explore the National Seashore where spectacular dunes, wild beaches and open heath greeted the Pilgrims. We also have time to wander through Provincetown, known for its artists' community and fine seafood restaurants. The next two days take us west on quiet lanes next to Cape Cod Bay and along an old towpath next to the Cape Cod Canal. The ferry sweeps us across Vineyard Sound on day six to the enchanting island of Martha's Vineyard. Miles of bike trails and lightly travelled roads connect the towns and villages. At day's end we ferry back to Falmouth. The final day's ride explores Woods Hole, where we can visit the National Fisheries Aquarium. The week ends with a ride on the Shining Sea Bike Path, along the beach from Woods Hole to Falmouth.

LENGTH OF TRIP: 7 days

DEPARTURE DATES: June 3, Sept. 9, Sept. 23

TOTAL COST: $495

TYPE OF PAYMENT ACCEPTED: Check, cash, credit card

RESERVATIONS/DEPOSIT: $150 deposit

CANCELLATION POLICY: Forfeit deposit

DEPARTURE LOCATION: Cape Cod

NEAREST AIRPORT: Hyannis, MA

TRANSPORTATION INFORMATION: 15-passenger van from NYC to Cape, $32 round trip

HEALTH, FITNESS OR AGE REQUIREMENTS: 18 years or older unless with guardian

TYPE OF WEATHER TO EXPECT: Mild late spring, late summer, early autumn

BEST TYPE OF CLOTHING AND FOOTWEAR: Comfortable, loose-fitting, layers

PERSONAL GEAR REQUIRED: Personal duffle

SPECIAL GEAR/EQUIPMENT REQUIRED: Bicycle

WHAT NOT TO BRING: Too much luggage

PHOTO POSSIBILITIES: Fantastic

FISHING POSSIBILITIES: Good

LICENSE REQUIREMENT: Visitor

BEST TYPE OF FISHING TACKLE: Varies for fresh and salt water

REPRESENTATIVE MENU—BREAKFAST: Full breakfast

LUNCH: Picnic on the road

DINNER: Sea food, fresh vegetables, homemade desserts and breads

CHORES/DUTIES GUESTS ARE EXPECTED TO HELP WITH: None

ADDITIONAL SPECIAL INFORMATION: Rules of bicycle safety sent upon confirmation

NAME OF OUTFITTER: Country Cycling Tours

ADDRESS: 140 W. 83 St.

CONTACT: Sherry Goldstein

CITY: New York

TITLE: Owner

STATE: New York   **ZIP:** 10025

TELEPHONE: (212) 874-5151

NUMBER OF YEARS IN BUSINESS: 7 **NUMBER OF STAFF:** 24

SPECIALIZING IN: Bicycling

SPECIAL PHILOSOPHY, CREDO, GOALS BEHIND BUSINESS: The joy of discovering the people and flavor of the regions and countries through which we cycle.

Photo: Peter Goldstein

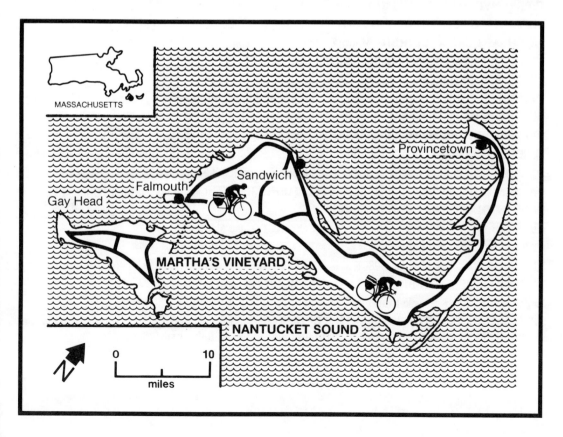

RUFF STUFF MOUNTAIN BICYCLE TOUR

As the western Montana sun crests the horizon and begins removing the nip from the air, we crawl from our tents into a silent world full of the scents of pine and—yes!—bacon frying! Later that morning, stomachs full and spirits soaring, we visit the Gildersleeves at their gold mining operations. They carved their homestead from the wilderness over 30 years ago. The next day finds us pedalling our fat-tire bikes along the top of a 7,000-foot-high ridge, the same one traversed by prehistoric Indians as they passed east over the Bitterroot Range en route to bison hunting grounds in what is now central Montana. We hike up the talus slopes of Chimney Butte and gaze westward into Idaho's prairie country, as did members of the Lewis and Clark party 200 years ago. From the top of this viewpoint, they realized that the deep mountain forest was at last about to release its grip on them. Our afternoon rest stops at Indian Post Office and Horse Sweat Pass conjure up pictures from a time now forgotten. By the final day, our rough road-riding skills are so honed that we fly down the 12-mile descent through ancient cedars to a special, hidden spot. As we soak in the natural hot springs, we are served scrumptious hors d'oeuvres and crisp white wine.

LENGTH OF TRIP: 7 days   **DEPARTURE DATES:** July 22, August 5, August 19

TOTAL COST: $400   **TYPE OF PAYMENT ACCEPTED:** Any

RESERVATIONS/DEPOSIT: $125 deposit; full payment due 30 days prior to trip

CANCELLATION POLICY: Money not refunded if person displaced others

DEPARTURE LOCATION: Missoula, MT   **NEAREST AIRPORT:** Missoula, MT

TRANSPORTATION INFORMATION: Will pick up at airport if notified in advance; taxi

HEALTH, FITNESS OR AGE REQUIREMENTS: Good physical condition

TYPE OF WEATHER TO EXPECT: Warm days, cool nights, possible rain

BEST TYPE OF CLOTHING AND FOOTWEAR: High altitude summer clothes; hiking boots

PERSONAL GEAR REQUIRED: Mountain bike, tent, sleeping bag, basic tool kit

SPECIAL GEAR/EQUIPMENT REQUIRED: See above

PHOTO POSSIBILITIES: Fantastic

FISHING POSSIBILITIES: Fantastic   **LICENSE REQUIREMENT:** Idaho

BEST TYPE OF FISHING TACKLE: Breakdown or telescoping rod, wet and dry flies

REPRESENTATIVE MENU—BREAKFAST: Huckleberry pancakes, sausage

LUNCH: Chicken salad on pita bread

DINNER: Chicken and veggies baked in foil, blueberry muffins, 3-bean salad

CHORES/DUTIES GUESTS ARE EXPECTED TO HELP WITH: Maintain personal equipment

NAME OF OUTFITTER: Bikecentennial

ADDRESS: P.O. Box 8308   **CONTACT:** Mac McCoy

CITY: Missoula   **TITLE:** Trips Coordinator

STATE: Montana   **ZIP:** 59801   **TELEPHONE:** (406) 721-1776

NUMBER OF YEARS IN BUSINESS: 9   **NUMBER OF STAFF:** 10

SPECIALIZING IN: Bicycle tours

SPECIAL PHILOSOPHY, CREDO, GOALS BEHIND BUSINESS: We are the bicycle travel association and attempt to make bicycle travel attractive to more and more individuals.

Photo: Stuart Crook

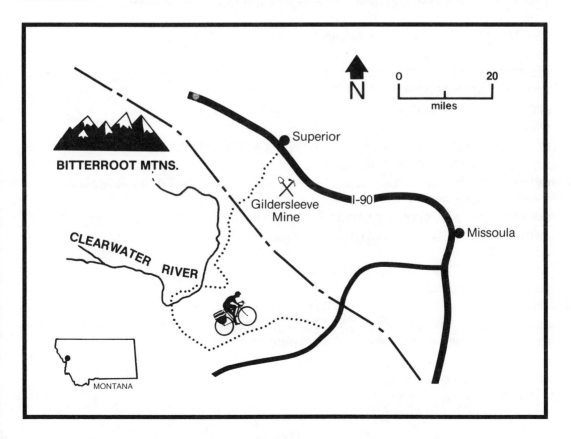

 COORS CLASSIC TOURPAK

In August of 1985 America's greatest bicycle race will celebrate the start of its second decade by conducting a two-week stage race that will begin in San Francisco, California and cross the western half of the United States with races in Sacramento, Lake Tahoe, Reno, Grand Junction, Aspen, Vail, Estes Park, Denver and Boulder. As part of the festivities race organizers are offering, for the second year, the very popular Coors Classic Tourpak. This unique travel adventure offers a limited number of spectators a chance to travel with Olympic and world-class cyclists from 14 nations as they tour the West. All transportation and housing requirements are provided along with several special benefits available only to Tourpak participants: exclusive front row seats, private interview and seminars conducted by professional cyclists and technicians, tickets to an amazing game called Cycleball, invitations to racer banquets, first person exposure to the winners of each race and much, much more! If you have ever wanted to experience world-class cycling and get a dynamite travel vacation to boot this is the adventure for you. Bring your bike if you want (we'll take care of it for you) and get ready for two weeks of the most exciting, scenic and spectacular cycling action of your life as you travel with one of the most pretigious events in America—The Coors International Bicycle Classic. Write for more details.

LENGTH OF TRIP: 15 days   **DEPARTURE DATES:** August 2, 1985

TOTAL COST: Approximately $800   **TYPE OF PAYMENT ACCEPTED:** Check, money order

RESERVATIONS/DEPOSIT: $400 deposit by June 1, balance by July 1

CANCELLATION POLICY: Full refund before July 1, no refund thereafter

DEPARTURE LOCATION: San Francisco, CA   **NEAREST AIRPORT:** San Francisco

TRANSPORTATION INFORMATION: Private shuttle from airport, air conditioned chartered comfort-coach throughout race

HEALTH, FITNESS OR AGE REQUIREMENTS: None

TYPE OF WEATHER TO EXPECT: Cool to hot

BEST TYPE OF CLOTHING AND FOOTWEAR: Casual, touring clothes for riding

PERSONAL GEAR REQUIRED: Personal duffle

SPECIAL GEAR/EQUIPMENT REQUIRED: Weather protection

PHOTO POSSIBILITIES: Fantastic

FISHING POSSIBILITIES: Very good   **LICENSE REQUIREMENT:** Out-of-state

BEST TYPE OF FISHING TACKLE: Trout flies and lures

REPRESENTATIVE MENU: Guests are on their own for daily meals but will be invited to join in four different banquets not open to the public

CHORES/DUTIES GUESTS ARE EXPECTED TO HELP WITH: Loading and unloading own bike

ADDITIONAL SPECIAL INFORMATION: Guests don't have to be cyclists or bring a bike to enjoy this special vacation.

NAME OF OUTFITTER: Coors International Bicycle Classic

ADDRESS: 1540 Lehigh   **CONTACT:** Joan Wood

CITY: Boulder   **TITLE:** Operations manager

STATE: Colorado   **ZIP:** 80303   **TELEPHONE:** (303) 499-1108

NUMBER OF YEARS IN BUSINESS: 10   **NUMBER OF STAFF:** 7

SPECIALIZING IN: International sporting events

SPECIAL PHILOSOPHY, CREDO, GOALS BEHIND BUSINESS: To offer an affordable package plan for anyone wishing to see the West in a unique fashion.

Photo: Michael Chritton

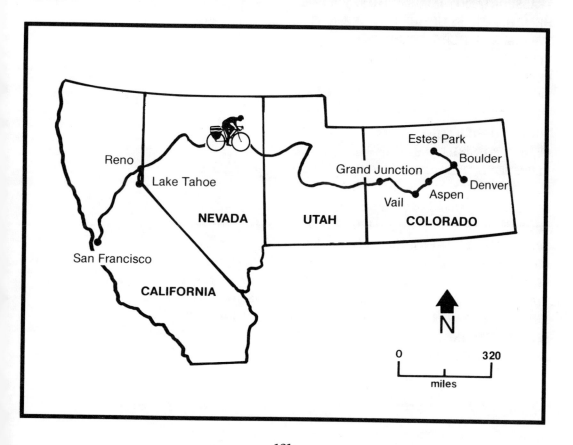

🚲 WINE COUNTRY BICYCLE TOUR

Experience the true diversity of California, from towering redwoods to rolling vineyards. Share the history created by explorers, homesteaders, Indians, conquistadors, and missionaries. Ride through charming towns hosting an array of antique shops, art galleries and unusual stores for browsing. Cycling on this wine country tour is ideal. Our routes are along some of the most scenic roads in northern California. In addition to acres of vineyards we'll pass lush pastures and stands of giant redwoods. While pedalling through the Napa, Sonoma, Alexander and Russian River valleys, we have ample time to enjoy the wine-tasting and tours offered at a variety of both famous and little-known wineries along the way. Your purchases will be carried in a van. From Geyserville to Calistoga and Sonoma to Occidental, we've selected a wonderful array of wine country inns and restaurants. Our first night is spent at the Isis Oasis. The second and third evenings find us at the elegant Mount View Hotel. We then ride off to the Sonoma Hotel for the fourth night. Our last night is in Occidental, where an Italian dinner at the famous Union Hotel awaits us. Swimming, hot tubs, excellent cuisine, wine tasting and camaraderie compelement this week of cycling in the California wine country.

LENGTH OF TRIP: 5 days

DEPARTURE DATES: May 6, June 17, July 15, July 29, Sept. 9, Sept. 23, Oct. 14

TOTAL COST: $523

TYPE OF PAYMENT ACCEPTED: Check, Visa, MC

RESERVATIONS/DEPOSIT: $150 deposit

CANCELLATION POLICY: Forfeit all deposit/payment

DEPARTURE LOCATION: Geyserville, CA   **NEAREST AIRPORT:** San Francisco

TRANSPORTATION INFORMATION: Van shuttle

HEALTH, FITNESS OR AGE REQUIREMENTS: Good physical athlete

TYPE OF WEATHER TO EXPECT: Warm

BEST TYPE OF CLOTHING AND FOOTWEAR: Touring clothing

PERSONAL GEAR REQUIRED: Bicycle

SPECIAL GEAR/EQUIPMENT REQUIRED: None

WHAT NOT TO BRING: Too much of anything

PHOTO POSSIBILITIES: Fantastic

FISHING POSSIBILITIES: None

REPRESENTATIVE MENU—BREAKFAST: Country inns, local restaurants

LUNCH: Picnic

DINNER: Country inns, local restaurants

CHORES/DUTIES GUESTS ARE EXPECTED TO HELP WITH: None

NAME OF OUTFITTER: Backroads Bicycle Touring Co.

ADDRESS: P.O. Box 5534   **CONTACT:** Tom Hale

CITY: Berkeley   **TITLE:** Owner/director/tour leader

STATE: California   **ZIP:** 94705   **TELEPHONE:** (415) 652-0786

NUMBER OF YEARS IN BUSINESS: 5   **NUMBER OF STAFF:** 12

SPECIALIZING IN: Bicycle tours

SPECIAL PHILOSOPHY, CREDO, GOALS BEHIND BUSINESS: Show guests the time of a lifetime

Photo: Backroads Bicycle Touring Co.

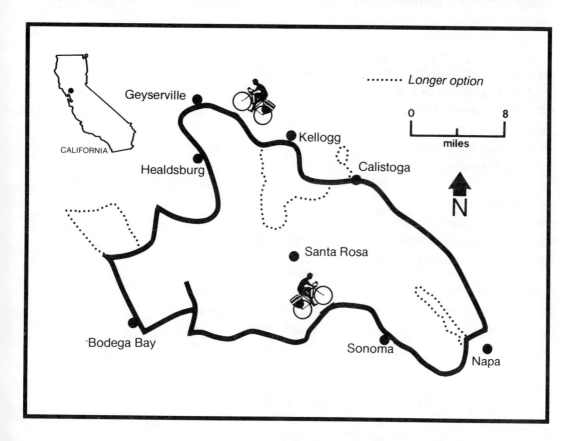

TOUR OF THE SCIUTO RIVER VALLEY

This event is not a race but a recreational and social rally for bicyclists. For most Tour of the Sciuto River Valley riders, the trip begins at the crack of dawn as they roll out of the Ohio Statehouse grounds for the 105-mile ride to Portsmouth on the Ohio River. Columbus is quiet and the downtown empty at this hour. As the sun burns away the morning mist, you become aware of the hundreds of cyclists sharing the road with you, representing veteran bike racers to novice cyclists. Riders come from every state in the Union and represent a cross-section of American society. Through the farm and woodlands of the southern Ohio countryside you enjoy the company of many people sharing the common goal of completing the 210-mile tour. The miles melt away as you are carried along in the bobbing mass of cyclists. At 25-mile intervals you can relax at food stops and refuel on picnic-style meals before continuing onward. Spring rains are inevitable on TOSRV but the foul weather tends to draw riders together as they help each other along with encouragement and good humor. A delicious chicken dinner awaits you in Portsmouth along with floor space in a gym for your sleeping bag. The next morning you mount up for the return to Columbus and another great day of bicycling.

LENGTH OF TRIP: 2 days

DEPARTURE DATES: Varies

TOTAL COST: American Youth Hostel members $19, others $22

TYPE OF PAYMENT ACCEPTED: Check, money order

RESERVATIONS/DEPOSIT: Paid in full with entry form

CANCELLATION POLICY: No refunds

DEPARTURE LOCATION: Columbus, OH   **NEAREST AIRPORT:** Columbus, OH

TRANSPORTATION INFORMATION: Various

HEALTH, FITNESS OR AGE REQUIREMENTS: Participants should have cycled a minimum of 300 miles prior to TOSRV

TYPE OF WEATHER TO EXPECT: Probably rainy

BEST TYPE OF CLOTHING AND FOOTWEAR: Wool; cycling shoes

PERSONAL GEAR REQUIRED: Basic tools for bike repairs, bicycle, sleeping bag

SPECIAL GEAR/EQUIPMENT REQUIRED: None

WHAT NOT TO BRING: Excess equipment

PHOTO POSSIBILITIES: Good

FISHING POSSIBILITIES: None

REPRESENTATIVE MENU—BREAKFAST: Picnic style food

LUNCH: Picnic style food

DINNER: Saturday night chicken dinner

CHORES/DUTIES GUESTS ARE EXPECTED TO HELP WITH: None

ADDITIONAL SPECIAL INFORMATION: It is especially important that cyclists prepare for TOSRV with good training miles and a proper choice of clothing

NAME OF OUTFITTER: Columbus Council of American Youth Hostels

ADDRESS: P.O. Box 2311

CONTACT: Charles Pace

CITY: Columbus

TITLE: TOSRV Tour Director

STATE: Ohio   **ZIP:** 43223

TELEPHONE: (614) 461-6648

NUMBER OF YEARS IN BUSINESS: 50+   **NUMBER OF STAFF:** 400 volunteers

SPECIALIZING IN: TOSRV is the major event of Columbus American Youth Hostels. Other activities include bicycling, hiking, canoeing, rafting, skiing, caving

Photo: TOSRV photo by Greg Siple

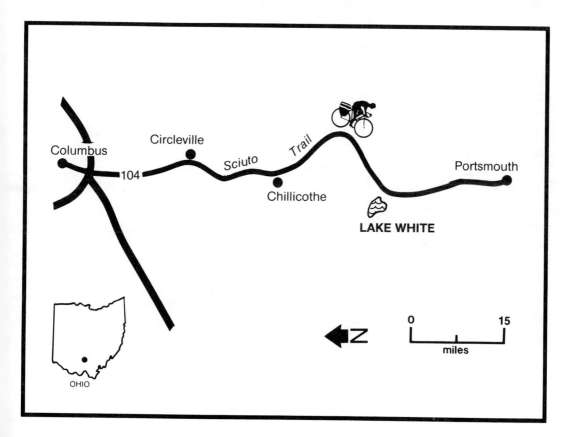

Columbus
Circleville
104
Sciuto
Trail
Chillicothe
LAKE WHITE
Portsmouth

OHIO

N

0
15
miles

MISTY FJORDS SALTWATER KAYAKING

The Misty Fjord cruise ship drops us off at the mouth of Rudyard Bay, a misnomer because this is a fjord, replete with 3,500-foot cliffs dwarfing our kayaks. Eagles are numerous and seals pop out of the water as if to check our progress into their domain. Our first night campsite is in Punchbowl Cove and we set a crab pot for possible crab delicacies later. In the meantime, Dolly Varden trout are easily caught on our spinning gear. Around noon we pull up the pot and find several nice specimens for dinner. We then quietly paddle north toward the head of the bay and view wildlife on shore, including a mink wrestling a carp onto the beach. We establish camp on the second night at the mouth of a salmon stream in the South Arm. Thousands of salmon mill in the water, waiting for the mystical urge to head up stream to spawn and die. Numerous eagles and seals feed on the fish. We push off the next morning towards the head of the inlet. Late in the morning we pass through the narrows and gaze upward in wonder at two arched caves. A pictograph awes us further downstream. By early afternoon, we are leisurely stretching our legs on a large grassy estuary, watching ducks feed. But the Misty Fjord rounds the bend to pick us up and return us to Ketchikan.

LENGTH OF TRIP: 3 days

TOTAL COST: $325

DEPARTURE DATES: Customized

TYPE OF PAYMENT ACCEPTED: Check, money order

RESERVATIONS/DEPOSIT: $100 deposit 30 days prior

CANCELLATION POLICY: Deposit refund negotiable

DEPARTURE LOCATION: Ketchikan, AK **NEAREST AIRPORT:** Ketchikan, AK

TRANSPORTATION INFORMATION: Bus, rent a car, taxi

HEALTH, FITNESS OR AGE REQUIREMENTS: None

TYPE OF WEATHER TO EXPECT: 50-85° F, occasional rain

BEST TYPE OF CLOTHING AND FOOTWEAR: Wool, rain gear, low boots, tennis shoes

PERSONAL GEAR REQUIRED: Sleeping bag

SPECIAL GEAR/EQUIPMENT REQUIRED: None

WHAT NOT TO BRING: Rigid frame pack

PHOTO POSSIBILITIES: Fantastic

FISHING POSSIBILITIES: Fantastic **LICENSE REQUIREMENT:** Sport fishing $10

BEST TYPE OF FISHING TACKLE: Spinning gear

REPRESENTATIVE MENU—BREAKFAST: Bacon, eggs

LUNCH: Soup, sandwiches

DINNER: Dungeness crab, trout

CHORES/DUTIES GUESTS ARE EXPECTED TO HELP WITH: Paddle kayak

NAME OF OUTFITTER: Outdoor Alaska

ADDRESS: Box 7814

CITY: Ketchikan

STATE: Alaska   **ZIP:** 99901

NUMBER OF YEARS IN BUSINESS: 6

CONTACT: Dale Pihlman

TITLE: Owner, manager

TELEPHONE: (907) 225-6044, 247-8444

NUMBER OF STAFF: 6

SPECIALIZING IN: Salt water kayaking, cruises

SPECIAL PHILOSOPHY, CREDO, GOALS BEHIND BUSINESS: Immersion in wilderness solitude with special attention to the intertidal marine ecosystem.

Photo: Outdoor Alaska

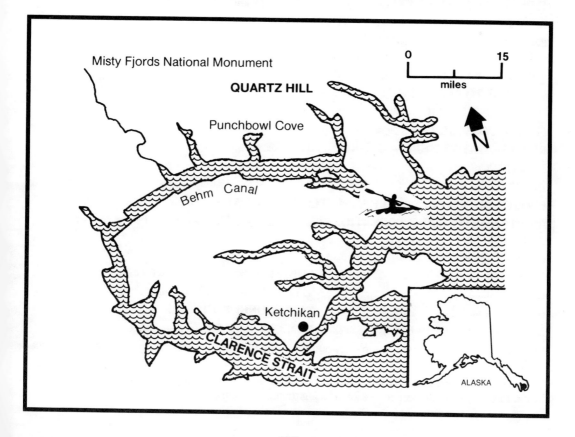

HUBBARD GLACIER KAYAK TRIP

This saltwater kayak adventure takes place at the base of Alaska's St. Elias range, one of the tallest coastal ranges in the world. Draining this mighty range is also one of the longest and most rapidly advancing glaciers in the world. The long, steep arms of Russell and Nunatak fjords form the pathway for this exciting trip. The scenery begins to unfold when we board the bushplane for the flight from Yakutat into the fjord. The next two days are spent learning to kayak and exploring the beaches of Russell Fjord as we move closer to the glacier. Even before they are in sight, we pass icebergs and hear the distant thundering of new ones being born as they break off the glacier's face and crash into the water. The high point of the trip is making camp opposite the glacier face and we visit the tiny island which lies in front. From here we have spectacular views of the seven-mile wall of blue glacier ice which averages 200-300 feet high. Seals and pelagic birds concentrate in this area, taking advantage of the upwellings caused by the falling ice. An exciting day hike will also take us up another glacier's outwash plain and allow us to walk on the moraine-covered fringe of the Hubbard glacier itself. The bushplane returns for us on the seventh day.

LENGTH OF TRIP: 7 days

DEPARTURE DATES: June 32; July 28; Aug. 25, 1984

TOTAL COST: $625 plus $150 floatplane

TYPE OF PAYMENT ACCEPTED: Any

RESERVATIONS/DEPOSIT: $200 deposit

CANCELLATION POLICY: Deposit credited to trip of choice in future

DEPARTURE LOCATION: Yakutat, AK

NEAREST AIRPORT: Junea or Anchorage

TRANSPORTATION INFORMATION: Jet plane to Yakutat, floatplane to glacier

HEALTH, FITNESS OR AGE REQUIREMENTS: Good health. No experience necessary.

TYPE OF WEATHER TO EXPECT: Temp in 60's; sunny and rainy

BEST TYPE OF CLOTHING AND FOOTWEAR: Warm clothing, rain gear, rubber boots

PERSONAL GEAR REQUIRED: Gear list mailed

SPECIAL GEAR/EQUIPMENT REQUIRED: Calf-high rubber boots are mandatory; can be rented with rain gear for $25. Sleeping bags $10.

WHAT NOT TO BRING: Pets, hair dryers

PHOTO POSSIBILITIES: Fantastic

FISHING POSSIBILITIES: None

REPRESENTATIVE MENU—BREAKFAST: Pancakes or eggs

LUNCH: Picnic style

DINNER: Pasta dish, fresh salad

CHORES/DUTIES GUESTS ARE EXPECTED TO HELP WITH: Set up tents, load boats, paddle

ADDITIONAL SPECIAL INFORMATION: 95% of guests have never kayaked before. Many are in their 50s.

NAME OF OUTFITTER: Alaska Discovery

ADDRESS: Box 26

CONTACT: Bonnie Kaden; Ken Leghorn

CITY: Gustavus

TITLE: Manager; assistant manager

STATE: Alaska   **ZIP:** 99826

TELEPHONE: (907) 586-1911

NUMBER OF YEARS IN BUSINESS: 13

NUMBER OF STAFF: 5 staff, 20 guides

SPECIALIZING IN: 2-3 week completely outfitted wilderness trips by raft, ocean kayak, canoe, backpack and cross country ski

SPECIAL PHILOSOPHY, CREDO, GOALS BEHIND BUSINESS: To promote wilderness preservation and to establish wilderness recreation as a legitimate alternative.

Photo: Hayden Kaden

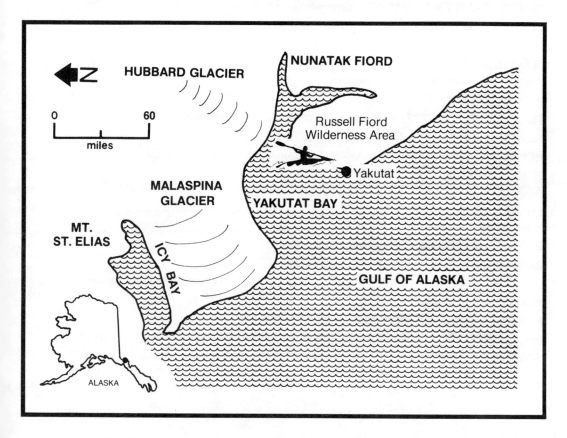

EASTERN AT SEA KAYAK TOURS

Our sea kayaking is based in the Deer Isle/Stonington coastal region, a peninsula jutting out between neighboring Penobscot and Jericho Bays in Maine. Camden is to the south and Acadia National Park is north. This coastal area is primarily a quiet fishing area and promises islands and coves which are removed from Maine's commercial pressures. Deer Isle's southern coves are ringed with small undeveloped islands, some sheltering sandy coves and wild grasses, others with rugged, rocky inlets and dense stands of pine hiding osprey nests. This region offers the opportunity to view seals, seabirds, harbor porpoise and infinite ocean life. Many of these islands are only a quarter-of-a-mile paddle from shore and depending on our paddlers' abilities and interests, we may visit and explore the waters and woods of Maine's protected offshore islands. Sea kayaking is for everyone who wants to explore our coastal environment and share in the sea's treasures and surprises. The menu will feature some of these treasures, including lobster, clams and mussels, as well as the all-American steak and potato fare with lemonade, fruit and vegetables. Trips run regardless of the weather, revealing all of the sea's many moods.

LENGTH OF TRIP: Varies

TOTAL COST: Varies

DEPARTURE DATES: Varies

TYPE OF PAYMENT ACCEPTED: Check, money order

RESERVATIONS/DEPOSIT: 50% deposit upon reservation, balance due 4 weeks prior to trip.

CANCELLATION POLICY: No refund

DEPARTURE LOCATION: Bangor, ME   **NEAREST AIRPORT:** Bangor, ME

TRANSPORTATION INFORMATION: None

HEALTH, FITNESS OR AGE REQUIREMENTS: Good physical condition, 12 years old min.

TYPE OF WEATHER TO EXPECT: Generally fair

BEST TYPE OF CLOTHING AND FOOTWEAR: Sneakers, wet suit, wind breaker

PERSONAL GEAR REQUIRED: Equipment list available

SPECIAL GEAR/EQUIPMENT REQUIRED: Guests are invited to bring own sea kayaks

WHAT NOT TO BRING: Tents, life jacket

PHOTO POSSIBILITIES: Fantastic

FISHING POSSIBILITIES: Fantastic   **LICENSE REQUIREMENT:** None

BEST TYPE OF FISHING TACKLE: Small reel and rod, 8 lb. test

REPRESENTATIVE MENU—BREAKFAST: Bacon, eggs, bread, juice, coffee

LUNCH: Fruit, rolls, cheese, juice

DINNER: Seafood, vegetables, lemonade, coffee

CHORES/DUTIES GUESTS ARE EXPECTED TO HELP WITH: Assisting in carrying equipment and sea kayaks

NAME OF OUTFITTER: Eastern River Expeditions

ADDRESS: Box 1173

CITY: Greenville

STATE: Maine   **ZIP:** 04441

NUMBER OF YEARS IN BUSINESS: 7

CONTACT: Joseph Fabin

TITLE: Director of Sea Kayak Program

TELEPHONE: (207) 675-2411

NUMBER OF STAFF: 2

SPECIALIZING IN: Sea kayaking and study of coastal and marine environment

SPECIAL PHILOSOPHY, CREDO, GOALS BEHIND BUSINESS: Sea kayaking is for everyone who wants to explore our coastal environment and share in the treasures the sea has given us.

Photo: Eastern River Expeditions

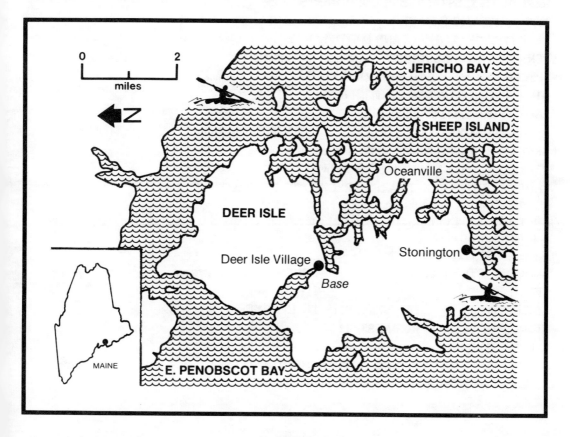

JERICHO BAY

SHEEP ISLAND

Oceanville

DEER ISLE

Stonington

Deer Isle Village

Base

MAINE

E. PENOBSCOT BAY

0   2
miles

N

♣ NORTHWEST WATERS

Go north this summer to Nootka Island and Esperanza Inlet on the west coast of Vancouver Island, British Columbia. Explore by canoe where the land meets the sea, gliding quietly and slowly through the deep fjords and along the calm waterways of a hundred island passages. Beginners and veterans can equally enjoy this 10-day expedition as they share the ocean environment with sea birds, deer, bear, otter and whales. Camping on small off-shore islands and travelling by water will immerse one in the moods and colors of sea and sky at dawn and sunset, and expose one to the energy of wind, wave and summer storm. The 12-person per group expeditions take the time to look and experience this wilderness setting with no stress and no haste. Fishing for salmon or hiking on the islands in search of wild blueberries are just two ways to idle away the hours. This is not a catered expedition but a guided one, allowing participants the freedom to eat what they want, and do what they want. All essential equipment is provided. All participants need to be concerned with is paddling a canoe after receiving instructions, and help with community chores at the campsites. A relaxed, refreshed mind and an appreciation of this rugged seascape will leave with you.

LENGTH OF TRIP: 10 days   **DEPARTURE DATES:** Varies

TOTAL COST: $385   **TYPE OF PAYMENT ACCEPTED:** Check

RESERVATIONS/DEPOSIT: $125 before May 15

CANCELLATION POLICY: See brochure

DEPARTURE LOCATION: Varies   **NEAREST AIRPORT:** Campbell River

TRANSPORTATION INFORMATION: Information sent upon receipt of deposit

HEALTH, FITNESS OR AGE REQUIREMENTS: None

TYPE OF WEATHER TO EXPECT: Northwest coastal

BEST TYPE OF CLOTHING AND FOOTWEAR: Equipment list available

PERSONAL GEAR REQUIRED: Equipment list available

SPECIAL GEAR/EQUIPMENT REQUIRED: Equipment list available

WHAT NOT TO BRING: Anything not on list

PHOTO POSSIBILITIES: Fantastic

FISHING POSSIBILITIES: Fantastic   **LICENSE REQUIREMENT:** CDN Non-resident

BEST TYPE OF FISHING TACKLE: Will send info

REPRESENTATIVE MENU: Supply your own

CHORES/DUTIES GUESTS ARE EXPECTED TO HELP WITH: Community choice; building fires, carrying canoes, gathering wood

ADDITIONAL SPECIAL INFORMATION: The fare reflects that this is NOT a catered expedition but a *guided* expedition

NAME OF OUTFITTER: Northwest Waters

ADDRESS: P.O. Box 212A   **CONTACT:** Robert Herman

CITY: Portland   **TITLE:** Owner

STATE: Oregon   **ZIP:** 97202/0212   **TELEPHONE:** (503) 242-0838

NUMBER OF YEARS IN BUSINESS: 11

SPECIALIZING IN: Ocean canoe expeditions

SPECIAL PHILOSOPHY, CREDO, GOALS BEHIND BUSINESS: Clients participate in the experience. No stress, slow movements. Seeing and enjoying nature.

Photo: Dorothy Haegert

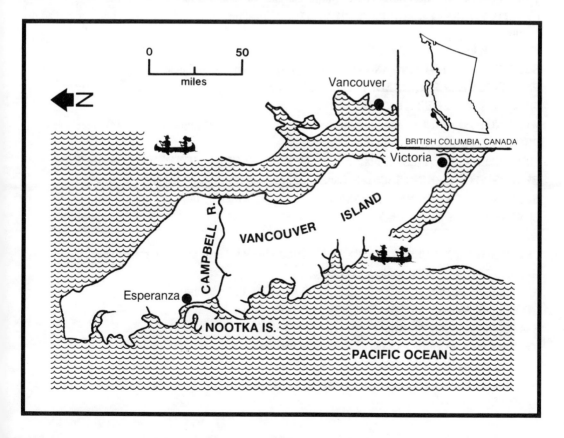

NORTH CANOE

This canoe expedition begins in the historic fishing village of Grand Marais and travels by car through Grand Portage, a one-time center of French and English fur trading. The ride continues inland past abandoned mining towns until the road ends at Northern Light Lake. Gear is loaded into canoes and the open expanse of water is entered. The first day's travel is light and the campsite that evening is comfortable, allowing everyone a chance to become familiarized with the equipment and procedure. The next day is a morning's paddle further into the scenic area and camp is pitched near prehistoric pictographs and a delightful sandy beach. Dinner that evening is a Dutch oven treat and a sweet bread improved with fresh-picked berries. The third day invites fishing the prime territory of small-mouth bass en route to our next camp, which we reach by carrying our canoes and gear a short distance to Saganaga Lake. On Saganaga, we paddle to a maze of islands where we have a choice of campsites. On the fourth day we complete two short portages, one of which skirts the beautiful Northern Light Falls, where we linger to fish and relax. On the fifth day we paddle back to Northern Light Lake and camp, and return to our starting point on day six to complete the expedition.

LENGTH OF TRIP: 6 days　　**DEPARTURE DATES:** May-Sept.

TOTAL COST: $1,000 for 5 people　　**TYPE OF PAYMENT ACCEPTED:** Check

RESERVATIONS/DEPOSIT: 25% at booking

CANCELLATION POLICY: Partial forfeit

DEPARTURE LOCATION: Grand Marais,　　**NEAREST AIRPORT:** Thunder Bay, Ontario
MN

TRANSPORTATION INFORMATION: Rental car, bus, or customer pickup by van

HEALTH, FITNESS OR AGE REQUIREMENTS: Normal physical condition; one child per two adults limit

TYPE OF WEATHER TO EXPECT: Varied

BEST TYPE OF CLOTHING AND FOOTWEAR: Equipment list available

PERSONAL GEAR REQUIRED: Equipment list available

SPECIAL GEAR/EQUIPMENT REQUIRED: None

WHAT NOT TO BRING: Stereos, radios, guns, cans, motorized equipment of any sort

PHOTO POSSIBILITIES: Fantastic

FISHING POSSIBILITIES: Fantastic　　**LICENSE REQUIREMENT:** MN & Ontario $15 each

BEST TYPE OF FISHING TACKLE: Rapala, mepps, twister jigs, pack rod and spinning gear

REPRESENTATIVE MENU—BREAKFAST: Pancakes, berries, syrup

LUNCH: Sausage, cheese, crackers

DINNER: Stroganoff, drink, Dutch oven cake, vegetable

CHORES/DUTIES GUESTS ARE EXPECTED TO HELP WITH: Everyone participates

NAME OF OUTFITTER: Wilderness Waters

ADDRESS: Box 1007Z　　**CONTACT:** P. Redmond

CITY: Grand Marais　　**TITLE:** Owner

STATE: Minnesota　　**ZIP:** 55604　　**TELEPHONE:** (218) 387-2525

NUMBER OF YEARS IN BUSINESS: 15　　**NUMBER OF STAFF:** 4+

SPECIALIZING IN: Wilderness canoe trips

SPECIAL PHILOSOPHY, CREDO, GOALS BEHIND BUSINESS: Wilderness emphasis, environment, pre-history, education, low impact.

Photo: Pigeon River Expeditions

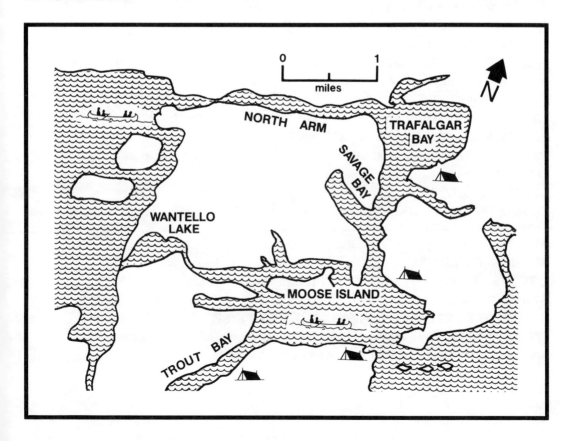

GUNFLINT GUIDED ADVENTURE TRIP

You and your trip companions and guide get acquainted over a dinner featuring platters of fish and meat, homemade breads, salad and dessert, and discuss the trip over a cup of coffee before the fireplace. After a night's rest and a big northwoods breakfast, the group heads to Seagull Lake and into the backcountry of the Boundary Waters Canoe Area of Minnesota. The next six days are spent paddling and exploring this vast, multi-million-acre water wonderland. Moose abound, as do beaver, mink, otter and eagles in the "paddle zone" of the wilderness where there are no buildings, roads or motors. The fishermen of the group catch walleye, northern or bass for dinner. This is the country of the Chippewa Indians and the French voyagers and it has changed little since they saw it years ago. This area forms the headwaters of the Arctic watershed in the glacial highlands of northeast Minnesota and all the lakes remain crystal clear and the fine drinking water is pure. When the party returns to the lodge, participants delight in hot showers, a sauna and a hearty farewell dinner. After a solid night's sleep and a big send-off breakfast, the adventurers return to their homes and wonder if the past seven days were only a dream.

LENGTH OF TRIP: 7 days   **DEPARTURE DATES:** July 21, Aug. 18, Sept. 1, Sept. 8

TOTAL COST: $295   **TYPE OF PAYMENT ACCEPTED:** Any

RESERVATIONS/DEPOSIT: $50 deposit payable up to 1 week before departure

CANCELLATION POLICY: Forfeit deposit

DEPARTURE LOCATION: Gunflint Lodge **NEAREST AIRPORT:** Duluth, MN

TRANSPORTATION INFORMATION: Bus $15; rental car $75; outfitter limo $100

HEALTH, FITNESS OR AGE REQUIREMENTS: None

TYPE OF WEATHER TO EXPECT: Hot days, cool nights

BEST TYPE OF CLOTHING AND FOOTWEAR: Equipment list available

PERSONAL GEAR REQUIRED: Equipment list available

SPECIAL GEAR/EQUIPMENT REQUIRED: Equipment list available

WHAT NOT TO BRING: Alcohol, firearms

PHOTO POSSIBILITIES: Fantastic

FISHING POSSIBILITIES: Fantastic   **LICENSE REQUIREMENT:** MN $15

BEST TYPE OF FISHING TACKLE: Light spinning gear

REPRESENTATIVE MENU—BREAKFAST: Orange drink, pancakes, hot beverage

LUNCH: Biscuits, sausage, cheese, beverage

DINNER: Freeze dried beef stroganoff, vegetable, cobbler, hot beverage

CHORES/DUTIES GUESTS ARE EXPECTED TO HELP WITH: Paddling, portage work, casual camp chores

NAME OF OUTFITTER: Gunflint Northwoods Outfitters

ADDRESS: Box 100-GTAA   **CONTACT:** Bruce Kerfoot

CITY: Grand Marais   **TITLE:** President

STATE: Minnesota   **ZIP:** 55604   **TELEPHONE:** (218) 388-2296, (800) 328-3325

NUMBER OF YEARS IN BUSINESS: 55   **NUMBER OF STAFF:** 45

SPECIALIZING IN: Canoe trips in the Boundary Waters Wilderness and the Quetico

SPECIAL PHILOSOPHY, CREDO, GOALS BEHIND BUSINESS: We emphasize low impact camping, leaving only our footprints.

Photo: Gunflint Northwoods Outfitters

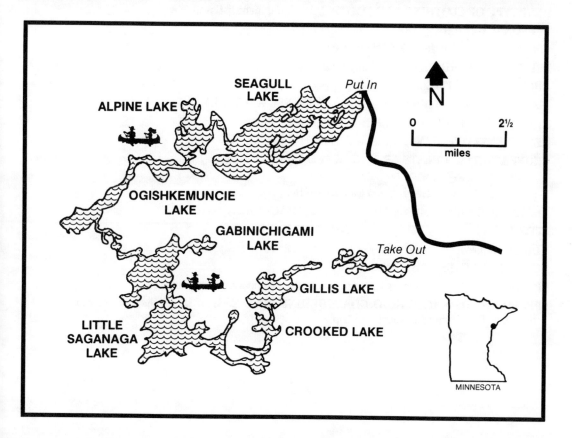

⚓ #11-KAWISHIWI TRIP

Are you independent enough to enjoy a true adventure? One that can be taken in one of the few remaining wilderness areas in the United States? This canoe trip demands self reliance and self confidence as you "get away from it all." There are no roads, no phones, no commercial distractions as you paddle and portage through pristine forests and sparkling lakes, stopping to camp overnight at lakeshore sites. Set your own pace—travel hard and put your endurance to the test, or travel leisurely, stopping to swim and laze on the beach. Catch some fish for dinner or breakfast, and enjoy the delicate flavor of a freshly caught lake trout. Evenings spent around the campfire are a soothing salve to a city-clogged mind, and calls of loons add a special note to the wilderness. You are on your own. There's no one telling you it's time to do this or that. Take a breather from the rat race and rediscover the world of the outdoors and rediscover yourself. All equipment and food is provided. Trippers simply need to provide normal good health and fitness and personal items.

LENGTH OF TRIP: 8-10 days   **DEPARTURE DATES:** May 15–Sept. 15

TOTAL COST: Varies   **TYPE OF PAYMENT ACCEPTED:** Any

RESERVATIONS/DEPOSIT: $20 deposit with booking

CANCELLATION POLICY: Forfeit deposit

DEPARTURE LOCATION: Tuscarora   **NEAREST AIRPORT:** Duluth, MN

TRANSPORTATION INFORMATION: Bus, rental car

HEALTH, FITNESS OR AGE REQUIREMENTS: Normal health

TYPE OF WEATHER TO EXPECT: Variable

BEST TYPE OF CLOTHING AND FOOTWEAR: Equipment list available

PERSONAL GEAR REQUIRED: Equipment list available

SPECIAL GEAR/EQUIPMENT REQUIRED: None

WHAT NOT TO BRING: Electrical anything

PHOTO POSSIBILITIES: Fantastic

FISHING POSSIBILITIES: Fantastic   **LICENSE REQUIREMENT:** MN

BEST TYPE OF FISHING TACKLE: Light spinning gear

REPRESENTATIVE MENU: Varies with trippers

CHORES/DUTIES GUESTS ARE EXPECTED TO HELP WITH: Trippers take care of all their own needs.

NAME OF OUTFITTER: Tuscarora Canoe Outfitters

ADDRESS: Gunflint Trail Box 110   **CONTACT:** Kerry Leeds

CITY: Grand Marais   **TITLE:** Outfitter

STATE: Minnesota   **ZIP:** 55604   **TELEPHONE:** (218) 388-2221

NUMBER OF YEARS IN BUSINESS: 10

SPECIALIZING IN: Wilderness canoe trips into the Boundary Waters Canoe Area

SPECIAL PHILOSOPHY, CREDO, GOALS BEHIND BUSINESS: To satisfy the customers by providing the needs for a happy and successful trip.

Photo: Tuscarora Canoe Outfitters

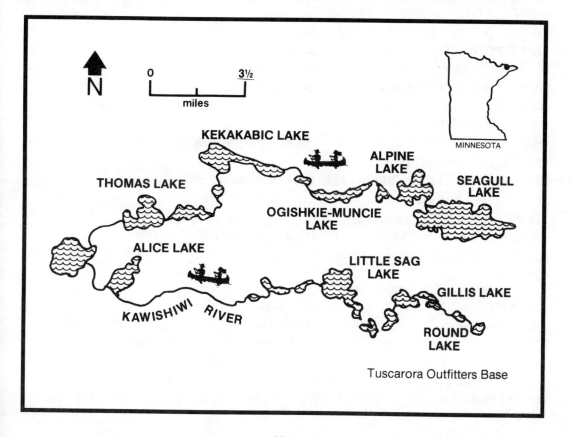

ALLAGASH WILDERNESS CANOE TRIP

The Allagash trip can begin at Chamberlain or Eagle lakes and continues for about 110 miles through the most notable waterways in the unorganized territories of Maine. We will visit the Tramway, hike to Priestly Lake and the fire tower on Priestly Mountain for a fantastic view of the state of Maine. We will take on the intricate section of whitewater known as Chase Rapids and several great stretches of whitewater on the St. John River between Allagash Village and the take-out point at St. Francis. A memorable highlight is the stopover at magnificent Allagash Falls for resting, basking in the sunshine and swimming. Although the Allagash Wilderness Waterway has many more visitors now that it is a state park, it is still the best canoeing area in the United States. The trip will last four to eight days and is well suited as a family expedition. It can be customized to fit your needs. Our food supply is a very important factor on our trips as we carry plenty of it for generous meals. When possible, fresh vegetables from our own organic garden are on the menu. Our equipment is selected for the kind of tripping to be encountered in each area. Guaranteed, you won't be bored!

LENGTH OF TRIP: 8 days

DEPARTURE DATES: June 23, July 7 and 28, August 5, 11, 19, 25

TOTAL COST: $395-$415 ($295-$315 for kids)

TYPE OF PAYMENT ACCEPTED: Check

RESERVATIONS/DEPOSIT: $100 ASAP

CANCELLATION POLICY: Deposit forfeited, but can apply to another trip

DEPARTURE LOCATION: Greenville, ME   **NEAREST AIRPORT:** Bangor, ME

TRANSPORTATION INFORMATION: Pick-up available at $20/person, $40 minimum

HEALTH, FITNESS OR AGE REQUIREMENTS: None

TYPE OF WEATHER TO EXPECT: Everything

BEST TYPE OF CLOTHING AND FOOTWEAR: Equipment list available

PERSONAL GEAR REQUIRED: Personal duffle, rain gear

SPECIAL GEAR/EQUIPMENT REQUIRED: Sleeping bag, pad

WHAT NOT TO BRING: Radios

PHOTO POSSIBILITIES: Fantastic

FISHING POSSIBILITIES: Good   **LICENSE REQUIREMENT:** 7 day

BEST TYPE OF FISHING TACKLE: Spinning

REPRESENTATIVE MENU—BREAKFAST: Hot cereal, blueberry muffins

LUNCH: Peanut butter, jam, cheese, dried fruit

DINNER: Broiled chicken, vegetables, potatoes, salad, cornmeal gingerbread

CHORES/DUTIES GUESTS ARE EXPECTED TO HELP WITH: Personal only

ADDITIONAL SPECIAL INFORMATION: Experience unnecessary, but bring a sense of adventure and a good attitude.

NAME OF OUTFITTER: Allagash Canoe Trips

ADDRESS: Box 713

CONTACT: Warren Cochrane

CITY: Greenville

TITLE: Director

STATE: Maine   **ZIP:** 04441

TELEPHONE: (207) 695-3668 after May

NUMBER OF YEARS IN BUSINESS: 31   **NUMBER OF STAFF:** 4

SPECIALIZING IN: Wilderness canoe trips into the Boundary Waters Canoe Area

SPECIAL PHILOSOPHY, CREDO, GOALS BEHIND BUSINESS: Real adventure, solid instruction, but not hardship for hardship's sake.

Photo: Allagash Canoe Trips

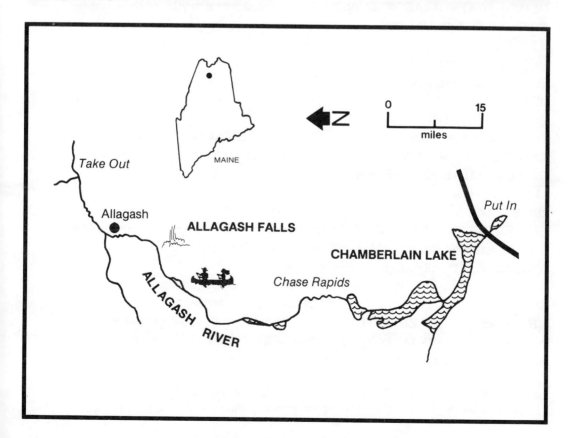

MAINE

N

0   15
miles

Take Out

Allagash

ALLAGASH FALLS

Put In

CHAMBERLAIN LAKE

Chase Rapids

ALLAGASH RIVER

VOYAGEUR CANOES ON THE MISSOURI

We will relive the days of the fur trade for seven days as we paddle in 26-foot reproductions of the French fur trader canoes. Each 10-person canoe is easy to paddle and stable enough to allow someone to stand on the gunwale. Optional side trips will explore old towns, mansions and wineries along the river. This is the river that won the West! We will hear tales and songs of the Indians, French and Germans who have lived in the area, and sagas about the river men and mountain men who lived, worked and fought their way up the Mighty Mo to the mountains. All participants will paddle and share in camp chores and be rewarded with beautiful vistas, fun experiences on the river and downhome cooking. The latter includes homemade doughnuts, bagels and lox, southern cured ham, hushpuppies, vegetables, salad, wine and homemade pie. No paddling experience is necessary. Guests just need to provide an interest in the outdoors, swimming skills, a positive attitude and the general fitness to paddle four to eight hours per day. The trip begins in St. Louis where we board a van and drive to the launch point near Arrow Rock. This trip is designed to be a learning experience for families and anyone who appreciates the outdoors and history.

LENGTH OF TRIP: 7 days **DEPARTURE DATES:** 2nd or 3rd week of June

TOTAL COST: $230 per person **TYPE OF PAYMENT ACCEPTED:** Check, money order

RESERVATIONS/DEPOSIT: Total paid 60 days before trip

CANCELLATION POLICY: Full refund 30 days before trip

DEPARTURE LOCATION: St. Charles, MO **NEAREST AIRPORT:** St. Louis

TRANSPORTATION INFORMATION: Will pick up at airport, bus or train

HEALTH, FITNESS OR AGE REQUIREMENTS: We require positive attitude about work

TYPE OF WEATHER TO EXPECT: Mild temps with possible thunderstorms

BEST TYPE OF CLOTHING AND FOOTWEAR: Long and short sleeved shirt, pants, tennis shoes

PERSONAL GEAR REQUIRED: Personal duffle and camping gear

SPECIAL GEAR/EQUIPMENT REQUIRED: Waterproof bags. Gear can be rented from outfitter.

WHAT NOT TO BRING: Recreational drugs, firearms, radios, large knife

PHOTO POSSIBILITIES: Good

FISHING POSSIBILITIES: Good **LICENSE REQUIREMENT:** Visitors

BEST TYPE OF FISHING TACKLE: Set lines or telescoping pole

REPRESENTATIVE MENU—BREAKFAST: Homemade doughnuts

LUNCH: Bagels and lox

DINNER: Southern cured ham, hushpuppies, vegetable salad, homemade pie

CHORES/DUTIES GUESTS ARE EXPECTED TO HELP WITH: Share camp chores on rotation

ADDITIONAL SPECIAL INFORMATION: Swimming skills required

NAME OF OUTFITTER: Adventures Unlimited

ADDRESS: P.O. Box 903 Mercer Blvd. **CONTACT:** Tom and Faye Sitzman

CITY: Omaha **TITLE:** Canoe outfitters

STATE: Nebraska **ZIP:** 68131 **TELEPHONE:** (402) 558-0210; 553-4010

NUMBER OF YEARS IN BUSINESS: 15 **NUMBER OF STAFF:** The Sitzman family of 5

SPECIALIZING IN: Family-type canoe trips; ocean kayak trips; voyageur canoe trips in 26-foot North Canoes

SPECIAL PHILOSOPHY, CREDO, GOALS BEHIND BUSINESS: Our trips are designed to be a learning experience well suited to families who appreciate history and the outdoors

Photo: Voyager Canoes

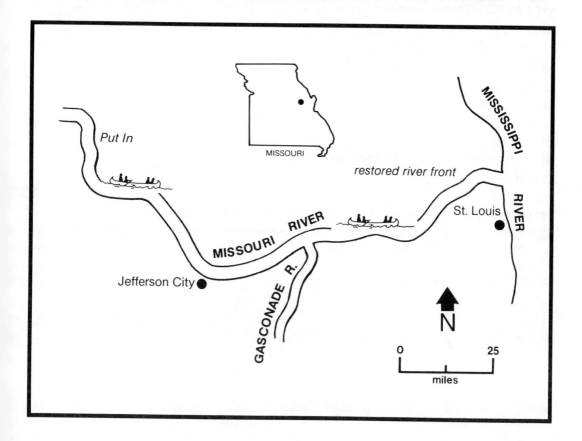

MISSISSIPPI

Put In

MISSOURI

restored river front

MISSOURI RIVER

MISSISSIPPI RIVER

St. Louis

Jefferson City

GASCONADE R.

N

0   25
miles

WILDERNESS WATERWAY EXPLORATION

The Everglades, never completely known, invites you to explore its mysteries during this 100-mile backcountry canoe trip. Your naturalist guide will lead you through areas few people have seen. Spot scarlet ibis, spoonbill, herons, egrets, storks, alligators and the elusive Everglades mink. After your arrival, we will travel through the Miccosukee Indian Reservation and the Big Cypress National Preserve to Everglades City where we'll spend the night at the Rod & Gun Club. After breakfast, we begin paddling from Chokoloskee Island, across its bay and oyster beds, and up the Lopez River. We may camp that evening at the historic Watson Homestead, the old home of the infamous frontiersman. Once on the Waterway, we begin each day with an early breakfast and then paddle through mangroves, past Indian mounds, and observe manatee, porpoise and otter at play. There will be time for fishing and exploring on foot. Our campsite may be at Lostman's Five, site of an old fishing camp; at Willie Willie, an Indian shell mound with high ground hardwood vegetation; at Camp Lonesome, where the Seminoles had a hunting camp and where tropical trees abound; and at Canepatch where wild sugarcane, bananas, avocados and guavas grow.

LENGTH OF TRIP: 9-12 days

DEPARTURE DATES: January–April

TOTAL COST: $549-$645

TYPE OF PAYMENT ACCEPTED: Check, MC, VISA

RESERVATIONS/DEPOSIT: $100 deposit with registration

CANCELLATION POLICY: Full refund less $25/person with written cancellation 30 days before trip.

DEPARTURE LOCATION: Everglades N.P. **NEAREST AIRPORT:** Miami, FL

TRANSPORTATION INFORMATION: Shuttle provided by outfitter, but cost depends on group size.

HEALTH, FITNESS OR AGE REQUIREMENTS: Good physical condition

TYPE OF WEATHER TO EXPECT: 40-80° dry season

BEST TYPE OF CLOTHING AND FOOTWEAR: Casual outdoor clothing

PERSONAL GEAR REQUIRED: Personal duffle

SPECIAL GEAR/EQUIPMENT REQUIRED: None

WHAT NOT TO BRING: Radios, weapons, illegal substances, axes

PHOTO POSSIBILITIES: Fantastic

FISHING POSSIBILITIES: Fantastic   **LICENSE REQUIREMENT:** None

BEST TYPE OF FISHING TACKLE: Saltwater

REPRESENTATIVE MENU—BREAKFAST: Varies

LUNCH: Picnic-style

DINNER: Fresh fish

CHORES/DUTIES GUESTS ARE EXPECTED TO HELP WITH: Paddling canoes

ADDITIONAL SPECIAL INFORMATION: Canoeing experience helpful but not necessary. Our natural guides have in-depth knowledge of ecological balance of Everglades and are experienced in backcountry camping.

NAME OF OUTFITTER: Everglades Canoe Outfitters, Inc.

ADDRESS: 39801 Ingraham Highway

CONTACT: Sheri M Leach

CITY: Homestead

TITLE: President

STATE: Florida   **ZIP:** 33034

TELEPHONE: (305) 246-1530

NUMBER OF YEARS IN BUSINESS: 4   **NUMBER OF STAFF:** 6

SPECIALIZING IN: Natural history tours, canoeing, biking, walking, hiking in Everglades, Ireland, Tortugas, Florida Keys

SPECIAL PHILOSOPHY, CREDO, GOALS BEHIND BUSINESS: Excellence as a standard in providing history tours

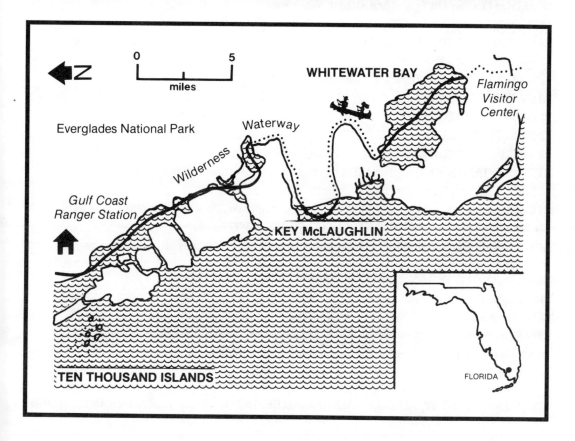

SMITH RIVER FLOAT FISHING EXPEDITION

Our float fishing expedition begins after a two- to three-hour drive across the beautiful Montana countryside of wide open spaces, mountains and small towns. Our 60-mile voyage through the Smith River Canyon will give anglers the opportunity to fish for wild Cutthroat, Rainbow and Brown trout in some of the most picturesque canyon settings imaginable. This small spring-fed river is an especially good dry fly stream. We think it is unquestionably one of the best "hopper" rivers in the West. Because there is no public access within the canyon, a wilderness atmosphere prevails and wildlife is abundant. Deer, black bear, eagles, mink and waterfowl are common sights. Elk, cougar and big horn sheep inhabit the high country. We often stop along the way to fish the better spots and take photos of the beautiful settings. We take pride in dishing out hearty meals of eggs, bacon, fruit, fresh bread, appetizers, steak and hot chocolate with schnapps for an after-dinner treat. Roomy tents, lawn chairs, massive tarps and even riverside saunas are standard gear. Three to seven days are spent amid this splendid outdoor lifestyle and nature cooperates with a lack of mosquitoes! The dry fly fishing is so outstanding that it is not uncommon for each guest to catch 20-50 fish *each*.

LENGTH OF TRIP: 3-7 days   **DEPARTURE DATES:** Anytime

TOTAL COST: $495-995   **TYPE OF PAYMENT ACCEPTED:** Any type

RESERVATIONS/DEPOSIT: 30% down 30 days before trip

CANCELLATION POLICY: Trip transferable to another date

DEPARTURE LOCATION: Great Falls, MT   **NEAREST AIRPORT:** Great Falls

TRANSPORTATION INFORMATION: Will pick up. Also hotel curb service.

HEALTH, FITNESS OR AGE REQUIREMENTS: None

TYPE OF WEATHER TO EXPECT: Moderate to hot; frequent thunderstorms

BEST TYPE OF CLOTHING AND FOOTWEAR: Cool and hot, raingear, river and hiking shoes

PERSONAL GEAR REQUIRED: Personal duffle, camp gear, fishing gear

SPECIAL GEAR/EQUIPMENT REQUIRED: None

WHAT NOT TO BRING: Limit gear to 100 lbs. per person

PHOTO POSSIBILITIES: Fantastic

FISHING POSSIBILITIES: Fantastic   **LICENSE REQUIREMENT:** Conservation/fishing $8-12

BEST TYPE OF FISHING TACKLE: Fly fishing, light spinning

REPRESENTATIVE MENU—BREAKFAST: Eggs, bacon, toast, fruit, juice, coffee

LUNCH: Fresh bread sandwiches, fresh meats, cookies, fruit, veggies

DINNER: Appetizers, wines, steak, broccoli, cheese, cheesecake, hot chocolate with schnapps

CHORES/DUTIES GUESTS ARE EXPECTED TO HELP WITH: None

ADDITIONAL SPECIAL INFORMATION: Guest ranch/float trip combo possible. Bring plenty of hopper fly patterns.

NAME OF OUTFITTER: Montana River Outfitters—Craig Madsen Outfitter

ADDRESS: 820 Central Ave.   **CONTACT:** E. Neale Streeks

CITY: Great Falls   **TITLE:** Outfitting manager

STATE: Montana   **ZIP:** 59401   **TELEPHONE:** (406) 761-1677

NUMBER OF YEARS IN BUSINESS: 7   **NUMBER OF STAFF:** 25

SPECIALIZING IN: Fishing guide service, whitewater and scenic river expeditions, hunting and wilderness pack trips

SPECIAL PHILOSOPHY, CREDO, GOALS BEHIND BUSINESS: To give guests a total river experience.

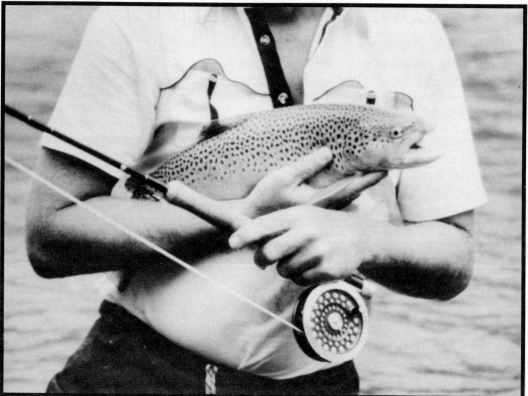

Photo: Montana River Outfitters

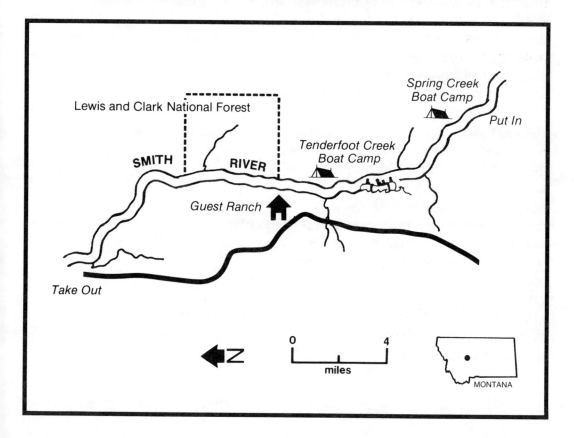

Spring Creek
Boat Camp

Put In

Lewis and Clark National Forest

Tenderfoot Creek
Boat Camp

SMITH   RIVER

Guest Ranch

Take Out

N

0   4
miles

MONTANA

LOWER GORGE STEELHEAD TRIP

At 7 a.m., we load last minute items into the vehicles and head for the Hammer Creek put-in on the Salmon River. When we pull away from the boat ramp in our 18-foot dory, our camp cook is still busily preparing his boat. We reach steelhead country by 9 a.m. the first morning but will arrive shortly after dawn on the next four days of fishing. Eventually the cook boat passes us and disappears around the bend. We find him shortly after noon, waiting with hot coffee and a deli-style lunch. After we finish the meal we pull ahead again in search of the crafty steelies. The cook boat will move on to the campsite, therefore enabling us to fish until dark if we so desire. When we arrive at camp, the wafting odors of sirloin steak, soup, corn, and strawberry shortcake greet us. All of the meals are produced from quality foods—no freeze-dried food here! The next few days feature the same fishing agenda with brief stops at points of interest, including Indian petroglyphs. If the weather takes a turn for the worse, we turn on the propane heaters in the front of the boats. But nothing warms you up better than hooking a steelhead, especially when it weighs between 10 and 20 lbs.

LENGTH OF TRIP: 5 days   **DEPARTURE DATES:** Varies

TOTAL COST: $525   **TYPE OF PAYMENT ACCEPTED:** Check, MC, Visa, AMEX

RESERVATIONS/DEPOSIT: $100 deposit when booking

CANCELLATION POLICY: Deposit retained—can be used within 2 years

DEPARTURE LOCATION: Riggins, ID   **NEAREST AIRPORT:** Boise, ID; Lewiston, ID; Slate Creek Air Strip, ID

TRANSPORTATION INFORMATION: Charter flight, bus, van

HEALTH, FITNESS OR AGE REQUIREMENTS: None

TYPE OF WEATHER TO EXPECT: Variable

BEST TYPE OF CLOTHING AND FOOTWEAR: Warm, preferably wool clothes; rubber boots

PERSONAL GEAR REQUIRED: Equipment list available

SPECIAL GEAR/EQUIPMENT REQUIRED: Fishing gear

WHAT NOT TO BRING: Radios, tape decks, valuables, pets

PHOTO POSSIBILITIES: Fantastic

FISHING POSSIBILITIES: Fantastic   **LICENSE REQUIREMENT:** Out of state $33

BEST TYPE OF FISHING TACKLE: We can supply

REPRESENTATIVE MENU—BREAKFAST: Ham, eggs

LUNCH: Deli-style lunch

DINNER: Steak, vegetables, salad, dessert

CHORES/DUTIES GUESTS ARE EXPECTED TO HELP WITH: Unload, load boats

ADDITIONAL SPECIAL INFORMATION: The boats are 18-foot dories with propane heat

NAME OF OUTFITTER: Salmon River Challenge

ADDRESS: Salmon River Route   **CONTACT:** Gerald P. Kooyers

CITY: Riggins   **TITLE:** Managing Partner

STATE: Idaho   **ZIP:** 83549   **TELEPHONE:** (208) 628-3264

NUMBER OF YEARS IN BUSINESS: 4

SPECIALIZING IN: Whitewater rafting and steelhead fishing

Photo: Salmon River Challenge

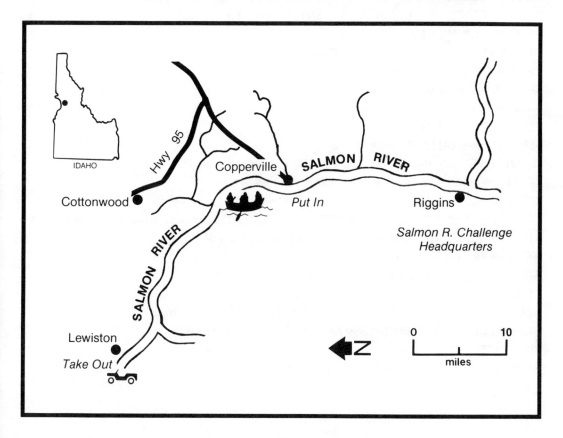

149

✒ SNAKE RIVER/BIRDS OF PREY TRIP

Our trip began in Boise. We were then driven two hours to our put-in on the Snake River near Grand View. As the gear was loaded, we had an opportunity to view hawks and owls on the nearby cliffs. Our morning float passed through farmland and we approached the canyon by lunch-time. We went ashore and hiked to see red-tailed hawk nests, and spotting scopes were set up to view the golden eagle nests across the river. Several varieties of waterfowl could be seen along the river, including terns and avocets. Orioles and tanagers thrived in the willows at the river's edge. By the second day we were well into the canyon. Prairie falcon and golden eagle sightings were frequent. A stop at Thomas Flat for lunch provided ample opportunity for the sharp-eyes to spot great horned owls, mallards and pheasants' nests. Down the river at Sinker Butte, long-eared owls could be found nesting early in the season. There was also an undetermined population of short-eared owls in the area, which could occasionally be seen overhead. Camp was across the river at Sinker Creek. There was a chorus of owls that night as we sat around the fire. After three more days of floating and birdwatching, we were driven the one-hour trip back to Boise.

LENGTH OF TRIP: 5 days

DEPARTURE DATES: Each Sunday and Tuesday in May

TOTAL COST: $499 adult + tax
$429 youth + tax

TYPE OF PAYMENT ACCEPTED: Check, cash, Visa, MC

RESERVATIONS/DEPOSIT: $100 deposit with reservation

CANCELLATION POLICY: No refund for no-shows

DEPARTURE LOCATION: Boise, ID   **NEAREST AIRPORT:** Boise, ID

TRANSPORTATION INFORMATION: Van service to and from airport; no charge

HEALTH, FITNESS OR AGE REQUIREMENTS: Good physical condition

TYPE OF WEATHER TO EXPECT: Mild with possible rain

BEST TYPE OF CLOTHING AND FOOTWEAR: Equipment list available

PERSONAL GEAR REQUIRED: Equipment list available

SPECIAL GEAR/EQUIPMENT REQUIRED: Tent and sleeping bag (can be rented from outfitter)

WHAT NOT TO BRING: Pets, radios, firearms

PHOTO POSSIBILITIES: Fantastic

FISHING POSSIBILITIES: Poor

REPRESENTATIVE MENU—BREAKFAST: Eggs, bacon, juice, muffins, fruit salad

LUNCH: Sandwiches, cookies, fruit, raw vegetables, juice

DINNER: Steak, corn, wine, salad, bread, Dutch oven dessert

CHORES/DUTIES GUESTS ARE EXPECTED TO HELP WITH: Be responsible for own gear

ADDITIONAL SPECIAL INFORMATION: This is not a whitewater trip.

NAME OF OUTFITTER: ECHO: The Wilderness Company, Inc.

ADDRESS: 6529 Telegraph Ave.   **CONTACT:** Joseph Daly

CITY: Oakland   **TITLE:** Co-owner

STATE: California   **ZIP:** 94609   **TELEPHONE:** (415) 652-1600

NUMBER OF YEARS IN BUSINESS: 12   **NUMBER OF STAFF:** 60

SPECIALIZING IN: Mountain river adventures in the western U.S.

SPECIAL PHILOSOPHY, CREDO, GOALS BEHIND BUSINESS: ECHO believes in running ecologically sound trips. We wish to share our appreciation for the wilderness in general and river rafting in particular.

Photo: Jerry Corsi

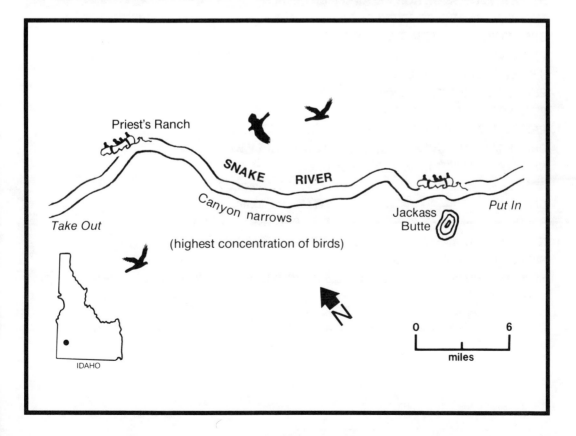

Priest's Ranch

SNAKE RIVER

Canyon narrows

Take Out

(highest concentration of birds)

Jackass Butte

Put In

IDAHO

N

0   6
miles

◌✿◌ GOURMET WHITEWATER

Spend half a day on a whitewater trip that features the original Jackson Hole gourmet picnic. Climb aboard and let our professional guide take you on an adventure through the Grand Canyon of the Snake River. Midway through the nine-mile trip, we'll stop along the bank of the Snake at our exclusive picnic site which overlooks the largest rapid in the canyon. Louise will have prepared a delicious lunch of Jackson Hole buffalo salami, Wyoming cheese and other local favorites with plenty of icy cold refreshment to wash it down. Afterwards you will have ample time to investigate the fascinating geological formations at riverside, as well as photograph family and friends against a picturesque backdrop. Then it is back on board the sturdy rafts and onto the biggest and best of Snake River whitewater. All you need to provide is shorts, sunglasses, hat, suntan lotion and soft-soled shoes such as sneakers. The trip fee includes lunch, round-trip transportation from Jackson, Wyoming, Coast Guard approved life jackets, rain gear and on-board storage. If you would like wine or beer, bring it along. The idea is to have a lot of fun, but watch out because this short trip may hook you on river running, encouraging you to sign up for longer and more dramatic expeditions in the future.

LENGTH OF TRIP: 1/2 day   **DEPARTURE DATES:** Daily

TOTAL COST: $20   **TYPE OF PAYMENT ACCEPTED:** Check, Visa, MC, AMEX

RESERVATIONS/DEPOSIT: Reservations taken up to departure

CANCELLATION POLICY: Forfeit money paid

DEPARTURE LOCATION: Jackson, WY   **NEAREST AIRPORT:** Jackson, WY

TRANSPORTATION INFORMATION: Public—$5; free transportation to put-in

HEALTH, FITNESS OR AGE REQUIREMENTS: None

TYPE OF WEATHER TO EXPECT: Mountain weather

BEST TYPE OF CLOTHING AND FOOTWEAR: Soft-soled shoes

PERSONAL GEAR REQUIRED: Shorts, sunglasses, hat, suntan lotion

SPECIAL GEAR/EQUIPMENT REQUIRED: None

PHOTO POSSIBILITIES: Great

FISHING POSSIBILITIES: None

REPRESENTATIVE MENU—LUNCH: Buffalo salami, Wyoming cheeses

CHORES/DUTIES GUESTS ARE EXPECTED TO HELP WITH: None

NAME OF OUTFITTER: Mad River Boat Trips

ADDRESS: Box 2222   **CONTACT:** Breck O'Neill

CITY: Jackson   **TITLE:** President

STATE: Wyoming   **ZIP:** 83001   **TELEPHONE:** (307) 733-6203

NUMBER OF YEARS IN BUSINESS: 8   **NUMBER OF STAFF:** 12

SPECIALIZING IN: Whitewater

SPECIAL PHILOSOPHY, CREDO, GOALS BEHIND BUSINESS: To increase knowledge of the flora, fauna and history of Jackson Hole and to have a lot of fun.

Photo: Mad River Boat Trips

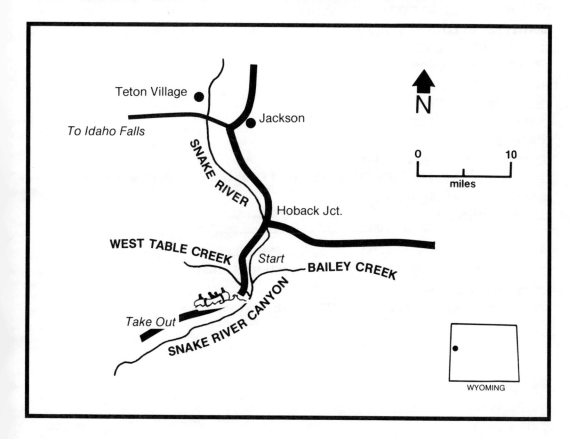

Teton Village ●

To Idaho Falls

Jackson ●

N

SNAKE RIVER

0   10
miles

Hoback Jct.

WEST TABLE CREEK

Start

BAILEY CREEK

SNAKE RIVER CANYON

Take Out

WYOMING

KENNEBEC WHITEWATER EXPEDITION

Our trip begins at East Outlet at Moosehead Lake, the source of the Kennebec River. We utilize six-man rafts to paddle three miles of Class III whitewater to Ledge Falls. At the falls, we stop for lunch, and inner tubes are provided for those wishing to tube this set of small rapids. After a leisurely lunch of deli cold cuts and cheese, we power our way up the 10-mile stretch to Indian Pond. Moose and loons are numerous and by midafternoon we arrive at our wilderness campsite. Maine lobster and homemade spaghetti are served with wine for dinner. The guides then prepare a large sauna with tarps and hot rocks from the campfire. The evening is spent socializing, relaxing and indulging in midnight swims. The next morning, we travel the remaining three miles to Harris Station Hydroelectric site, which is the beginning of the Kennebec Gorge, the biggest whitewater in the East. We switch to eight-man rafts and each is guided by a professional Maine registered guide to tackle rapids such as the Three Sisters, the Alley Way and Magic Falls. After a steak cookout at noon on the shores of the Kennebec, we continue through the biggest, steepest gorge in New England to arrive at The Forks . . . and civilization.

LENGTH OF TRIP: 2 days

DEPARTURE DATES: Throughout summer

TOTAL COST: $140

TYPE OF PAYMENT ACCEPTED: Visa, MC

RESERVATIONS/DEPOSIT: $70 deposit 30 days prior to trip

CANCELLATION POLICY: Lose deposit

DEPARTURE LOCATION: The Forks, ME

NEAREST AIRPORT: Waterville, Maine

TRANSPORTATION INFORMATION: Rental car, or outfitter picks up with advance notice.

HEALTH, FITNESS OR AGE REQUIREMENTS: Normal good health; 12 years old minimum

TYPE OF WEATHER TO EXPECT: Very warm to cool

BEST TYPE OF CLOTHING AND FOOTWEAR: Sneakers, wool pile clothing

PERSONAL GEAR REQUIRED: Personal duffle, sleeping bag

SPECIAL GEAR/EQUIPMENT REQUIRED: None

PHOTO POSSIBILITIES: Photographers on all trips

FISHING POSSIBILITIES: None

REPRESENTATIVE MENU—BREAKFAST: Eggs, bacon, coffee

LUNCH: Steak, cold cuts

DINNER: Complete menu at our lodge

CHORES/DUTIES GUESTS ARE EXPECTED TO HELP WITH: Wash dishes, set up tent

NAME OF OUTFITTER: Northern Outdoors

ADDRESS: Route 201

CONTACT: Wayne Hockmeyer

CITY: The Forks

TITLE: President

STATE: Maine   **ZIP:** 04985

TELEPHONE: (207) 663-4466

NUMBER OF YEARS IN BUSINESS: 9

NUMBER OF STAFF: 40

SPECIALIZING IN: Whitewater raft trips

SPECIAL PHILOSOPHY, CREDO, GOALS BEHIND BUSINESS: The establishment of the best outdoor center in the Northeast.

Photo: Jeff Proctor

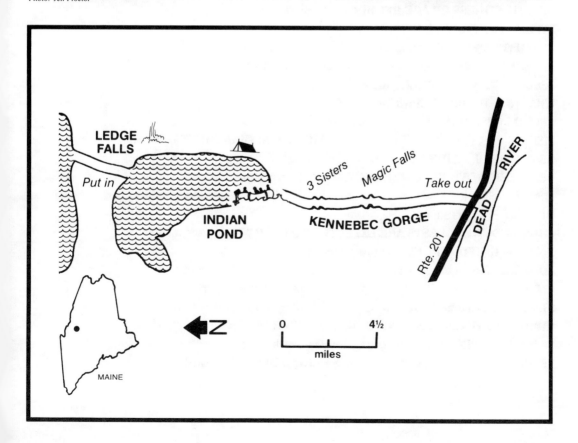

3-DAY PRIMITIVE NEW RIVER TRIP

The New River's headwaters begin in North Carolina. Fed by mountain streams, the New River flows northward, growing in volume and velocity, carving its way through a thousand-foot deep gorge toward the foothills of West Virginia. For immense power, size and beauty, the New River can be compared to no other river east of the Mississippi. After checking in at our office in Lansing, West Virginia, this trip begins with a bus ride to the put-in site. The river offers more than whitewater excitement. On the three-day primitive New River trip we take time to swim the pools, explore old mining towns, hike the two beautiful waterfalls on Fern Creek and simply relax. Halfway down the gorge we set up camp approximately one mile above one of the major rapids. Evening brings more leisure time for hiking, fishing for small mouth bass and taking it easy as your guide prepares a hearty meal of steak or fish, vegetables and other delicacies. On the second day we travel through the wildest eight miles of the river. The third day allows time for more relaxing, floating and swimming. The rafting season is from April 1st to November 1st, but the most exciting season is the spring due to the big water. Summer months are an escape from the heat and fall brings dramatic foliage.

LENGTH OF TRIP: 3 days

DEPARTURE DATES: April-November

TOTAL COST: $205 plus 5% sales tax

TYPE OF PAYMENT ACCEPTED: Check, cash, m.o.

RESERVATIONS/DEPOSIT: Full payment 1 month before departure

CANCELLATION POLICY: After 30 days, forfeit deposit

DEPARTURE LOCATION: Lansing, WV   **NEAREST AIRPORT:** Charleston, NC

TRANSPORTATION INFORMATION: Bus, rental, car, small plane, cab

HEALTH, FITNESS OR AGE REQUIREMENTS: None

TYPE OF WEATHER TO EXPECT: Varies upon season

BEST TYPE OF CLOTHING AND FOOTWEAR: Equipment list available

PERSONAL GEAR REQUIRED: Personal duffle, sleeping bag, tent, rainsuit

SPECIAL GEAR/EQUIPMENT REQUIRED: None

WHAT NOT TO BRING: Anything not on list

PHOTO POSSIBILITIES: Professional photographer on river

FISHING POSSIBILITIES: Excellent   **LICENSE REQUIREMENTS:** WV $5

BEST TYPE OF FISHING TACKLE: Fly or spin cast

REPRESENTATIVE MENU—BREAKFAST: Eggs, french toast

LUNCH: Deli-style

DINNER: Steak or fish, vegetable, salad

CHORES/DUTIES GUESTS ARE EXPECTED TO HELP WITH: Paddling

NAME OF OUTFITTER: Class VI River Runners, Inc.

ADDRESS: Box 78, Ames Heights Rd.   **CONTACT:** Sheri Kettering

CITY: Lansing   **TITLE:** Office manager

STATE: West Virginia   **ZIP:** 25862   **TELEPHONE:** (304) 574-0704

NUMBER OF YEARS IN BUSINESS: 6   **NUMBER OF STAFF:** 35

SPECIALIZING IN: Whitewater rafting, kayaking, rock climbing

SPECIAL PHILOSOPHY, CREDO, GOALS BEHIND BUSINESS: Quality

Photo: Northern Outdoors

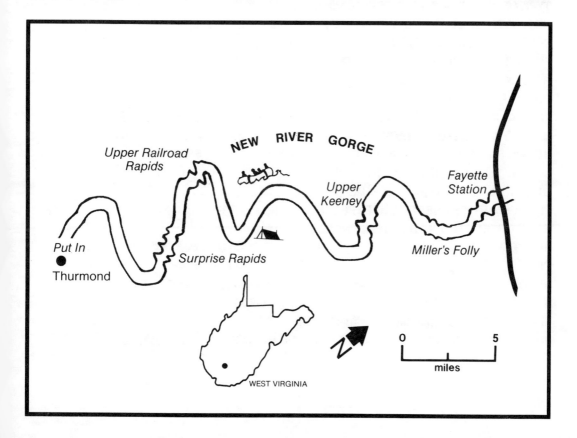

NEW RIVER GORGE

Upper Railroad
Rapids

Upper
Keeney

Fayette
Station

Put In

Surprise Rapids

Miller's Folly

Thurmond

WEST VIRGINIA

0   5

miles

YAMPA RIVER RAFT TRIP

Don Hatch River Expeditions pioneered the Yampa and Green rivers in 1929. With over 53 years of experience, nobody else has run as many people down the western rivers as Hatch has. The expedition down the Yampa River is especially unique because its running season is so short. The Yampa is a free-flowing river, the last remaining undammed major drainage of the Colorado River system. Hence, the Yampa has a short but wild runable season from early April to July. This trip begins at the Dinosaur National Monument's eastern border and ends at the Split Mountain Gorge boat ramp at its southern border. En route, you will hike, enjoy solitude and join friends around the campfire for cocktails. You may see deer, mountain sheep and an occasional mountain lion. The Yampa Gorge is typified by sheer white sandstone cliffs overhanging the river with black streaking called desert varnish, caused by run-off that leaches manganese from the rocks to be oxidized. Because the Yampa is a free-flowing river, the peak flows are often very high. This river offers one of the West's toughest rapids in Warm Springs. You may be asked to walk around this one! The Yampa joins the Green River below the Canyon of Lodore.

LENGTH OF TRIP: 3, 4, 5 days   **DEPARTURE DATES:** Varies

TOTAL COST: Varies   **TYPE OF PAYMENT ACCEPTED:** Check, cash, t.c.

RESERVATIONS/DEPOSIT: $100 deposit 10 days after booking

CANCELLATION POLICY: Policy varies

DEPARTURE LOCATION: Vernal, UT   **NEAREST AIRPORT:** Vernal, UT

TRANSPORTATION INFORMATION: Provided

HEALTH, FITNESS OR AGE REQUIREMENTS: None

TYPE OF WEATHER TO EXPECT: Warm, sunny

BEST TYPE OF CLOTHING AND FOOTWEAR: Equipment list available

PERSONAL GEAR REQUIRED: Equipment list available

SPECIAL GEAR/EQUIPMENT REQUIRED: Sleeping bag, ground cloth, duffle bags

WHAT NOT TO BRING: Expensive jewelry and watches

PHOTO POSSIBILITIES: Fantastic

FISHING POSSIBILITIES: Good   **LICENSE REQUIREMENT:** Utah 5-day, $5

BEST TYPE OF FISHING TACKLE: Trout/spinner flies, catfish/stinkbait, #2 hook

REPRESENTATIVE MENU—BREAKFAST: Eggs, bacon, sausage, french toast

LUNCH: Deli sandwiches, fruit, chips, pickles, cookies

DINNER: Steaks or chops, cakes, salads, vegetable

CHORES/DUTIES GUESTS ARE EXPECTED TO HELP WITH: None

NAME OF OUTFITTER: Don Hatch River Expeditions

ADDRESS: P.O. Box C   **CONTACT:** Todd Gordon

CITY: Vernal   **TITLE:** Operations manager

STATE: Utah   **ZIP:** 84078   **TELEPHONE:** (901) 789-4316; 1566

NUMBER OF YEARS IN BUSINESS: 54   **NUMBER OF STAFF:** 50

SPECIALIZING IN: Whitewater river trips

SPECIAL PHILOSOPHY, CREDO, GOALS BEHIND BUSINESS: The original river running company; no other outfitter has run as many people down the western rivers as Hatch has. We match or beat competitors' prices.

Photo: George Henry

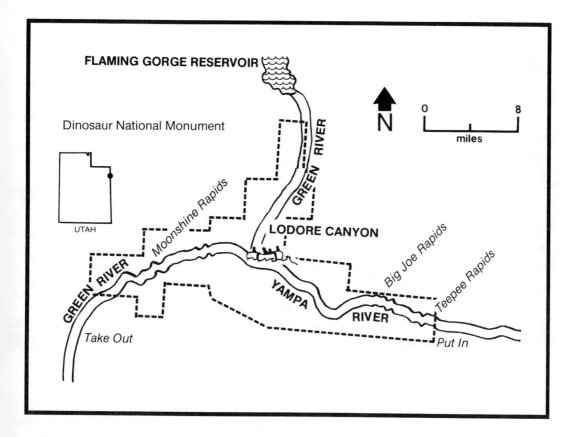

FLAMING GORGE RESERVOIR

Dinosaur National Monument

UTAH

GREEN RIVER

Moonshine Rapids

LODORE CANYON

GREEN RIVER

YAMPA RIVER

Big Joe Rapids

Teepee Rapids

Take Out

Put In

N

0   8
miles

ᕕᕗ CANYONLANDS/CATARACT CANYON

This legendary gorge is buried in the heart of Utah's Canyonlands National Park. Nowhere in its entire course does the Colorado River descend more precipitously than through the Cataract. We begin our six-day Cataract run 48 miles above the famous confluence on the Colorado River, or we'll launch 52 miles above the confluence on the Green River where either of the rivers makes a grand entrance into the canyon country. The first part of the trip finds us quietly riding the current past brilliantly colored cliffs and towering table-top mesas. We walk to points of interest such as the Doll House in the Land of Standing Rock, the Loop, and various ruins of the ancient Anasazi. Later in the trip we reach the dramatic confluence of the Green and Colorado rivers. Beyond are the thrilling rapids of Cataract Canyon, which we reach the next day. The hours in the boat that day are filled with the roar of a wild river. Participants are responsible for keeping their boats well-bailed! On the final morning, after running 65 miles of this glorious river, we empty onto Lake Powell where "Hayduke" power boat is waiting to take us to Hite Marina. This trek emphasizes high value wilderness trips with a high guide-to-guest ratio for maximum learning and safety.

LENGTH OF TRIP: 5, 6 days

DEPARTURE DATES: Every Monday, May-June; every Sunday, July-Aug.

TOTAL COST: $440 (group discounts available)

TYPE OF PAYMENT ACCEPTED: Check, wire transfers, money order

RESERVATIONS/DEPOSIT: $220 deposit

CANCELLATION POLICY: Call for info

DEPARTURE LOCATION: Green River, UT   **NEAREST AIRPORT:** Salt Lake City, UT

TRANSPORTATION INFORMATION: Various types available

HEALTH, FITNESS OR AGE REQUIREMENTS: Good physical condition; 16 years old minimum in high-water May and June trips

TYPE OF WEATHER TO EXPECT: Warm to hot

BEST TYPE OF CLOTHING AND FOOTWEAR: Equipment list available

PERSONAL GEAR REQUIRED: Sleeping bag, foam pad, ground cloth—can be rented from outfitter for $15/unit.

SPECIAL GEAR/EQUIPMENT REQUIRED: None

PHOTO POSSIBILITIES: Fantastic

FISHING POSSIBILITIES: Good   **LICENSE REQUIREMENT:** Utah

BEST TYPE OF FISHING TACKLE: Line, hook and our food scraps

REPRESENTATIVE MENU—BREAKFAST: Varies

LUNCH: Varies

DINNER: Varies

CHORES/DUTIES GUESTS ARE EXPECTED TO HELP WITH: Bailing boats, packing own gear.

NAME OF OUTFITTER: Holiday River Expeditions, Inc.

ADDRESS: 519 Malibu Dr.   **CONTACT:** Dee and Sue Holladay

CITY: Salt Lake City   **TITLE:** Owner

STATE: Utah   **ZIP:** 84107   **TELEPHONE:** (801) 266-2087

NUMBER OF YEARS IN BUSINESS: 18   **NUMBER OF STAFF:** 25

SPECIALIZING IN: Wilderness river expeditions primarily in small oar-powered rafts. Secondarily in kayaks, canoes and inflatable kayaks.

SPECIAL PHILOSOPHY, CREDO, GOALS BEHIND BUSINESS: High-value wilderness trips, no motors, high guide-to-guest ratio to provide maximum learning and safety.

Photo: Holiday River Expeditions

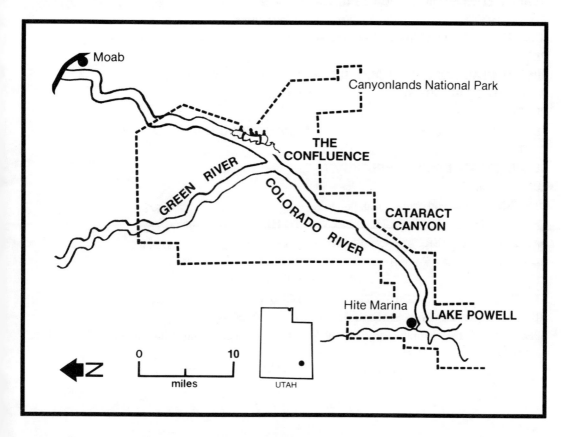

Moab

Canyonlands National Park

THE
CONFLUENCE

GREEN RIVER

COLORADO RIVER

CATARACT
CANYON

Hite Marina

LAKE POWELL

N

0   10

miles

UTAH

SAN JUAN RIVER WILDERNESS

The San Juan River is a tributary of the mighty Colorado and is the fastest major waterway in the United States. For the first few miles, the river courses through a wild flood plain, abruptly entering a series of remarkable close-walled canyons descending 1,000-2,500 feet deep and adorned with piñon and juniper pine that guard ancient ruins and petroglyphs. Farther downstream, the river flows through a gorge where maidenhair fern and columbine flowers grow profusely in sharp contrast to the sandstone walls. It is a beautiful area well worth exploring. We will take a hike to Slickhorn Canyon, Grand Gulch and Honaker Trail and have fun on the small but swift rapids of the San Juan River in this canyon country adventure. Departures leave from Bluff, Utah or Flagstaff, Arizona in June and July. All river equipment is provided but don't forget your camera because of the picture-perfect scenes you will encounter. They are worth capturing. If fishing interests you, bring a rod and try to lure the catfish out of the river. Meals are included and dinners will be enjoyed around a blazing campfire.

LENGTH OF TRIP: 7 days   **DEPARTURE DATES:** June 23, July 7

TOTAL COST: $550   **TYPE OF PAYMENT ACCEPTED:** Check, money order, cashier's check

RESERVATIONS/DEPOSIT: 30% deposit 60 days prior to departure

CANCELLATION POLICY: No refund unless replacement found

DEPARTURE LOCATION: Bluff, Utah or Flagstaff, AZ   **NEAREST AIRPORT:** Bluff, Flagstaff

TRANSPORTATION INFORMATION: Free shuttle from airport to lodging

HEALTH, FITNESS OR AGE REQUIREMENTS: None

TYPE OF WEATHER TO EXPECT: Warm, possible showers

BEST TYPE OF CLOTHING AND FOOTWEAR: Light clothing, rain gear, tennis shoes

PERSONAL GEAR REQUIRED: Personal duffle, camping gear

SPECIAL GEAR/EQUIPMENT REQUIRED: All river equipment supplied by outfitter

WHAT NOT TO BRING: No guns, radios, pets; pack light.

PHOTO POSSIBILITIES: Fantastic

FISHING POSSIBILITIES: Fair   **LICENSE REQUIREMENT:** Utah

BEST TYPE OF FISHING TACKLE: Stinkbait

REPRESENTATIVE MENU—BREAKFAST: Eggs, cereal, coffee

LUNCH: Cold cuts

DINNER: Steak or porkchops, salad, potatoes

CHORES/DUTIES GUESTS ARE EXPECTED TO HELP WITH: None

NAME OF OUTFITTER: American Wilderness Alliance

ADDRESS: 4260 East Evans Ave., #3   **CONTACT:** Regan Mallett

CITY: Denver   **TITLE:** Trip Coordinator

STATE: Colorado   **ZIP:** 80222   **TELEPHONE:** (303) 758-5018

NUMBER OF YEARS IN BUSINESS: 7   **NUMBER OF STAFF:** 6

SPECIALIZING IN: Rafting, sportyak, dory, horseback, backpack, fishing, kayak, hike with packstock, canoe, sailing, educational

SPECIAL PHILOSOPHY, CREDO, GOALS BEHIND BUSINESS: Working to preserve wild America, its free-flowing rivers and wildlands.

Photo: John Running

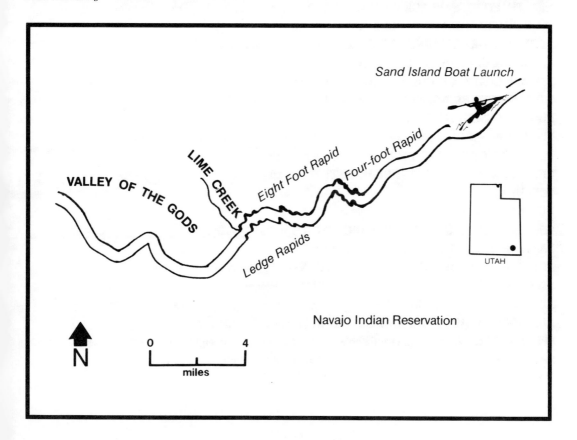

Sand Island Boat Launch

VALLEY OF THE GODS

LIME CREEK

Eight Foot Rapid

Four-foot Rapid

Ledge Rapids

UTAH

Navajo Indian Reservation

N

0   4
miles

 # KLAMATH HOT SHOT

Feel like a true outdoorsman by learning a new skill, the kind that takes you through whitewater. Historical Happy Camp, California is the meeting place for the thrilling Klamath Hot Shot inflatable kayaking river adventure. The skills are easily learned and allow you to navigate a remote river in the Northwest. The first day is spent paddling 17 miles through spectacular scenic canyon country where bear, deer, osprey, otters, blue heron and bald eagle live. A bountiful lunch of selected cold cuts, fresh fruits and homebaked cookies refuel paddlers for the afternoon's endeavors. When camp is made that evening in the great forests, river travelers relate their whitewater conquests as steak sizzles on the grill. The next morning they awake to steaming hot coffee and bacon frying over an open fire. A motor coach takes them to the Little Salmon River for a thrilling inflatable kayak run down to the confluence of the Klamath River. They again set up camp and enjoy a riverside barbecue amid tall pines. The biggest challenges of the trip still lie in store, and the guests face them on the third and final day of the expedition. After surviving the thrills and chills, ice-cold drinks and cold watermelon await them at the take-out site.

LENGTH OF TRIP: 3 days   **DEPARTURE DATES:** Mon., Fri., June & July

TOTAL COST: $280   **TYPE OF PAYMENT ACCEPTED:** Check, credit card

RESERVATIONS/DEPOSIT: $150 within 30 days of reservation

CANCELLATION POLICY: Forfeit all funds

DEPARTURE LOCATION: Happy Camp,   **NEAREST AIRPORT:** Medford
Calif.; Grants Pass, Ore.

TRANSPORTATION INFORMATION: Airport Transit $6

HEALTH, FITNESS OR AGE REQUIREMENTS: Active, healthy, 14 years old minimum

TYPE OF WEATHER TO EXPECT: Dry and warm

BEST TYPE OF CLOTHING AND FOOTWEAR: Tennis shoes

PERSONAL GEAR REQUIRED: Personal duffle

SPECIAL GEAR/EQUIPMENT REQUIRED: None

WHAT NOT TO BRING: All gear is provided except for personal items

PHOTO POSSIBILITIES: Good

FISHING POSSIBILITIES: Good   **LICENSE REQUIREMENT:** CA-variable

BEST TYPE OF FISHING TACKLE: Flies, hot shot lures

REPRESENTATIVE MENU—BREAKFAST: Bacon, eggs

LUNCH: Cold cuts, fruit

DINNER: Steak, salad, garlic bread

CHORES/DUTIES GUESTS ARE EXPECTED TO HELP WITH: None

NAME OF OUTFITTER: Orange Torpedo Trips

ADDRESS: P.O. Box 1111   **CONTACT:** Myrna or Don Stevens

CITY: Grants Pass   **TITLE:** Proprietors

STATE: Oregon   **ZIP:** 97526   **TELEPHONE:** (503) 479-5061

NUMBER OF YEARS IN BUSINESS: 16   **NUMBER OF STAFF:** 70

SPECIALIZING IN: Whitewater inflatable kayaking adventures on eight major western rivers.

SPECIAL PHILOSOPHY, CREDO, GOALS BEHIND BUSINESS: Adventures for active people; we teach you what you need to know and the skills are easily learned.

Photo: Orange Torpedo Trips

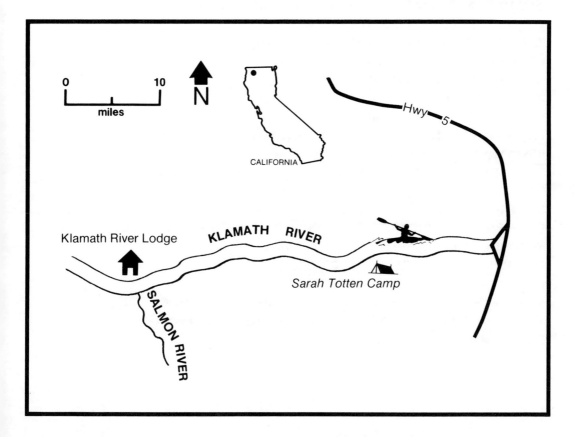

165

⚜ HELLS CANYON RAFT TRIP

The evening before the raft trip begins, an orientation session is held at the Holiday Inn in Boise, Idaho where your sleeping bag units will be issued and last-minute questions are answered. The next morning everyone is transported to the river put-in just below Hells Canyon Dam. You have just entered the steepest and narrowest gorge in North America, Hells Canyon. Its dark granite mountains seem to extend to the sky. After a robust lunch, the float trip begins and you promptly get splashed with whitewater from the first rapid. Looming ahead are Idaho's two biggest rapids, Wild Sheep and Granite Creek, which toss rafts around like bobbing corks. The principle behind running these rapids is to enter, hang on and hope you come out right side up! In addition to floating the river there are opportunities to take side canyon hikes, explore abandoned mines, visit old homesteads, observe ancient Indian pictographs, fish or simply relax and enjoy the scenery once in camp. Delicious meals of sourdough surprises and Dutch oven delights will satisfy the hearty appetites everyone develops in the great outdoors. When the six days have elapsed, the participants are transported to Boise via Lewiston, flying over the impressive area they have just rafted.

LENGTH OF TRIP: 6 days　　**DEPARTURE DATES:** Weekly May-Oct.

TOTAL COST: $710　　**TYPE OF PAYMENT ACCEPTED:** Check, cash, money order

RESERVATIONS/DEPOSIT: $100 deposit upon confirmation

CANCELLATION POLICY: Forfeit money paid

DEPARTURE LOCATION: Boise, ID　　**NEAREST AIRPORT:** Boise, ID

TRANSPORTATION INFORMATION: Included in price

HEALTH, FITNESS OR AGE REQUIREMENTS: Normal health, 8 years old minimum

TYPE OF WEATHER TO EXPECT: Cool to hot, depending upon season

BEST TYPE OF CLOTHING AND FOOTWEAR: Casual

PERSONAL GEAR REQUIRED: Personal duffle

SPECIAL GEAR/EQUIPMENT REQUIRED: Rain suit

WHAT NOT TO BRING: Firearms, cassette players, radios

PHOTO POSSIBILITIES: Fantastic

FISHING POSSIBILITIES: Fantastic　　**LICENSE REQUIREMENT:** Utah 7-day, $14.50

BEST TYPE OF FISHING TACKLE: Light weight spinning

REPRESENTATIVE MENU—BREAKFAST: Eggs, bacon, sourdough pancakes

LUNCH: Hoagie sandwich

DINNER: Barbequed chicken, rice, gravy, cole slaw, apple crunch

CHORES/DUTIES GUESTS ARE EXPECTED TO HELP WITH: Set up own tent, load and unload raft

NAME OF OUTFITTER: Idaho Adventures River Trips

ADDRESS: P.O. Box 834-GA　　**CONTACT:** Hank Miller

CITY: Salmon　　**TITLE:** President

STATE: Idaho　　**ZIP:** 83467　　**TELEPHONE:** (208) 756-2986

NUMBER OF YEARS IN BUSINESS: 14　　**NUMBER OF STAFF:** 15

SPECIALIZING IN: River raft trips on Idaho's famous rivers.

SPECIAL PHILOSOPHY, CREDO, GOALS BEHIND BUSINESS: To provide complete river experience that everybody can enjoy.

Photo: Hank Miller

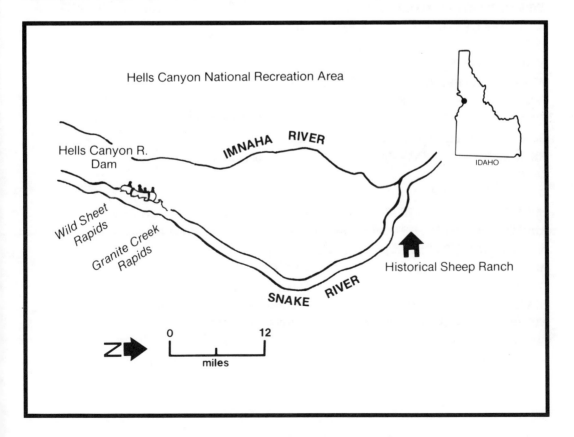

Hells Canyon National Recreation Area

IMNAHA RIVER

Hells Canyon R. Dam

IDAHO

Wild Sheet Rapids

Granite Creek Rapids

Historical Sheep Ranch

SNAKE RIVER

N

0   12
miles

MIDDLE FORK OF THE SALMON RIVER

Idaho's Middle Fork has qualities that no other river has. Boatmen who know the river intimately invite you to get acquainted with its personality as well. The Middle Fork of the Salmon River rips through 105 miles of the most inaccessible, primitive country in the U.S. It is wild, untamed, rugged and still relatively untouched by roads. The ideal access to the land of the Tukudeka Indians, the Sheepeaters, is by the river itself. Three and six day river trips can be taken through Rocky Mountain River Tours of Hailey, Idaho, whose philosophy is to have fun and do it right. Naturalist guides open up the area's secrets to the river runners, and wild animals occasionally allow you to glimpse them. Trout fishing is a dream because of the lack of annoying mosquitoes. This popular trip exposes participants to blue skies, and 90° F temperatures while floating cool waters amid mountain terrain. Running rapids, swimming, hiking and relaxing in natural hot springs fill the days. Volleyball games at the camp site, Dutch oven cuisine (including crab-stuffed chicken breasts), and lively conversation under the star-studded sky further exemplify the good life of the outdoorsman.

LENGTH OF TRIP: 3, 6 days   **DEPARTURE DATES:** Every 8 days June-Sept.

TOTAL COST: $450, $825   **TYPE OF PAYMENT ACCEPTED:** Check

RESERVATIONS/DEPOSIT: $150 at least 60 days prior to departure

CANCELLATION POLICY: No refund

DEPARTURE LOCATION: Stanley, ID   **NEAREST AIRPORT:** Boise, ID

TRANSPORTATION INFORMATION: Transportation/accommodation forms supplied by outfitter

HEALTH, FITNESS OR AGE REQUIREMENTS: 8 years old minimum

TYPE OF WEATHER TO EXPECT: Hot

BEST TYPE OF CLOTHING AND FOOTWEAR: Shorts, t-shirt, tennis shoes

PERSONAL GEAR REQUIRED: Equipment list available

SPECIAL GEAR/EQUIPMENT REQUIRED: None

WHAT NOT TO BRING: Tape deck, radio

PHOTO POSSIBILITIES: Fantastic

FISHING POSSIBILITIES: Fantastic   **LICENSE REQUIREMENTS:** 7 day $14.50

BEST TYPE OF FISHING TACKLE: Fly fishing

REPRESENTATIVE MENU—BREAKFAST: Fondue, coffee cake

LUNCH: Salmon-stuffed tomatoes

DINNER: Crab-stuffed chicken breasts

CHORES/DUTIES GUESTS ARE EXPECTED TO HELP WITH: Having fun

ADDITIONAL SPECIAL INFORMATION: Make reservations 6 months early; much repeat clientele

NAME OF OUTFITTER: Rocky Mountain River Tours

ADDRESS: P.O. Box 126   **CONTACT:** David and Sheila Mills

CITY: Hailey   **TITLE:** Owners

STATE: Idaho   **ZIP:** 83333   **TELEPHONE:** (208) 788-9300

NUMBER OF YEARS IN BUSINESS: 14   **NUMBER OF STAFF:** 12

SPECIALIZING IN: Whitewater rafting

SPECIAL PHILOSOPHY, CREDO, GOALS BEHIND BUSINESS: Doing it right

Photo: Rocky Mountain River Tours

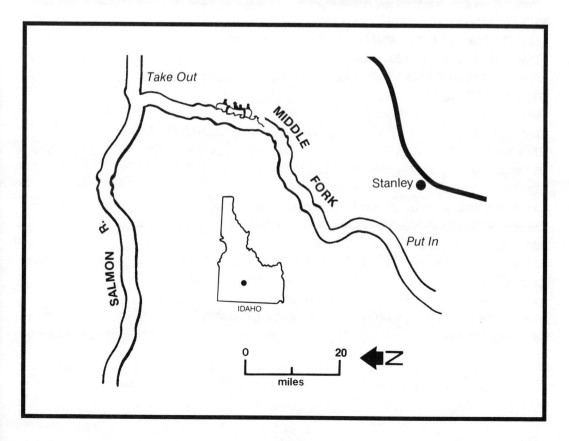

169

RIVER OF NO RETURN WILDERNESS TRIP

Eighty miles of river through 2.2 million acres of wilderness in Idaho will fill six memorable days of your life. It begins innocently enough at a riverside lodge in Salmon where the curious watch the rafts get rigged for the journey down the River of No Return. This waterway carved the second deepest gorge in North America and this group's rafts and kayaks will trespass it. Time is whiled away that afternoon with swimming, hiking and then a family-style dinner. During a moonlit walk through the soothing solitude, wristwatches beep or tick like unfriendly aliens. The next morning, the first on the river, rafts quietly follow the currents until the river explodes in the Gun Barrel Rapid. The universal exclamation "Yahoooooo!" rings from the boats. Tales are recounted at camp that evening while wine is sipped and the sunset bounces colors off canyon walls. Each day unfolds with more events. Exploration up side canyons stirs imaginations as hikers find relics of another time. Fresh-picked apples and cherries appear in baked wonders that evening. Excited muscles tight from a day on the water unkink in natural hot springs. The river runners relax on the sandy banks as celestial illumination silhouettes tall canyon walls. The river reassuringly gurgles.

LENGTH OF TRIP: 6 days

DEPARTURE DATES: April-Sept.

TOTAL COST: $700 adults

TYPE OF PAYMENT ACCEPTED: Check, cash, trade

RESERVATIONS/DEPOSIT: $150 deposit

CANCELLATION POLICY: Make special arrangements

DEPARTURE LOCATION: Salmon, ID   **NEAREST AIRPORT:** Boise, ID

TRANSPORTATION INFORMATION: Variety; outfitter will help make arrangements

HEALTH, FITNESS OR AGE REQUIREMENTS: "Our passengers must be emotionally capable of handling six days of putting wet tennis shoes on in the morning and forgetting what time it is."

TYPE OF WEATHER TO EXPECT: Cool to hot, occasional shower

BEST TYPE OF CLOTHING AND FOOTWEAR: Equipment list available

PERSONAL GEAR REQUIRED: Personal duffle, eating utensils

SPECIAL GEAR/EQUIPMENT REQUIRED: Compact sleeping equipment

WHAT NOT TO BRING: Jewelry

PHOTO POSSIBILITIES: Fantastic

FISHING POSSIBILITIES: Good   **LICENSE REQUIREMENTS:** 7 day $14.50

BEST TYPE OF FISHING TACKLE: Spinning tackle with mepps spinners/lures

REPRESENTATIVE MENU—BREAKFAST: Souffle, coffee cake, fresh fruit, coffee

LUNCH: Salmon-stuffed tomatoes, assorted crackers/breads, fruit

DINNER: Chicken enchiladas, spanish rice, lemon mousse, wine

CHORES/DUTIES GUESTS ARE EXPECTED TO HELP WITH: Making camp

NAME OF OUTFITTER: Salmon River Outfitters

ADDRESS: P.O. Box 307   **CONTACT:** Steven Shephard, Marietta Gilman-Shephard

CITY: Columbia   **TITLE:** Owners, managers

STATE: California   **ZIP:** 95310   **TELEPHONE:** (209) 532-2766

NUMBER OF YEARS IN BUSINESS: 4   **NUMBER OF STAFF:** 7

SPECIALIZING IN: River wilderness trips, plans to run women's backpacking program in works, winter cross-country ski trekking

SPECIAL PHILOSOPHY, CREDO, GOALS BEHIND BUSINESS: To provide gentle yet stimulating entry and temporary residence with the wilderness so every average asphalt-bound citizen can get the most from themselves and the outdoors.

Photo: Salmon River Outfitters

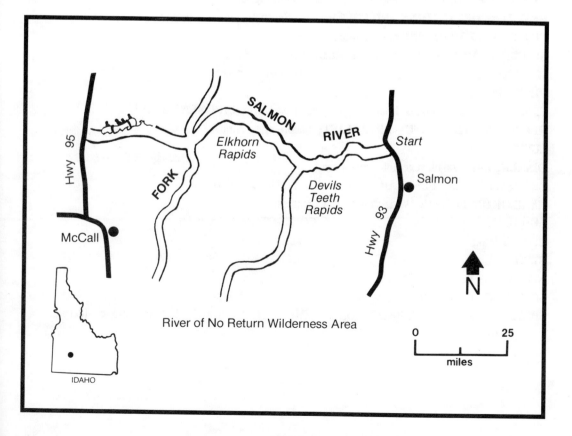

BRUNEAU RIVER TRIP

Radios, newspapers, magazines and tape players will have no place on this five-day river trip through the dramatic mountain country of Salmon, Idaho. The deliberately small-sized group of participants stresses the wilderness experience offered by living on the Bruneau River. The trip begins with a scenic one-hour flight from Boise over the Bruneau Canyon en route to the river launch site. Upon landing, river running begins immediately as the remainder of the day is spent shooting the exciting rapids on the upper Bruneau River. The next four days will be filled with the spectacular beauty of the desert canyon's basalt cliffs towering overhead and thrilling whitewater plunges underneath at a 50-foot per mile gradient on its way to joining the mighty Snake River. The narrow chutes and fast moving rapids dictate small maneuverable rafts with one guest and one guide per boat. When on shore, participants can explore the serene side canyons, soak in natural hot springs and camp on lush grassy bars. Sky wildlife is abundant. The final day is capped with whitewater excitement on Five Mile Rapids—five miles of continuous class III, IV and V rapids. The trip concludes with a quiet, short drive by van back to Boise and civilization.

LENGTH OF TRIP: 5 days

DEPARTURE DATES: May 21, 18; June 4, 8

TOTAL COST: $1,100

TYPE OF PAYMENT ACCEPTED: Check, cash

RESERVATIONS/DEPOSIT: $25 with booking

CANCELLATION POLICY: Forfeit deposit if cancelled within 30 days of trip

DEPARTURE LOCATION: Boise, ID

NEAREST AIRPORT: Boise, ID

TRANSPORTATION INFORMATION: Included in trip fee

HEALTH, FITNESS OR AGE REQUIREMENTS: Good general health

TYPE OF WEATHER TO EXPECT: Warm days, cool nights

BEST TYPE OF CLOTHING AND FOOTWEAR: Synthetic fabrics; hiking boots

PERSONAL GEAR REQUIRED: Equipment list available

SPECIAL GEAR/EQUIPMENT REQUIRED: None

WHAT NOT TO BRING: Radio, tape player, newspaper, magazine

PHOTO POSSIBILITIES: Fantastic

FISHING POSSIBILITIES: Poor

LICENSE REQUIREMENTS: ID $7

REPRESENTATIVE MENU—BREAKFAST: Bacon, eggs, pancakes

LUNCH: Sandwiches

DINNER: Steak, salad, vegetable, cheesecake

CHORES/DUTIES GUESTS ARE EXPECTED TO HELP WITH: None

NAME OF OUTFITTER: Wilderness River Outfitters

ADDRESS: P.O. Box 871

CONTACT: Joe Tonsmeire

CITY: Salmon

TITLE: Owner

STATE: Idaho   **ZIP:** 83467

TELEPHONE: (208) 756-3959

NUMBER OF YEARS IN BUSINESS: 14

SPECIALIZING IN: Rafting, backpacking, backcountry ski tours

SPECIAL PHILOSOPHY, CREDO, GOALS BEHIND BUSINESS: Small groups stress wilderness experience.

Photo: Wilderness River Outfitters

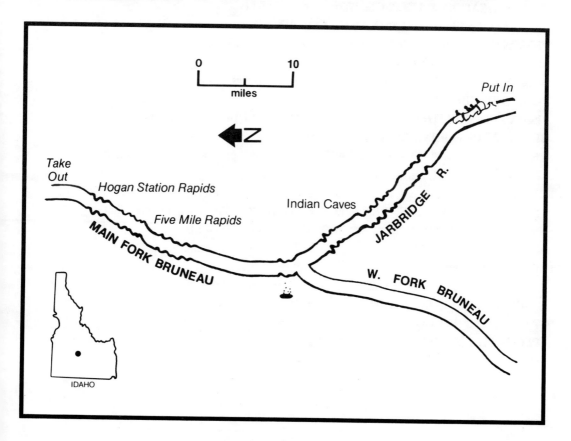

0   10

miles

N

Put In

Take Out

Hogan Station Rapids

Five Mile Rapids

Indian Caves

JARBRIDGE R.

MAIN FORK BRUNEAU

W. FORK BRUNEAU

IDAHO

2-DAY TUOLUMNE RIVER TRIP

Aptly named the queen of the California rivers, the Tuolumne serves a banquet of whitewater fit for any royalty. "Appetizer" rapids lick and splash the raft, preparing us for the "salad," "soup" and then the "main course," the thunderous Clavey Falls. This impressive Class V river dishes out more than extraordinary whitewater, however. It also offers the pristine, unspoiled beauty of the Tuolumne Canyon, nestled in the foothills near Yosemite National Park, and some of the best trout fishing on any California waterway. Anglers have ample opportunity to try their luck when we're camped and our guides are busily preparing the gourmet meals for which we are famous. The next morning, after wetting our feet in Rock Garden and a few other notable rapids, we stop for a robust lunch of burritos and then try some exploring. Back on the river we face Ram's Head rapids and the infamous Clavey Falls. After the Falls, we pull over to camp for the night and toast our newfound status as true Class V river runners. The next day, after challenging and beating Power House, Grey's Grindstone, Steam Boat and Hell's Kitchen rapids, we reluctantly leave the river at Ward's Ferry. We are two days older but infinitely wiser in the ways of the wild Tuolumne.

LENGTH OF TRIP: 2 days

DEPARTURE DATES: Varies

TOTAL COST: $245

TYPE OF PAYMENT ACCEPTED: Any

RESERVATIONS/DEPOSIT: $60 deposit 10 days after reservation

CANCELLATION POLICY: No refund

DEPARTURE LOCATION: Groveland, CA   **NEAREST AIRPORT:** Modesto or San Francisco

TRANSPORTATION INFORMATION: Rental car, $22-55/day

HEALTH, FITNESS OR AGE REQUIREMENTS: 12 years old minimum

TYPE OF WEATHER TO EXPECT: Warm days, cool nights

BEST TYPE OF CLOTHING AND FOOTWEAR: Wetsuit bodies and shorts

PERSONAL GEAR REQUIRED: Personal duffle, sleeping bag, ground cloth

SPECIAL GEAR/EQUIPMENT REQUIRED:

WHAT NOT TO BRING: Firearms, alcohol in glass containers, electrical appliances

PHOTO POSSIBILITIES: Fantastic

FISHING POSSIBILITIES: Fantastic   **LICENSE REQUIREMENT:** CA—trout stamp $15

BEST TYPE OF FISHING TACKLE: Lures, salmon eggs

REPRESENTATIVE MENU—BREAKFAST: Eggs, biscuits, pancakes, sausages, juice

LUNCH: Fresh avocado burritos or cold cuts, fruit, juice

DINNER: Charbroiled steaks, baked potatoes, salad, wine, cake, fruit, cheese

CHORES/DUTIES GUESTS ARE EXPECTED TO HELP WITH: Loading, unloading gear into boat

NAME OF OUTFITTER: Outdoor Adventure River Specialists (OARS)

ADDRESS: P.O. Box 67

CONTACT: George Wendt

CITY: Angels Camp

TITLE: President

STATE: California   **ZIP:** 95222

TELEPHONE: (209) 736-4677

NUMBER OF YEARS IN BUSINESS: 14   **NUMBER OF STAFF:** 22

SPECIALIZING IN: Whitewater rafting

SPECIAL PHILOSOPHY, CREDO, GOALS BEHIND BUSINESS: We aim to please using small oar-powered boats.

Photo: O.A.R.S.

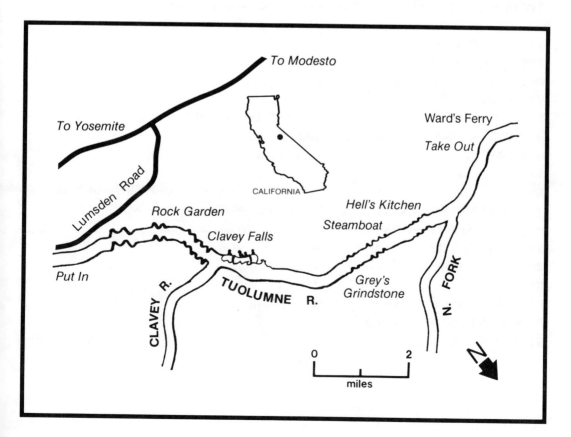

5-DAY SELWAY RIVER TRIP

We launch onto the crystal-clear waters of the Selway River near Whitecap Creek and soon we are immersed in the beauty, grandeur, isolation and silence of this compact canyon. For the first two days we float downstream through rapids which, on any other river, would be the highlight of the trip, but on the Selway are merely warmups to the real thing. Day three finds us camped on a sandy beach opposite the Moose Creek confluence, just one mile upstream of the major rapids. It seems like an odd place to spend the day trying to relax but we manage to occupy our minds with thoughts of the Selway's other unique attractions, such as her wildness, thick pine forests, lush moss and fern grottoes, wide wildflower meadows and scenic vistas. Wildlife ranging from bear to eagle inhabit the shores and the fishing for native trout is splendid. We find it easy to relax. The major rapids of days four and five are even more exciting and exhilarating than we had imagined. Giant waves, tight passages and thunder holes keep us well occupied for five continuous miles. The biggest of the big—Double Drop, Ladle, Little Niagara and Wolf Creek—are all classics in the whitewater world. In fact, Selway is in a class of its own.

LENGTH OF TRIP: 5 days

DEPARTURE DATES: June 22, 30, July 8, 15

TOTAL COST: $645 per person

TYPE OF PAYMENT ACCEPTED: Check

RESERVATIONS/DEPOSIT: $200 deposit on March 1 of previous year

CANCELLATION POLICY: No refund

DEPARTURE LOCATION: Salmon, ID

NEAREST AIRPORT: Boise, ID

TRANSPORTATION INFORMATION: Charter plane or rent car from Boise to Salmon

HEALTH, FITNESS OR AGE REQUIREMENTS: 12 years minimum age

TYPE OF WEATHER TO EXPECT: Cool, sunny, occasional thunderstorm

BEST TYPE OF CLOTHING AND FOOTWEAR: Farmer John wetsuit with booties

PERSONAL GEAR REQUIRED: All camping gear

SPECIAL GEAR/EQUIPMENT REQUIRED: Wetsuits, tents recommended

WHAT NOT TO BRING: Radios, pets, expensive jewelry, extensive fishing gear

PHOTO POSSIBILITIES: Fantastic

FISHING POSSIBILITIES: Fantastic

LICENSE REQUIREMENT: Idaho

BEST TYPE OF FISHING TACKLE: Light spinning and fly outfits

REPRESENTATIVE MENU—BREAKFAST: Eggs, bacon, muffins, juice, coffee

LUNCH: Cold cut sandwiches, fresh fruit drinks

DINNER: Steaks, chicken, fresh salad, rice, potatoes, bread, wine, fresh-baked Dutch oven dessert.

CHORES/DUTIES GUESTS ARE EXPECTED TO HELP WITH: None

ADDITIONAL SPECIAL INFORMATION: Expect to get wet and have fun.

NAME OF OUTFITTER: American River Touring Association

ADDRESS: 445 High St.

CONTACT: N/A

CITY: Oakland

TITLE: N/A

STATE: California   **ZIP:** 95601

TELEPHONE: (415) 465-9355

NUMBER OF YEARS IN BUSINESS: 20+

SPECIALIZING IN: Whitewater rafting vacations

SPECIAL PHILOSOPHY, CREDO, GOALS BEHIND BUSINESS: To preserve and protect our nation's waterways through the education of the people.

Photo: American River Touring Association

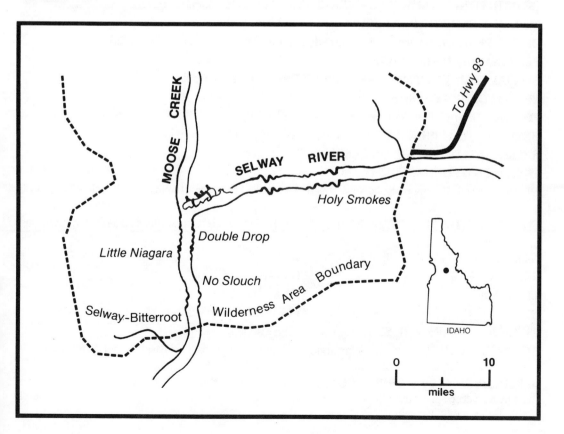

MOOSE CREEK

SELWAY RIVER

To Hwy 93

Holy Smokes

Double Drop

Little Niagara

No Slouch

Selway-Bitterroot

Wilderness Area Boundary

IDAHO

0 10
miles

COPPER RIVER BY DORY

See Alaska by dory, a graceful and elegant boat that withstands the rigors of whitewater. Gary Lane and Karen Wells offer the only dory trips in the state and they attempt to offer treks with class. With few rapids, a normally mellow character and awesome grandeur, the Copper River is an ideal family trip to undertake by dory. The river flows through the spectacular Wrangell–Saint Elias National Park and Preserve. With mountainous terrain blanketed by fields of ice and snow more profound than any other glacial area outside of the poles, and with greater relief than even the Himalayas, this area has been declared a world heritage site. Highlights include campsites established near waterfalls and glaciers, salmon fishing, hikes to explore historical railway trestles, walks on glaciers to study moraines, devil stones, moulin holes and seracs. You can also hike along the face of two active glaciers, see the Million Dollar Bridge and calving glaciers drop blocks that become icebergs. Bald eagles, grizzlies, seals and other wildlife may even make appearances. The excitement of the days are topped only by the gourmet meals prepared over an open fire and served with champagne and select wines. These nine-day trips begin and end in Anchorage.

LENGTH OF TRIP: 9 days

DEPARTURE DATES: Aug. 1 and 15

TOTAL COST: $949 per person

TYPE OF PAYMENT ACCEPTED: Check, money order

RESERVATIONS/DEPOSIT: $200 deposit 1 month prior to trip

CANCELLATION POLICY: All money, except nonrefundable deposit, will be refunded if given a written 2-week notice.

DEPARTURE LOCATION: Anchorage, AK   **NEAREST AIRPORT:** Anchorage, AK

TRANSPORTATION INFORMATION: Free van transportation from motel

HEALTH, FITNESS OR AGE REQUIREMENTS: 6 years old minimum

TYPE OF WEATHER TO EXPECT: Sunshine and rain, 40-80° F

BEST TYPE OF CLOTHING AND FOOTWEAR: Pile garments and knee-high rubber boots

PERSONAL GEAR REQUIRED: 2 sets of everything

SPECIAL GEAR/EQUIPMENT REQUIRED: Equipment list available

PHOTO POSSIBILITIES: Fantastic

FISHING POSSIBILITIES: Fantastic   **LICENSE REQUIREMENT:** 1-day, $5

BEST TYPE OF FISHING TACKLE: Heavy lures, mepps, silver spoons

REPRESENTATIVE MENU—BREAKFAST: Eggs Elegant

LUNCH: Pocket bread sandwiches

DINNER: Smoked salmon steaks, fresh green salad, baked potatoes, champagne, chocolate fantasy dessert

CHORES/DUTIES GUESTS ARE EXPECTED TO HELP WITH: Unload/load boats from trailers, wash own dishes.

NAME OF OUTFITTER: Eclipse Expeditions, Inc.

ADDRESS: Rt. 1 Box 72

CONTACT: Gary Lane

CITY: Cove

TITLE: Director

STATE: Oregon   **ZIP:** 97824

TELEPHONE: (503) 568-4663

NUMBER OF YEARS IN BUSINESS: 5

NUMBER OF STAFF: 2

SPECIALIZING IN: River trips by dory and raft. Combination trips: backpacking/raft/dory and horseback/raft/dory. Hunting trips: elk.

SPECIAL PHILOSOPHY, CREDO, GOALS BEHIND BUSINESS: ". . . to provide a superb service and generate a deep appreciation for the numerous animals, wondrous country, and powerful natural forces that we respectfully encounter."

Photo: Eclipse Expeditions

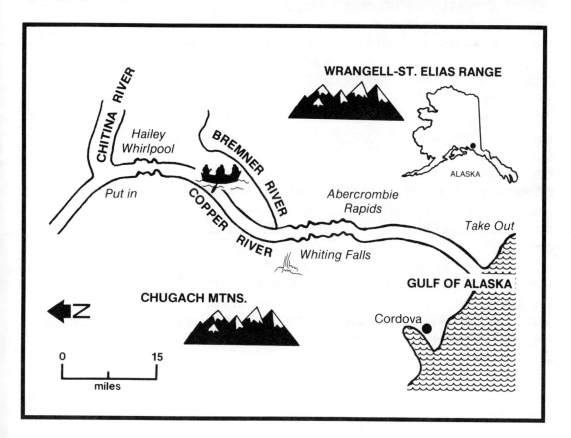

TATSHENSHINI-ALSEK EXPEDITION

The Tatshenshini River valley is a wild and pristine habitat for an abundance of wildlife, including bald eagles, grizzly bear, mountain goats and wolves. The 12-day whitewater rafting trip through this unspoiled, primordial world begins in Haines, Alaska. A 106-mile van trip takes participants to Dalton Post where they make camp for the night on a riverside beach. After an Alaskan breakfast the next morning, river touring and techniques will be explained before the group paddles downriver. The third day begins with a short hike with the expedition naturalist who explains the unique plant and animal communities of the area. As the trip progresses, glaciers seen in the distance move closer and the river widens as its pace quickens. The group camps one night in the center of immense icefield-capped mountains that resemble Pakistan on one side of the river and Hawaii's lush Nepali coast on the other. On the ninth day, the boats drift down an avenue of glaciers with nearly two dozen ice rivers in sight simultaneously. A rest day allows for exploration around the iceberg-filled bay. The eleventh day is exhilarating as the boats sneak past icebergs and flotsam during the final 11 miles. After arrival in Dry Bay, the group camps one more night on the riverbank and then flies back to Juneau.

LENGTH OF TRIP: 12 days

DEPARTURE DATES: July 31, 1984

TOTAL COST: $1,450

TYPE OF PAYMENT ACCEPTED: Check

RESERVATIONS/DEPOSIT: $200 deposit 2-4 months prior to trip

CANCELLATION POLICY: No refunds for no shows

DEPARTURE LOCATION: Juneau, AK   **NEAREST AIRPORT:** Juneau, AK

TRANSPORTATION INFORMATION: Bus, taxi

HEALTH, FITNESS OR AGE REQUIREMENTS: Good physical condition

TYPE OF WEATHER TO EXPECT: Varied

BEST TYPE OF CLOTHING AND FOOTWEAR: Equipment list available

PERSONAL GEAR REQUIRED: Equipment list available

SPECIAL GEAR/EQUIPMENT REQUIRED: Equipment list available

PHOTO POSSIBILITIES: Fantastic

FISHING POSSIBILITIES: Fair

REPRESENTATIVE MENU—BREAKFAST: All gourmet and plenty of it

LUNCH: Same

DINNER: Same

CHORES/DUTIES GUESTS ARE EXPECTED TO HELP WITH: Wash own dishes after meals.

NAME OF OUTFITTER: James Henry River Journeys

ADDRESS: P.O. Box 807   **CONTACT:** James Katz

CITY: Bolinas   **TITLE:** Director

STATE: California   **ZIP:** 94924   **TELEPHONE:** (415) 868-1836

NUMBER OF YEARS IN BUSINESS: 12   **NUMBER OF STAFF:** 3-12

SPECIALIZING IN: River rafting, trekking, natural history, art work shops

SPECIAL PHILOSOPHY, CREDO, GOALS BEHIND BUSINESS: Migrations, treading lightly, environmental concerns, quality of life.

Photo: James Katz

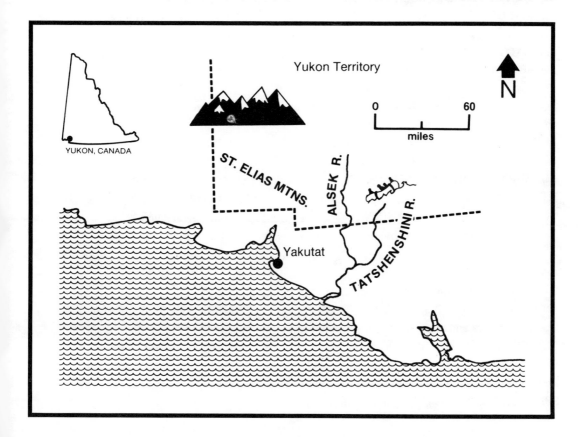

Yukon Territory

YUKON, CANADA

ST. ELIAS MTNS.

ALSEK R.

TATSHENSHINI R.

Yakutat

0   60
miles

N

 # FLOATING THE COLORADO

We drive to the put-in point at Lee's Ferry, Arizona, last road access to the Grand Canyon. We help load our duffel onto a cargo raft that will follow us, then clamber into our boats and push away from the sandy bank. The river is flat and calm here. We round a bend, jiggle over a riffle and depart civilization. Suddenly I begin to realize that a trip down the Grand Canyon of the Colorado River is one of the premier adventures in the world, a voyage into the past, to the dinosaurs and beyond. The river is a time machine taking us into a primeval world. We stare in awe at the stairstep formations above us, terrace upon terrace, pinnacle upon butte, ridge upon cornice. And late that day, an ominous downstream rumble reminds us that whitewater is near. Our guide tells us to hold on, tightens his grip on the oars, inhales deeply and directs the boat into the frothy white center of a rapid. The boat bobs crazily, lurching and heaving. The river dashes icy water in our faces and we shriek like happy, frightened children. I see that the guide is in control, attacking each wave, hitting its crest cleanly to give his passengers maximum ride. But I also realize that one missed stroke, one bad swipe with the oar and the boat could lurch sideways, get tipped over by a wave and we would get very wet. For the next two weeks we live in this wonderful mix of natural grandeur, intense excitement, desert solitude, comic relief, growing partnerships and personal rejuvenation. Truly the king of river trips!

NAME OF TRIP: 14-Day All Paddle Grand Canyon Raft Trip
OUTFITTER: Arizona Raft Adventures
ADDRESS: P.O. Box 697G, Flagstaff, AZ 86002   **TELEPHONE:** (602) 526-8200
CONTACT: Rob Elliott, president
NUMBER OF YEARS IN BUSINESS: 18   **NUMBER OF STAFF:** 30
LENGTH OF TRIP: 14 days   **DEPARTURE LOCATION:** Flagstaff, AZ
COST: $1,185   **RESERVATIONS/DEPOSIT:** $200 1-10 months prior to trip
SPECIALIZING IN: Oar-powered, paddle-powered, oar & paddle powered (hybrid), and motor-powered whitewater raft trips in the Grand Canyon.

* * *

NAME OF TRIP: 8-Day Motorized Full-Length Grand Canyon Raft Trip
OUTFITTER: Diamond River Adventures, Inc.
ADDRESS: Box 1316/916 Vista Ave., Page, AZ 86040   **TELEPHONE:** (602) 645-8866
CONTACT: Bill Diamond, owner/president
NUMBER OF YEARS IN BUSINESS: 15   **NUMBER OF STAFF:** 3-30
LENGTH OF TRIP: 8 days   **DEPARTURE LOCATION:** Lee's Ferry, AZ
COST: $760 plus tax   **RESERVATIONS/DEPOSIT:** $150 with reservation
SPECIALIZING IN: Raft trips through the Grand Canyon on the Colorado

* * *

NAME OF TRIP: Kayak Support Trip
OUTFITTER: Expeditions Inc./Grand Canyon Youth Expeditions
ADDRESS: Rt. 4 Box 755, Flagstaff, AZ 86001   **TELEPHONE:** (602) 774-8176, 779-3769
CONTACT: Dick and Susie McCallum, president and vice-president
NUMBER OF YEARS IN BUSINESS: 14   **NUMBER OF STAFF:** 10
LENGTH OF TRIP: 12, 14, 16, 18 days   **DEPARTURE LOCATION:** Flagstaff, AZ
COST: $935-$1,063   **RESERVATIONS/DEPOSIT:** $200 with reservation
SPECIALIZING IN: Grand Canyon river trips

* * *

Photo: Grand Canyon Dories

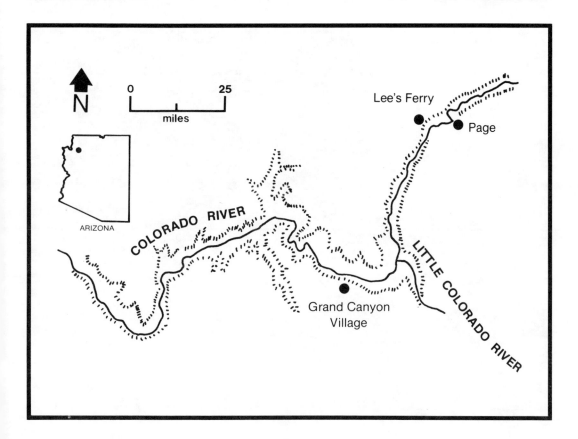

Photo: Joseph Daniel

Photo: Holiday River Expeditions

Photo: Joseph Daniel

Photo: Joseph Daniel

NAME OF TRIP: Thrill Boat Trip
OUTFITTER: Georgie's Royal River Rats
ADDRESS: Box 12057, Las Vegas, NV 89112   **TELEPHONE:** (702) 451-5588
CONTACT: Georgie Clark, owner
NUMBER OF YEARS IN BUSINESS: 40   **NUMBER OF STAFF:** Varies
LENGTH OF TRIP: 7 days   **DEPARTURE LOCATION:** Las Vegas, NV
COST: $727.25 (including bus, plane, helicopter)
RESERVATIONS/DEPOSIT: $100 with reservation
SPECIALIZING IN: Whitewater

*   *   *

NAME OF TRIP: Grand Canyon Motorized Raft Trip
OUTFITTER: Grand Canyon Expeditions, Inc.
ADDRESS: P.O. Box O, Kanab, UT 84741   **TELEPHONE:** (801) 644-2691
CONTACT: Ron, Marc or Jana Smith, president, manager, secretary-treasurer
NUMBER OF YEARS IN BUSINESS: 20   **NUMBER OF STAFF:** 7-10
LENGTH OF TRIP: 9 days   **DEPARTURE LOCATION:** Las Vegas, NV
COST: $985—adult, $886—8 to 14 years   **RESERVATIONS/DEPOSIT:** $325 with reservation
SPECIALIZING IN: River running

*   *   *

NAME OF TRIP: Grand Canyon River Expeditions
OUTFITTER: Sleight Expeditions
ADDRESS: P.O. Box 118, Laverkin, UT 84745   **TELEPHONE:** (801) 635-2177
CONTACT: Mark P. Sleight, president
NUMBER OF YEARS IN BUSINESS: 4   **NUMBER OF STAFF:** 10
LENGTH OF TRIP: 13 days—rowing/8 days—motor   **DEPARTURE LOCATION:** Lee's Ferry, AZ
COST: $1,100—rowing/$750—motor   **RESERVATIONS/DEPOSIT:** $100 with reservation
SPECIALIZING IN: Grand Canyon river trips

*   *   *

NAME OF TRIP: All the Way Through the Grand Canyon By Dory
OUTFITTER: Martin Litton's Grand Canyon Dories Inc.
ADDRESS: Box 3029, Stanford, CA 94305   **TELEPHONE:** (415) 851-0411
CONTACT: Martin Litton, president
NUMBER OF YEARS IN BUSINESS: 19   **NUMBER OF STAFF:** Varies
LENGTH OF TRIP: 18 days   **DEPARTURE LOCATION:** Lee's Ferry, AZ
COST: $1,560   **RESERVATIONS/DEPOSIT:** 25% with reservation
SPECIALIZING IN: Motorless float trips on wilderness rivers and associated activities

*   *   *

NAME OF TRIP: Grand Canyon River Trips
OUTFITTER: White Water River Expeditions, Inc.
ADDRESS: P.O. Box 1269, Mariposa, CA 95388   **TELEPHONE:** (209) 742-6633
CONTACT: Jeanne Schulz, assistant office manager
NUMBER OF YEARS IN BUSINESS: 20   **NUMBER OF STAFF:** Varies
LENGTH OF TRIP: 7 days   **DEPARTURE LOCATION:** Las Vegas, NV
COST: $895 deluxe/$1,125 super deluxe   **RESERVATIONS/DEPOSIT:** $200 with reservation
SPECIALIZING IN: River trips through the Grand Canyon

HAWAII SUN & SAIL CRUISE

If you desire a bit of adventure and the romance of Pacific trade wind sailing among incomparable tropical islands, if you enjoy starting off the day with a swim in warm crystal clear waters of a quiet anchorage, if you search for a natural paradise without crowds, if you like to float lazily over beautiful coral formations surrounded by clouds of butterflies, damsel and parrot fish, if you wish to explore ancient Hawaiian heiaus (temples) and petroglyphs, then run away to the sea. Our sleek 33-foot and 35-foot sloops allow you to venture back to the old Hawaii. Our suggested itinerary allows us five evenings aboard the sailboat as we set sail from Manele Bay, Lanai and cross the Auau and Kalohi Channels to Maui and Molokai. Fresh seafood and native dishes are enjoyed each evening as we like to anchor in a quiet cove immersed in the soft rays of the Hawaiian sunset. The black velvet tropical sky full of stars invites us to camp on deck or nestle below in a comfortable berth at day's end. Our small group orientation creates a very personalized vacation opportunity. Should you be traveling alone, we can match you with others seeking to enjoy the "other" side of Hawaii. Our congenial skippers and crews easily transform strangers into a gathering of friends.

LENGTH OF TRIP: 6 days   **DEPARTURE DATES:** Sundays all year

TOTAL COST: $720   **TYPE OF PAYMENT ACCEPTED:** Check

RESERVATIONS/DEPOSIT: $100/person with reservation

CANCELLATION POLICY: Full refund

DEPARTURE LOCATION: Lanai, HI   **NEAREST AIRPORT:** Lanai, HI

TRANSPORTATION INFORMATION: Provided

TYPE OF WEATHER TO EXPECT: 75°-80°F—excellent!

BEST TYPE OF CLOTHING AND FOOTWEAR: Swimsuits, rubber sandals

PERSONAL GEAR REQUIRED: Equipment list available

SPECIAL GEAR/EQUIPMENT REQUIRED: None

WHAT NOT TO BRING: Excessive baggage

PHOTO POSSIBILITIES: Fantastic

FISHING POSSIBILITIES: Fantastic   **LICENSE REQUIREMENT:** None

BEST TYPE OF FISHING TACKLE: Supplied

REPRESENTATIVE MENU—BREAKFAST: Fruit, eggs, local breads

LUNCH: Fruit, cheese, meats, fish, breads

DINNER: Seafood, steak, chicken, sunshine, mahi mahi; Hawaiian-style gourmet cooking

CHORES/DUTIES GUESTS ARE EXPECTED TO HELP WITH: Relax or join in

ADDITIONAL SPECIAL INFORMATION: Bring sunscreen and cotton coverups

NAME OF OUTFITTER: Adrift Adventures

ADDRESS: P.O. Box 577 Dept. J   **CONTACT:** Kerry Richardson

CITY: Glenwood Springs   **TITLE:** Director

STATE: Colorado   **ZIP:** 81602   **TELEPHONE:** (303) 945-2281

NUMBER OF YEARS IN BUSINESS: 9   **NUMBER OF STAFF:** 6

SPECIALIZING IN: Sailing charters and whitewater rafting

SPECIAL PHILOSOPHY, CREDO, GOALS BEHIND BUSINESS: To introduce the first-time and experienced sailor to the non-commercial "other" Hawaii.

Photo: Kerry Richardson

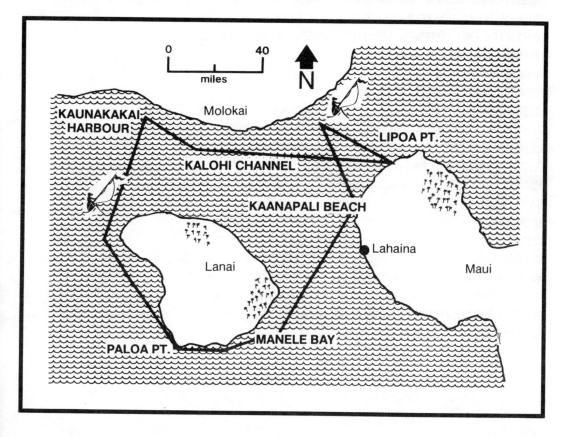

SAILING/FORAGING FOR NATURAL FOODS

This is an opportunity to forage for wild foods while sailing North America's last unspoiled cruising grounds. Guests may fish for flounder, halibut, cod, rockfish and salmon while surrounded by the spectacular wilderness scenery of Prince William Sound. In certain anchorages, we will drop crab and shrimp pots for coon stripe and spotted shrimp or dungeness, tanner and king crab. The shores may be foraged on low tide for butter clams, cockles and blue mussels. Nancy Lithcoe, an expert on native plants of the area, will lead trips ashore to gather wild edible plants and berries. The fresh food will be incorporated into daily meals. The combination of sailing and gathering your own food provides an escape from the hectic pace of modern life to a slower, more simplified and basic existence. A certain satisfaction also comes from gathering your own food supply. This six-day trip will encourage a self-sufficiency rarely developed in a high-tech world. Guests are expected to help with the cooking and cleaning while under way. Clothing should be practical and include knee-high rubber boots and sneakers. This excursion's effects and new knowledge will last a lifetime.

LENGTH OF TRIP: 6 days

TOTAL COST: Varies according to size of boat

DEPARTURE DATES: Varies

TYPE OF PAYMENT ACCEPTED: Check

RESERVATIONS/DEPOSIT: $300 deposit immediately

CANCELLATION POLICY: Deposit is forfeited with less than 1 month's notice

DEPARTURE LOCATION: Whittier, AK   **NEAREST AIRPORT:** Anchorage

TRANSPORTATION INFORMATION: Bus to train

HEALTH, FITNESS OR AGE REQUIREMENTS: None

TYPE OF WEATHER TO EXPECT: Temps 50-80° F, some rain

BEST TYPE OF CLOTHING AND FOOTWEAR: Knee-high rubber boots, tennis shoes

PERSONAL GEAR REQUIRED: Sleeping bag

SPECIAL GEAR/EQUIPMENT REQUIRED: N/A

PHOTO POSSIBILITIES: Fantastic

FISHING POSSIBILITIES: Good   **LICENSE REQUIREMENT:** Alaska $20

BEST TYPE OF FISHING TACKLE: Medium weight spinning gear

REPRESENTATIVE MENU: Varies

CHORES/DUTIES GUESTS ARE EXPECTED TO HELP WITH: Cooking, cleaning

ADDITIONAL SPECIAL INFORMATION: Guests must wear life jackets while under way

NAME OF OUTFITTER: Alaskan Wilderness Sailing Safaris

ADDRESS: Box 701   **CONTACT:** James Lithcoe

CITY: Whittier   **TITLE:** Owner

STATE: Alaska   **ZIP:** 99686   **TELEPHONE:** (907) 338-2134

NUMBER OF YEARS IN BUSINESS: 10   **NUMBER OF STAFF:** 4

SPECIALIZING IN: Flotilla sailing cruises in Prince William Sound

SPECIAL PHILOSOPHY, CREDO, GOALS BEHIND BUSINESS: To introduce others to America's last unspoiled cruising area.

Photo: Alaskan Wilderness Sailing Safari

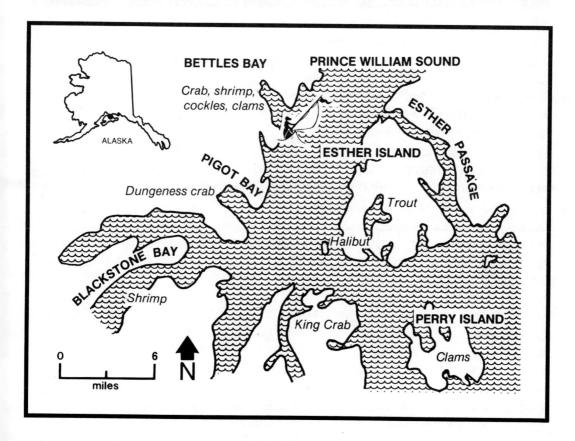

BAHAMAS SAILING CRUISE

Ship's Log, 1000: After breakfast, we sailed for Eleuthera. The winds were still blowing strong, and in expectation of their forces, we had reefed our mainsail before leaving. All hands were ready to assist with hoisting the jib, mainsail and the mizzen. Then, for the next hour, the motion of the wind, the salty sea spray and the sound of Beethoven coming over the ship's stereo system soothes us with a feeling of peace.

1300: We cleared off the deck as the Dolphin made way across a very shallow bank to Dunmoretown. We were now under the power of the motor. Ginny got the real test of strength with the lead line this day as we went from 11 feet to 5 feet. The Dolphin draws 4½ feet! Once Captain Gene etched our mark on the bottom, just enough to say "The Dolphin was here." Then we spun off to find deeper waters.

1400: We found a beautiful shallow coral reef, perfect for snorkeling and diving. The reef was alive with yellow and purple sea fans and fishes of every size and color.

1600: We docked at Harbour Island where we received a warm welcome from the Dock Master. First stop was Willie's Tavern where the beer is cold and refreshing and Willie friendly and receptive to a bunch of grubby-looking seamen.

LENGTH OF TRIP: 7-14 days　　**DEPARTURE DATES:** Whenever group reserves

TOTAL COST: $325 per person per week　　**TYPE OF PAYMENT ACCEPTED:** Check

RESERVATIONS/DEPOSIT: $400 when booking

CANCELLATION POLICY: Lose deposit

DEPARTURE LOCATION: Bahamas　　**NEAREST AIRPORT:** Miami, FL

TRANSPORTATION INFORMATION: Drive to Miami or fly into airport and rent car to drive to boat.

HEALTH, FITNESS OR AGE REQUIREMENTS: Should be able to swim

TYPE OF WEATHER TO EXPECT: Mostly warm and sunny

BEST TYPE OF CLOTHING AND FOOTWEAR: Casual

PERSONAL GEAR REQUIRED: Personal duffle

SPECIAL GEAR/EQUIPMENT REQUIRED: Snorkeling gear, sheets, sleeping bag, air mattress

WHAT NOT TO BRING: Anything valuable

PHOTO POSSIBILITIES: Fantastic

FISHING POSSIBILITIES: Fantastic　　**LICENSE REQUIREMENT:** None

BEST TYPE OF FISHING TACKLE: Heavy duty ocean tackle

REPRESENTATIVE MENU—BREAKFAST: Bacon, eggs, toast, coffee, hot cereal

LUNCH: Sandwiches, cheese, fruit, vegetable plate

DINNER: Spaghetti, salad, strawberry shortcake

CHORES/DUTIES GUESTS ARE EXPECTED TO HELP WITH: Cooking, cleaning, handling sails, etc.

ADDITIONAL SPECIAL INFORMATION: Eight mm. videotape (VHS or Beta) available of cruise. Voters registration card, passport, or birth certificate required to enter Bahamas.

NAME OF OUTFITTER: Windward Bound, Inc.

ADDRESS: 1535 Snapfinger　　**CONTACT:** Wiliam Chiappini

CITY: Decatur　　**TITLE:** President

STATE: Georgia　　**ZIP:** 30032　　**TELEPHONE:** (404) 288-1259

NUMBER OF YEARS IN BUSINESS: 5　　**NUMBER OF STAFF:** 3

SPECIALIZING IN: Sailing, snorkeling, living on a boat, all types of ocean/island adventures.

SPECIAL PHILOSOPHY, CREDO, GOALS BEHIND BUSINESS: Do-it-yourself cruises, i.e. the group buys and prepares food, helps the captain handle the boat, etc.

Photo: Cheri Baird

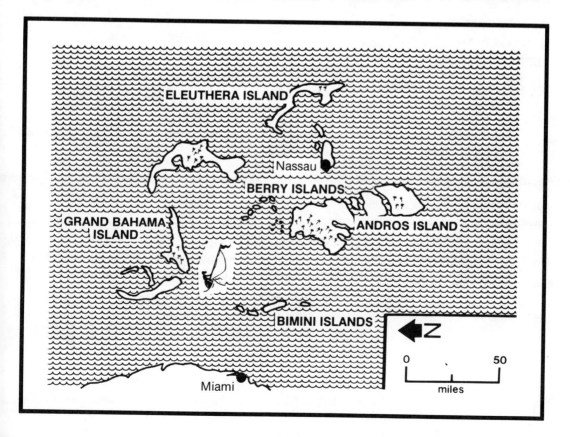

ELEUTHERA ISLAND

Nassau

BERRY ISLANDS

GRAND BAHAMA
ISLAND

ANDROS ISLAND

BIMINI ISLANDS

N

0   50

miles

Miami

WINDJAMMER CRUISES

The ship slides across the gentle harbor swell as we leave the port in the early morning light. The captain calls "halyard crews, line up!" The mains'l is hoisted first, then the tops'l, fores'l and jibs. Gently at first and then with more strength, the vessel cuts through the water. Look astern, the wake is a mixture of deep green and white. Look aloft, the lines are taut and the big mains'l seems to ride up forever in the sparkling air. Look around the salty vista and see other schooners, islands, and perhaps porpoise surfacing close by to breathe, or seals sunning themselves on nearby rock ledges. To a great extent, the wind and tide determine each day's course and destination. Often we slide through narrow passages or weave through clusters of granite-based islands. The fresh air cultivates hearty appetites and they are appeased with Maine blueberry pancakes, muffins, fresh fish and chowders, oven-hot pies and even homemade ice cream. Dinner could consist of rowing ashore to a deserted beach and cooking a huge lobster dinner over an open fire with drawn butter, hors d'oeuvres and all the trimmings. The days rush by as guests enjoy exciting sailing, the spray splashing over the windward rail and the sun beaming down from the bright blue sky.

NAME OF TRIP: Windjammer "Angelique"

OUTFITTER: Yankee Packet Company   **TELEPHONE:** (207) 236-8873

ADDRESS: Box 736, Camden, ME 04843

CONTACT: Mike Anderson, owner/operator   **NUMBER OF STAFF:** 7

LENGTH OF TRIP: 6 days   **DEPARTURE LOCATION:** Camden, ME

COST: $360-$410   **RESERVATIONS/DEPOSIT:** $150 with reservation

SPECIALIZING IN: Windjammer vacations

*   *   *

NAME OF TRIP: September Foliage Cruise

OUTFITTER: Sylvina W. Beal Schooner Cruises   **TELEPHONE:** (207) 548-2922

ADDRESS: Box 509N, Belfast, ME 04915

CONTACT: Capt. John D. Worth, owner   **NUMBER OF STAFF:** 6

LENGTH OF TRIP: 6 days   **DEPARTURE LOCATION:** Belfast, ME

COST: $375   **RESERVATIONS/DEPOSIT:** $150 with reservation

SPECIALIZING IN: We take 18 guests on windjammer adventures along the Maine coast. Great food, lively sailing and new friends.

*   *   *

NAME OF TRIP: Schooner J. & E. Riggin

OUTFITTER: Schooner J. & E. Riggin

ADDRESS: Box 571, Rockland, ME 04841   **TELEPHONE:** (207) 594-2923

CONTACT: Capt. Dave and Sue Allen, owners/operators

NUMBER OF YEARS IN BUSINESS: 7   **NUMBER OF STAFF:** 6

LENGTH OF TRIP: 6 days   **DEPARTURE LOCATION:** Rockland, ME

COST: $340-$415   **RESERVATIONS/DEPOSIT:** $150 with reservation

SPECIALIZING IN: Weekly windjammer cruises along the Maine coast.

*   *   *

Photo: Maine Windjammer Cruises

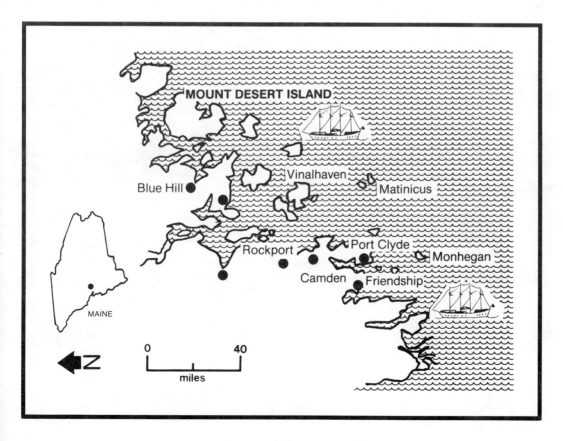

MOUNT DESERT ISLAND

Blue Hill

Vinalhaven

Matinicus

Rockport

Port Clyde

Monhegan

Camden

Friendship

MAINE

N

0   40
miles

Photo: Maine Windjammer Cruises

Photo: Maine Windjammer Cruises

Photo: Maine Windjammer Cruises

NAME OF TRIP: Windjammer Coastal Cruise
OUTFITTER: Schooner Stephen Taber
ADDRESS: 70 Elm St., Camden, ME 04843   **TELEPHONE:** (207) 236-3520
CONTACT: Capt. Ken and Ellen Barnes, owners
NUMBER OF YEARS IN BUSINESS: 38   **NUMBER OF STAFF:** 6
LENGTH OF TRIP: 6 days   **DEPARTURE LOCATION:** Camden, ME
COST: $360-425   **RESERVATIONS/DEPOSIT:** $150 with reservation
SPECIALIZING IN: Windjamming off the rugged coast of Maine

*   *   *

NAME OF TRIP: Schooner Cruises
OUTFITTER: Yankee Schooner Cruises
ADDRESS: Box 696, Camden, ME 04843   **TELEPHONE:** (207) 236-4449
CONTACT: Capt. Jim Sharp, owner
NUMBER OF YEARS IN BUSINESS: 20   **NUMBER OF STAFF:** 7 per schooner
LENGTH OF TRIP: 6 days   **DEPARTURE LOCATION:** Camden, ME
COST: $395   **RESERVATIONS/DEPOSIT:** $100 with reservation
SPECIALIZING IN: Windjammer cruises

*   *   *

NAME OF TRIP: Virgin Islands Cruise
OUTFITTER: Dirigo Cruises   **TELEPHONE:** (203) 669-7068
ADDRESS: 39 Waterside Lane, Clinton, CT
CONTACT: Whitcomb   **NUMBER OF STAFF:** 2
LENGTH OF TRIP: 6 days   **DEPARTURE LOCATION:** St. Thomas, VI
COST: $535   **RESERVATIONS/DEPOSIT:** $150 with reservation
SPECIALIZING IN: Vacation windjammer cruises

*   *   *

NAME OF TRIP: Schooner Timberwind Cruise
OUTFITTER: Schooner Timberwind   **TELEPHONE:** (207) 437-2851
ADDRESS: Box 247, Rockport, ME 04856
CONTACT: Bill Alexander   **NUMBER OF STAFF:** 6
LENGTH OF TRIP: 6 days   **DEPARTURE LOCATION:** Rockport, ME
COST: $360-395   **RESERVATIONS/DEPOSIT:** $120 with reservation
SPECIALIZING IN: Weekly Windjammer Cruises

BAJA LONG-RANGE SPORTFISHING

The ocean waters south of San Diego, California along the Pacific Coast of Baja are home to innumerable game fish. Sportfishing this rich area almost guarantees you a trophy catch, done off the decks of the 95-foot Executive. From June through December, groups of 38 or fewer anglers head south to enjoy some of the finest fishing anywhere. Depending upon the length of the trip and the time of year, fishermen test their skills against yellowtail, bass, albacore, yellowfin tuna, bluefin tuna, dorado, grouper, wahoo, black sea bass and more. Since the species range from scrappy 3 lb. calico bass to tackle-testing 300-plus lb. tuna, the trips suit both experts and beginners. The experienced captain and crew are always available to help, too. Since their boat is your home for the entire trip, the maximum amount of time possible is spent fishing. You unpack once and relax in comfortable air-conditioned and carpeted cabins, a roomy salon for lounging or feasting on top quality meals, such as french toast for breakfast and prime rib with all the trimmings for dinner. There are no chores expected of you except to catch your intended quota of fish and make provisions to transport the haul home.

LENGTH OF TRIP: 2-10 days **DEPARTURE DATES:** June through Dec.

TOTAL COST: $220-1,080 **TYPE OF PAYMENT ACCEPTED:** Any

RESERVATIONS/DEPOSIT: 50% to confirm

CANCELLATION POLICY: Forfeit deposit unless trip is completely booked at departure

DEPARTURE LOCATION: H&M Landing, **NEAREST AIRPORT:** San Diego, CA
San Diego, CA

TRANSPORTATION INFORMATION: Cab

HEALTH, FITNESS OR AGE REQUIREMENTS: Normal good health

TYPE OF WEATHER TO EXPECT: Generally mild and fair

BEST TYPE OF CLOTHING AND FOOTWEAR: Casual, comfortable

PERSONAL GEAR REQUIRED: Equipment list available

SPECIAL GEAR/EQUIPMENT REQUIRED: Adequate fishing tackle for length of trip

PHOTO POSSIBILITIES: Fantastic

FISHING POSSIBILITIES: Fantastic **LICENSE REQUIREMENT:** Mexican (included in
trip fee)

BEST TYPE OF FISHING TACKLE: Medium to heavy saltwater tackle

REPRESENTATIVE MENU—BREAKFAST: Eggs, french toast

LUNCH: Fresh soup, fish sandwich, salad

DINNER: Prime rib dinner, all the trimmings, dessert

CHORES/DUTIES GUESTS ARE EXPECTED TO HELP WITH: None

ADDITIONAL SPECIAL INFORMATION: Provisions must be made for transporting your fresh frozen catch home.

NAME OF OUTFITTER: M. V. Executive Inc.

ADDRESS: 2445 Morena Blvd., Suite 200 **CONTACT:** Rich Allee

CITY: San Diego **TITLE:** Manager

STATE: California **ZIP:** 92110 **TELEPHONE:** (619) 275-4253

NUMBER OF STAFF: 1-2

SPECIALIZING IN: Baja long range sportfishing and Baja natural history vacation cruises

Photo: M. V. Executive, Inc.

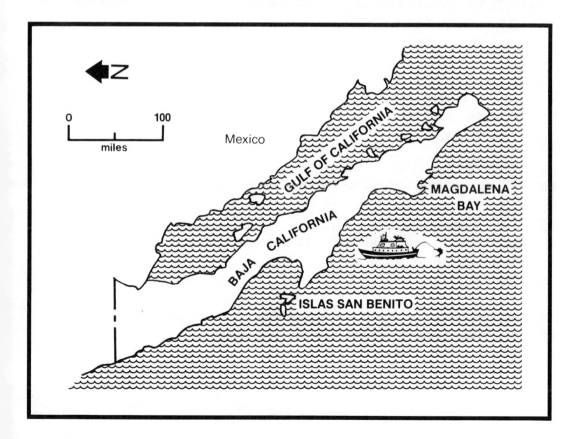

SAN IGNACIO SEA FARI

As we cruised south by boat for two days, we were escorted by sleek dolphin gracefully riding our bow wave in a friendly salute. We also encountered large numbers of elephant seals and sea lions on San Martin and San Benitos islands, which have been rookery sites for hundreds of years. We entered San Ignacio Lagoon at high tide and were surrounded by gray whales as we anchored. Breaching whales displayed almost human-like exhilaration as they lifted their 40-ton bodies almost completely out of the water, then hitting the surface with a resounding splash time and time again. Later, inside the lagoon, the exquisite calm was broken only by the gentle breathing of the whales, the raucous cries of gulls and a constant hum from our ship's generator. We had sailed 400 miles to make this contact. That afternoon we were rewarded. A "friendly" whale and her calf surfaced under our 15-foot skiff. Our excitement grew and was barely contained until at last the calf moved closer. He looked at us with wide, intelligent eyes, inviting contact. Straining over the side of the skiff, I rubbed his smooth and as yet unbarnacled skin. He smiled at me, a big toothy grin, and then dove, leaving only a whale print.

LENGTH OF TRIP: 9 days

DEPARTURE DATES: Dec.-May

TOTAL COST: $1,120

TYPE OF PAYMENT ACCEPTED: Any

RESERVATIONS/DEPOSIT: 50% to confirm

CANCELLATION POLICY: No refund

DEPARTURE LOCATION: H&M Landing, San Diego, CA

NEAREST AIRPORT: San Diego, CA

TRANSPORTATION INFORMATION: Taxi

HEALTH, FITNESS OR AGE REQUIREMENTS: None

TYPE OF WEATHER TO EXPECT: Moderate

BEST TYPE OF CLOTHING AND FOOTWEAR: Casual

PERSONAL GEAR REQUIRED: Personal duffle

SPECIAL GEAR/EQUIPMENT REQUIRED: Equipment list available

WHAT NOT TO BRING: Evening wear

PHOTO POSSIBILITIES: Fantastic

FISHING POSSIBILITIES: Fantastic

LICENSE REQUIREMENT: Mexico (included in trip fee)

BEST TYPE OF FISHING TACKLE: Provided

REPRESENTATIVE MENU—BREAKFAST: Eggs, bacon, pancakes

LUNCH: Sandwiches, fresh fish

DINNER: Prime rib, steak, lobster, chicken, salads

CHORES/DUTIES GUESTS ARE EXPECTED TO HELP WITH: Observe water conservation

NAME OF OUTFITTER: Pacific Sea Fari Tours

ADDRESS: 2803 Emerson

CONTACT: Dale Sydenstricker

CITY: San Diego

TITLE: Natural History Coordinator

STATE: California   **ZIP:** 92106

TELEPHONE: (619) 226-8224

NUMBER OF YEARS IN BUSINESS: 15

NUMBER OF STAFF: 20

SPECIALIZING IN: Natural history

SPECIAL PHILOSOPHY, CREDO, GOALS BEHIND BUSINESS: To preserve the natural environment and to become a close part of it.

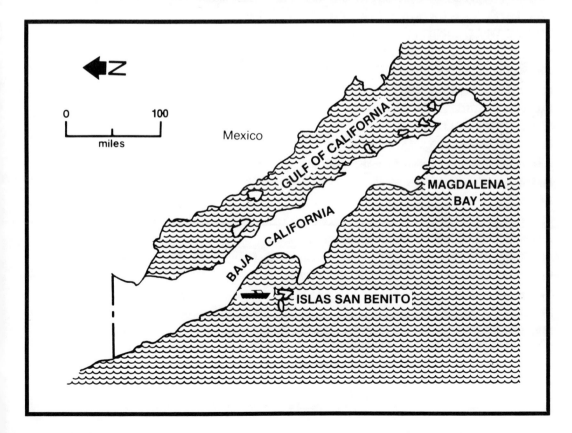

MAGDALENA BAY WHALE WATCHING

Every year the California grey whale migrates 5,000 miles from the Bering Strait to the protected lagoons of Baja California, Mexico. They come to these quiet waters to breed, calve, and teach their newborns the rudimentary skills necessary for survival. Magdalena Bay is the southernmost lagoon where the whales drift lazily with the changing tides in this narrow channel. Whale-watching is enjoyed from the Don Jose as well as oar-powered skiffs. You will have the opportunity to gently drift with them and come silently upon a sleeping whale to observe this magnificent mammal. Hear them breathe, watch them spyhop, breach and fluke. This is a unique peaceful area and is ideal for observing and sharing with the others the feeling you receive of serenity from these graceful giants. Experience the awesome yet gentle power of the grey whale in its graceful movements. There is also time to explore Magdalena Island with its rolling sand dunes and long isolated beaches strewn with shells and driftwood. The miles of mangrove channels in Magdalena Bay provide marvelous birdwatching opportunities as a wide variety of migrating shore and sea birds gather in the low dense trees or search for food at the water's edge. The final night is spent in the port city of La Paz.

LENGTH OF TRIP: 8 days   **DEPARTURE DATES:** January-March

TOTAL COST: $895 plus airfare   **TYPE OF PAYMENT ACCEPTED:** Check

RESERVATIONS/DEPOSIT: $150 deposit with reservation

CANCELLATION POLICY: Forfeit deposit if not notified

DEPARTURE LOCATION: La Paz, B.C.S,   **NEAREST AIRPORT:** La Paz
Mexico

TRANSPORTATION INFORMATION: Charter bus to Magdalena Bay

HEALTH, FITNESS OR AGE REQUIREMENTS: Good health

TYPE OF WEATHER TO EXPECT: Warm sunny days, cool nights

BEST TYPE OF CLOTHING AND FOOTWEAR: Casual

PERSONAL GEAR REQUIRED: None

SPECIAL GEAR/EQUIPMENT REQUIRED: Tent, sleeping bags

PHOTO POSSIBILITIES: Fantastic

FISHING POSSIBILITIES: Fair   **LICENSE REQUIREMENT:** Provided

BEST TYPE OF FISHING TACKLE: Provided

REPRESENTATIVE MENU—BREAKFAST: American/Mexican

LUNCH: American/Mexican

DINNER: American/Mexican

CHORES/DUTIES GUESTS ARE EXPECTED TO HELP WITH: Just have a good time

NAME OF OUTFITTER: Baja Expeditions, Inc.

ADDRESS: P.O. Box 3725   **CONTACT:** Penny

CITY: San Diego   **TITLE:** Manager

STATE: California   **ZIP:** 92103   **TELEPHONE:** (619) 297-0506

NUMBER OF YEARS IN BUSINESS: 10   **NUMBER OF STAFF:** 6

SPECIALIZING IN: Whale-watching expeditions, diving and natural history cruises in the Sea of Cortez, muleback camping expeditions to view cave art.

SPECIAL PHILOSOPHY, CREDO, GOALS BEHIND BUSINESS: We offer unique travel for unique people.

Photo: Baja Expeditions

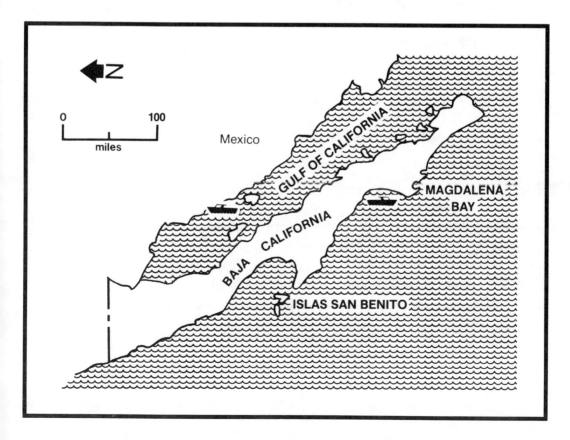

NORTHWEST ADVENTURE

Have you ever wanted to crash through boiling rapids in a whitewater raft? Or stand atop a 10,000-foot peak surrounded by tumbling glaciers? How about exploring an offshore island chain by bicycle, learning to telemark on cross-country skis or skipping across the waves on a sailboard? Now you can do all this and more on the Northwest Adventure. We begin by taking our bicycles on the ferry to San Juan Island for two days of cycling along the ocean. Then it is back to the mainland and up to 10,700-foot Mt. Baker, a dormant volcano at the northern end of the Cascades, for skiing and snow climbing. From there we head east over the mountains to our base camp in Mazama for a rest day before heading down the Methow River for whitewater rafting and kayaking lessons. Then back to the mountains for an easy yet spectacular climb up Early Winters Spire after a rock climbing lesson. We fish for trout in Blue Lake, enjoy a day of windsurfing and then head back to Seattle. Sounds like a lot? It is, but there is plenty of time for relaxing along the way since we won't be moving all of the time. Sounds like fun? It is the ultimate! This two-week program includes all meals, accommodations, transportation and equipment. No experience necessary.

LENGTH OF TRIP: 14 days   **DEPARTURE DATES:** Varies

TOTAL COST: $895   **TYPE OF PAYMENT ACCEPTED:** Check

RESERVATIONS/DEPOSIT: $100 deposit with reservation

CANCELLATION POLICY: No refunds

DEPARTURE LOCATION: Seattle, WA   **NEAREST AIRPORT:** Seattle, WA

TRANSPORTATION INFORMATION: Free van pickup

HEALTH, FITNESS OR AGE REQUIREMENTS: 16 years old minimum

TYPE OF WEATHER TO EXPECT: Moderate days, cool nights

BEST TYPE OF CLOTHING AND FOOTWEAR: Equipment list available

PERSONAL GEAR REQUIRED: Personal duffle

SPECIAL GEAR/EQUIPMENT REQUIRED: None

PHOTO POSSIBILITIES: Good

FISHING POSSIBILITIES: Good   **LICENSE REQUIREMENTS:** WA $15

BEST TYPE OF FISHING TACKLE: Fly or light spinning

REPRESENTATIVE MENU—BREAKFAST: Varies

LUNCH: Varies

DINNER: Varies

CHORES/DUTIES GUESTS ARE EXPECTED TO HELP WITH: Minimal

NAME OF OUTFITTER: Liberty Bell Alpine Tours

ADDRESS: Star Rt. Box A   **CONTACT:** Eric Sanford

CITY: Mazama   **TITLE:** Director

STATE: Washington   **ZIP:** 98833   **TELEPHONE:** (509) 996-2250

NUMBER OF YEARS IN BUSINESS: 8   **NUMBER OF STAFF:** 20

SPECIALIZING IN: Backpacking, climbing, skiing, bicycling, rafting, kayaking, boardsailing

Photo: Eric Sanford

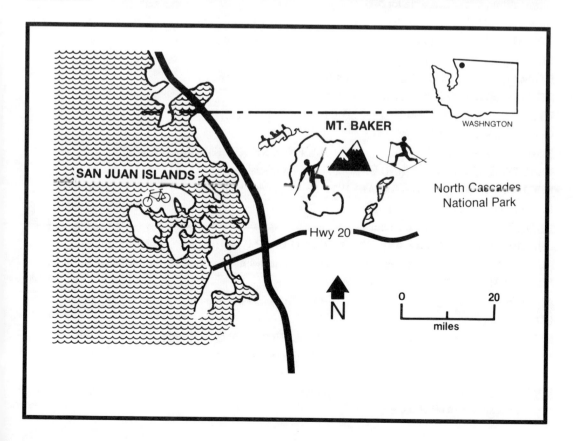

SAN JUAN ISLANDS

MT. BAKER

WASHNGTON

North Cascades
National Park

Hwy 20

N

0   20
      miles

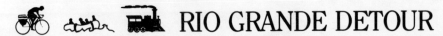 # RIO GRANDE DETOUR

Day 1: Wave goodbye to Santa Fe and cycle out to peaceful high country roads in rustic northern New Mexico. Visit remote Spanish villages and churches of Chimayo, Truchas and Cordova. Enjoy snow-capped mountain scenery and wildflowers. Try your luck maneuvering bikes across icy mountain streams and then camp along river. Day 2: Thrilling whitewater rafting through famed "Taos Box" of the Rio Grande. If you like roller coasters, you'll love Powerline Falls, Sunset Rapids and the Rock Garden stretches of this wild river. You've earned dinner and a warm bed in town tonight. Day 3: Cycle back-road to Taos Indian Pueblo this morning. Sample yummy fry bread and get a close look at the arts and crafts. Exhilarating afternoon ride high in the San Antonio Mountains (we shuttle you up there). Camp along the river. Day 4: All aboard for a scenic morning train ride on the narrow gauge Cumbres-Toltec railway. Depart the train at 10,015 feet for an extra long descent cycle into Chama. Relax in a rustic lodge tonight. Day 5 and 6: More great cycling in the San Juan mountains and a luxurious soak in the crystal clear hot springs of Ojo Caliente before returning to Santa Fe. A gala farewell dinner and night's lodging wrap up a great trip.

LENGTH OF TRIP: 6 days   **DEPARTURE DATES:** June 9, June 17, July 3

TOTAL COST: $675 ($495 camping only)   **TYPE OF PAYMENT ACCEPTED:** Check, Visa, MC

RESERVATIONS/DEPOSIT: $150 deposit 50 days prior

CANCELLATION POLICY: No deposits are refunded

DEPARTURE LOCATION: Santa Fe, NM   **NEAREST AIRPORT:** Santa Fe, NM

TRANSPORTATION INFORMATION: Bicycle Detours will pick up Santa Fe arrivals. Public shuttle from Albuquerque available for $20.

HEALTH, FITNESS OR AGE REQUIREMENTS: 18 years old minimum; advanced beginner

TYPE OF WEATHER TO EXPECT: 75-80° F days, cool evenings, possible showers

BEST TYPE OF CLOTHING AND FOOTWEAR: Warm-ups, shorts, t-shirts, warm sweater, sneakers

PERSONAL GEAR REQUIRED: Sleeping bag

SPECIAL GEAR/EQUIPMENT REQUIRED: None

WHAT NOT TO BRING: No 10-speed bikes (mountain bikes only)

PHOTO POSSIBILITIES: Fantastic

FISHING POSSIBILITIES: Fair   **LICENSE REQUIREMENT:** NM $14

BEST TYPE OF FISHING TACKLE: Fly and small artificial lures

REPRESENTATIVE MENU—BREAKFAST: Fruit, granola, pancakes

LUNCH: Deli style sandwiches, salad, dessert

DINNER: Appetizer, chicken enchiladas, beans and salsa, salad, wine, beer, Mexican bread pudding

CHORES/DUTIES GUESTS ARE EXPECTED TO HELP WITH: None

ADDITIONAL SPECIAL INFORMATION: Trip includes whitewater rafting, narrow-gauge train ride

NAME OF OUTFITTER: Bicycle Detours

ADDRESS: Box 44078   **CONTACT:** Frank and Sarah Lister

CITY: Tucson   **TITLE:** Owners

STATE: Arizona   **ZIP:** 85733   **TELEPHONE:** (602) 326-1624

NUMBER OF YEARS IN BUSINESS: 2   **NUMBER OF STAFF:** 5

SPECIALIZING IN: Off-road bicycle tours, river rafting, horseback riding, hiking

SPECIAL PHILOSOPHY, CREDO, GOALS BEHIND BUSINESS: Touring on all-terrain bicycles brings out the explorer in all of us.

Photo: Bicycle Detours

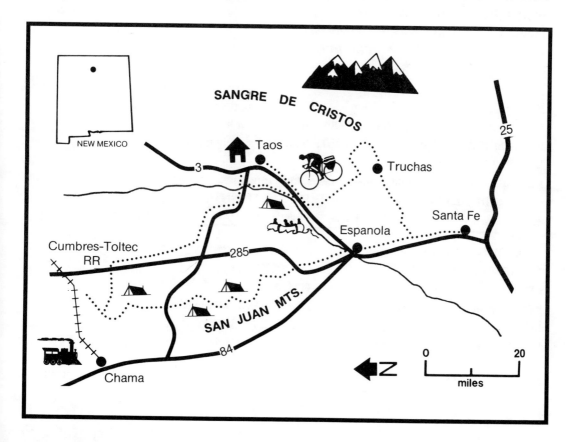

205

YELLOWSTONE CANOE/BACKPACK

Paddle a 26-foot voyageur canoe into the remote arms of Yellowstone Lake, stopping occasionally to catch 15-19 inch cutthroat trout, and to photograph moose, elk, eagles with a backdrop of geysers, steaming hot pots, forests and meadows. At a new camp each afternoon, we set up tents, relax, explore beaches and take a refreshing swim to soothe muscles while dinner is being prepared. On the fourth day we rendezvous with the backpackers of the trip and we celebrate the half-way point with a great feast. Over the next four days we swap modes of travel with the packers and stretch new muscles as we shoulder 40-50 pound packs to explore the mountains, rivers, high lakes, geyser basins and wildlife of Yellowstone back country. We will hike on routes once used by early explorers like Jim Bridger and John Colter. Lightweight freeze-dried cuisine will be our fare for this part of the expedition. These eight days of wilderness travel leave you with a new-found appreciation of the "other side" of Yellowstone, America's greatest national park. The best way to appreciate Old Faithful is to understand the environs of this unique area.

LENGTH OF TRIP: 8 days   **DEPARTURE DATES:** Sat. through Sun. in August

TOTAL COST: $650   **TYPE OF PAYMENT ACCEPTED:** Check

RESERVATIONS/DEPOSIT: $130 with reservation

CANCELLATION POLICY: Forfeit deposit

DEPARTURE LOCATION: Bozeman, MT   **NEAREST AIRPORT:** Bozeman, MT

TRANSPORTATION INFORMATION: Provided

HEALTH, FITNESS OR AGE REQUIREMENTS: Must be physically able to do trip.

TYPE OF WEATHER TO EXPECT: 45-85° F; mostly sun; occasional shower

BEST TYPE OF CLOTHING AND FOOTWEAR: Shorts, long pants, jacket, running, hiking shoes

PERSONAL GEAR REQUIRED: Personal duffle

SPECIAL GEAR/EQUIPMENT REQUIRED: None

WHAT NOT TO BRING: Guns

PHOTO POSSIBILITIES: Fantastic

FISHING POSSIBILITIES: Fantastic   **LICENSE REQUIREMENT:** Provided

BEST TYPE OF FISHING TACKLE: Light spinning gear or fly rod

REPRESENTATIVE MENU—BREAKFAST: Bacon, eggs, granola, coffee

LUNCH: Gorp, sandwiches, juice

DINNER: Lasagne, corn, fruit, smoked oysters, fresh fish, drinks

CHORES/DUTIES GUESTS ARE EXPECTED TO HELP WITH: Pitch tents, help in kitchen, paddle

ADDITIONAL SPECIAL INFORMATION: Energetic people who enjoy the wilderness enjoy this trip the most.

NAME OF OUTFITTER: Sunburst Adventures

ADDRESS: 3038 Candy Lane   **CONTACT:** Terry Johnson

CITY: Bozeman   **TITLE:** Owner

STATE: Montana   **ZIP:** 59715   **TELEPHONE:** (406) 586-3212

NUMBER OF YEARS IN BUSINESS: 3   **NUMBER OF STAFF:** 4

SPECIALIZING IN: Horses, backpacking, canoeing, ski touring in Yellowstone National Park and Montana wilderness areas.

SPECIAL PHILOSOPHY, CREDO, GOALS BEHIND BUSINESS: Sunburst—a bright spot in one's life and adventure. We stress the adventure.

Photo: Terry Johnson

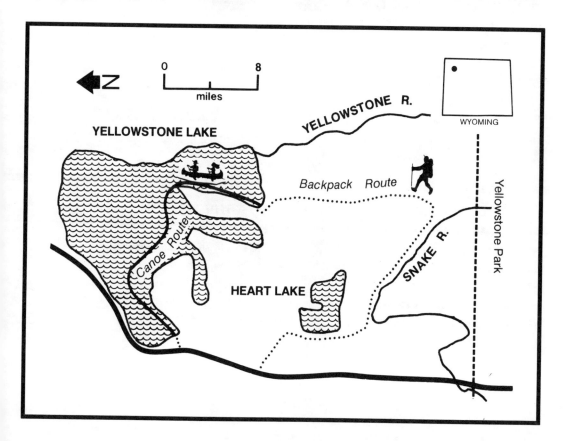

VANCOUVER ISLAND SAFARI

A northwestern safari does not explore steamy jungles of lions and tigers, but snow-capped mountains and remote coastal areas inhabited by seals and otters. Spend five days hiking in the alpine interior of Strathcona Park near Campbell River, British Columbia, and thrill to the wonderland of flowers, limestone formations and peaceful lakes that show no sign that man has visited there before. From the summit of a lofty peak, look east over Buttle Lake and west to the Golden Hinde and a mountain panorama. After two days of relaxation at the Lodge and practicing basic paddling, travel to historic Nootka Sound. Canoe from Hisnit where Captain Cook first set foot in North America. Sneak your canoe into creek mouths and rocky caves behind the reefs at Escalante. Plenty of food is taken on the trip, but a pleasant part of a west coast safari is foraging for wild food. Nootka Sound offers a banquet of salmon, clams, oysters and berries. Return after five days on the coast on the Uchuck III, a converted minesweeper, renowned for its delicious Nanaimo Bars served on board to the hungry explorers, a just reward upon return from a safari in the Northwest wilderness.

LENGTH OF TRIP: 14 days   **DEPARTURE DATES:** July 2, Aug. 20, Sept. 8

TOTAL COST: $785 Canadian   **TYPE OF PAYMENT ACCEPTED:** Any

RESERVATIONS/DEPOSIT: $290 deposit

CANCELLATION POLICY: Deposit can be transferred to a future trip

DEPARTURE LOCATION: Strathcona Lodge   **NEAREST AIRPORT:** Campbell River

TRANSPORTATION INFORMATION: Lodge van from airport

HEALTH, FITNESS OR AGE REQUIREMENTS: Good physical condition

TYPE OF WEATHER TO EXPECT: Variable, usually sunny

BEST TYPE OF CLOTHING AND FOOTWEAR: Warm, waterproof

PERSONAL GEAR REQUIRED: Personal duffle

SPECIAL GEAR/EQUIPMENT REQUIRED: None

WHAT NOT TO BRING: Valuables, pets

PHOTO POSSIBILITIES: Fantastic

FISHING POSSIBILITIES: Good   **LICENSE REQUIREMENT:** Salt water

BEST TYPE OF FISHING TACKLE: Salmon

REPRESENTATIVE MENU—BREAKFAST: Buffet

LUNCH: Buffet

DINNER: Two entrees, vegetables

CHORES/DUTIES GUESTS ARE EXPECTED TO HELP WITH: Light duties

NAME OF OUTFITTER: Strathcona Park Lodge and Education Centre

ADDRESS: Box 2160   **CONTACT:** Jim and Myrna Boulding

CITY: Campbell River   **TITLE:** Owners, managers

STATE: B.C., Canada   **ZIP:** V9W 5C9   **TELEPHONE:** Radio phone N693546

NUMBER OF YEARS IN BUSINESS: 27

SPECIALIZING IN: Wilderness adventures/outdoor education

Photo: Strathcona Park Lodge

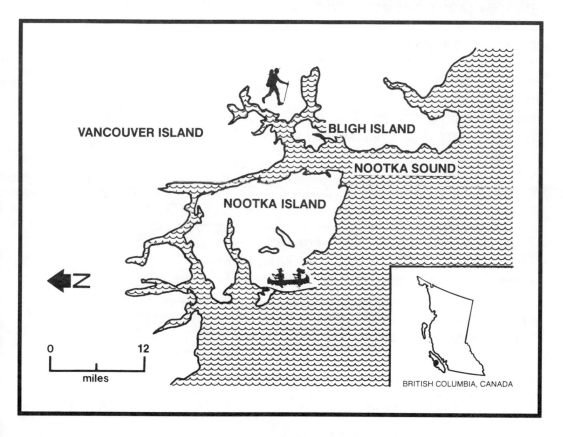

VANCOUVER ISLAND

BLIGH ISLAND

NOOTKA SOUND

NOOTKA ISLAND

N

0   12
miles

BRITISH COLUMBIA, CANADA

 # SOUTHWEST WING SAFARI

Southwest Safaris specialize in taking people by unique forms of travel to the most remote and exciting corners of the Great American Southwest—New Mexico, Colorado, Utah and Arizona. The focus is to combine five days of adventure with education, accommodating small groups of up to five people to maximize personal attention. Air travel to destinations is emphasized because it eliminates days of travelling time and also provides perspectives on time, landscapes and human activities on a much broader scale that cannot be comprehended from the ground alone. After tour members land at respective locations of interest, whether the Grand Canyon, a remote travelling post, Canyonlands National Park, or the Goosenecks of the San Juan River, they are met by four-wheel-drive vehicles or rafts, as appropriate to the area of study and exploration. There participants will more closely examine the natural and cultural aspects of this relatively untouched frontier called the Four Corners Region. All tours emphasize the study of geology, archaeology, ecology and American history. Participants enjoy an intensive field study while revelling in the dry, clean air and warm sunshine of this southwestern safari.

LENGTH OF TRIP: 5 days   **DEPARTURE DATES:** Varies

TOTAL COST: $1,495   **TYPE OF PAYMENT ACCEPTED:** Check, Visa, MC, AMEX

RESERVATIONS/DEPOSIT: $200 deposit 45 days prior to departure

CANCELLATION POLICY: Forfeit full payment

DEPARTURE LOCATION: Santa Fe, NM   **NEAREST AIRPORT:** Santa Fe, NM

TRANSPORTATION INFORMATION: Taxi, rental car

HEALTH, FITNESS OR AGE REQUIREMENTS: Good physical condition

TYPE OF WEATHER TO EXPECT: Hot days, cool nights

BEST TYPE OF CLOTHING AND FOOTWEAR: Equipment list available

PERSONAL GEAR REQUIRED: Equipment list available

SPECIAL GEAR/EQUIPMENT REQUIRED: None

WHAT NOT TO BRING: Anything not on list

PHOTO POSSIBILITIES: Fantastic

FISHING POSSIBILITIES: Fair

REPRESENTATIVE MENU—BREAKFAST: Varies

LUNCH: Varies

DINNER: Varies

CHORES/DUTIES GUESTS ARE EXPECTED TO HELP WITH: Pitching/striking camp, cooking, cleanup

NAME OF OUTFITTER: Southwest Safaris

ADDRESS: P.O. Box 945   **CONTACT:** Bruce Adams

CITY: Santa Fe   **TITLE:** President

STATE: New Mexico   **ZIP:** 87504-0945   **TELEPHONE:** (505) 988-4246

NUMBER OF YEARS IN BUSINESS: 10

SPECIALIZING IN: Air/land/river natural history expeditions in the Four Corners

SPECIAL PHILOSOPHY, CREDO, GOALS BEHIND BUSINESS: We attempt to combine adventure with education, accommodating small groups only to maximize personal attention.

Photo: Southwest Safari

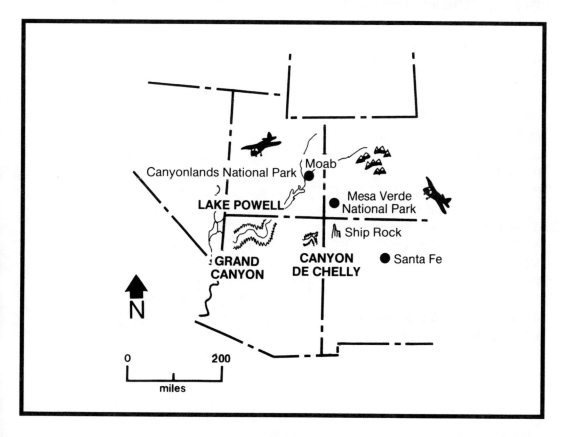

211

 # DESOLATION CANYON TRIP

If you are looking for an authentic Western experience integrating the history of the cowboys with the rich tradition of river exploration, this combination river trip/trail ride is the answer. The expedition begins at Green River, Utah at the Tavaputs Ranch which sits 10,000 feet above sea level. This historic working cattle ranch is owned and operated by Don and Jeanette Wilcox, third and fourth generation cowboys running a "cow outfit" originally established in the 1800s by Don's grandfather. The Wilcoxes serve as your hosts and share tales and recollections of the early Indians, cowboys and outlaws who roamed this country. Two days on the ranch will be filled with horseback riding and jeep touring as you explore the Tavaputs Plateau, investigate ancient Indian ruins and enjoy the abundance of wildlife. The morning of the third day, you ride down the historic cattle drive trail to meet the rafts on the Green River. During the ride, you will drop 5,000 feet through various climatic zones on the way to the canyon bottom. Dinner will be served shortly after meeting the boat crew at the river. The following morning, the group embarks on three days of exciting river running and seeing the old West from a different perspective.

LENGTH OF TRIP: 6 days

DEPARTURE DATES: Summer

TOTAL COST: $3595

TYPE OF PAYMENT ACCEPTED: Check, cash

RESERVATIONS/DEPOSIT: $100 with reservation

CANCELLATION POLICY: Call

DEPARTURE LOCATION: Green River, UT   **NEAREST AIRPORT:** Grand Junction, CO

TRANSPORTATION INFORMATION: Bus, train, charter air taxi

HEALTH, FITNESS OR AGE REQUIREMENTS: Normal good health

TYPE OF WEATHER TO EXPECT: Hot

BEST TYPE OF CLOTHING AND FOOTWEAR: Lightweight clothing that dries quickly

PERSONAL GEAR REQUIRED: Equipment list available

SPECIAL GEAR/EQUIPMENT REQUIRED: None

WHAT NOT TO BRING: Pets, firearms, electronic gear

PHOTO POSSIBILITIES: Fantastic

FISHING POSSIBILITIES: Poor

REPRESENTATIVE MENU—BREAKFAST: Eggs, ham, coffee

LUNCH: Sandwiches, fruit, beer, punch

DINNER: Steak, potatoes, salad

CHORES/DUTIES GUESTS ARE EXPECTED TO HELP WITH: Load and unload boats

ADDITIONAL SPECIAL INFORMATION: Guests should be comfortable around horses and mules, and have previous riding experience

NAME OF OUTFITTER: Moki Mac River Expeditions, Inc.

ADDRESS: P.O. Box 21242

CONTACT: Richard S. Quist

CITY: Salt Lake City

TITLE: Owner

STATE: Utah   **ZIP:** 84121

TELEPHONE: (801) 942-0254

NUMBER OF YEARS IN BUSINESS: 30

SPECIALIZING IN: River trips, combination river/trail trips

SPECIAL PHILOSOPHY, CREDO, GOALS BEHIND BUSINESS: "It's your own damn fault if you have no fun!"

Photo: M. Patterson

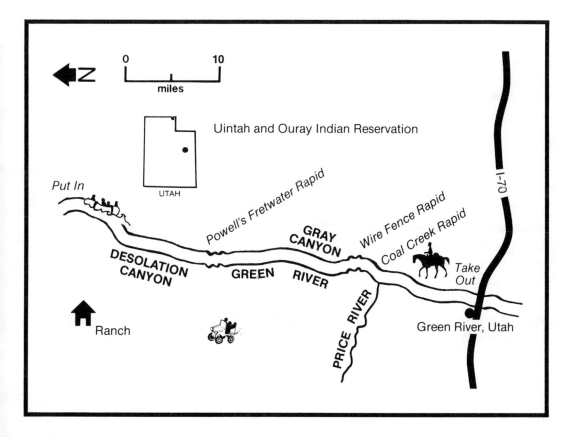

213

GATES OF THE ARCTIC

It often takes a week of hiking with no roads for hundreds of miles, where the only trails are those made by caribou or moose, to realize what true, remote wilderness is. We have to fly to our starting point which begins in the small village of Bettles and then fly by floatplane to Summit Lake at the crest of the Arctic Divide. The backpacking distance we need to cover is only 20 miles, so we have lots of time to explore this captivating country on day hikes. The scenery is spectacular—uninterrupted vistas and jagged mountains, deep gorges, hanging valleys and waterfalls. Then at the base of Mt. Doonerak, we take to the river in rafts and float through the grand peaks of Frigid Crags and Boreal Mountain, which gave Gates of the Arctic its name. After some exciting whitewater on the first day where everyone shares in the paddling, the river flattens and widens, slowing down to a leisurely flow. We spend a week floating along at this speed, even in the evening when the river turns liquid gold in the land of the midnight sun. The gravel bars we camp on often tell a story with animal tracks, sometimes of passing moose, caribou, wolves, grizzlies and lynxes. Fifteen days later, we find ourselves all too soon back in civilization.

LENGTH OF TRIP: 15 days

DEPARTURE DATES: July 6 and Aug. 8

TOTAL COST: $1450

TYPE OF PAYMENT ACCEPTED: Check, money order

RESERVATIONS/DEPOSIT: $200 deposit at least 30 days prior to departure

CANCELLATION POLICY: Forfeit $200 deposit

DEPARTURE LOCATION: Fairbanks, AK   **NEAREST AIRPORT:** Fairbanks

TRANSPORTATION INFORMATION: Free pickup from hotel to charter plane

HEALTH, FITNESS OR AGE REQUIREMENTS: Physically fit, experienced backpacker, minimum 16 years old

TYPE OF WEATHER TO EXPECT: Temps range from 30-80°F.

BEST TYPE OF CLOTHING AND FOOTWEAR: Synthetic or wool clothing, boots

PERSONAL GEAR REQUIRED: Backpack and camping gear

SPECIAL GEAR/EQUIPMENT REQUIRED: Equipment list provided

WHAT NOT TO BRING: Anything not on list

PHOTO POSSIBILITIES: Fantastic

FISHING POSSIBILITIES: Good   **LICENSE REQUIREMENTS:** 10-day visitor's

BEST TYPE OF FISHING TACKLE: Packrod with flies or spinners

REPRESENTATIVE MENU—BREAKFAST: Granola, hot cereal

LUNCH: Cheese, sausage, crackers

DINNER: All natural backpack dinners with fresh vegetables

CHORES/DUTIES GUESTS ARE EXPECTED TO HELP WITH: Setting up camp, meals, cleanup

NAME OF OUTFITTER: Arctic Treks

ADDRESS: Box 73452

CONTACT: Carol Kasza

CITY: Fairbanks

TITLE: Owner/guide

STATE: Alaska   **ZIP:** 99707

TELEPHONE: (907) 455-6502

NUMBER OF YEARS IN BUSINESS: 6   **NUMBER OF STAFF:** 5-6

SPECIALIZING IN: Backpacking and rafting. We design and lead our trips as we would for a group of our friends.

SPECIAL PHILOSOPHY, CREDO, GOALS BEHIND BUSINESS: Each person is expected to contribute to the well-being of the group and the trip and in return reap the rewards of a true adventure.

Photo: Arctic Treks

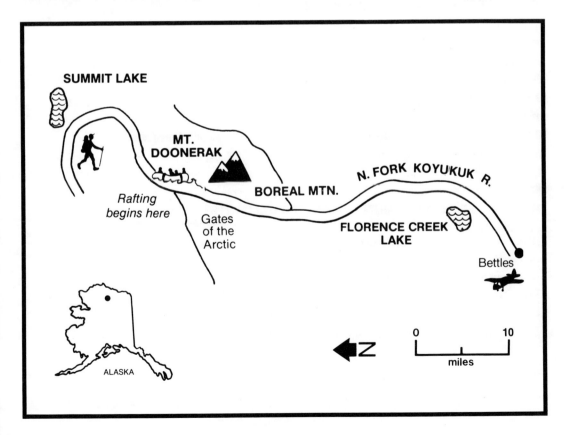

SUMMIT LAKE

MT. DOONERAK

BOREAL MTN.

N. FORK KOYUKUK R.

Rafting begins here

Gates
of the
Arctic

FLORENCE CREEK
LAKE

Bettles

ALASKA

N

0   10
     miles

LAKE POWELL ADVENTURE

On the morning of the trip, our main group will be divided into two separate parties. One-half will leave Wahweap Marina for three days of houseboating on Lake Powell. Along the 1800 miles of shoreline we will explore such places as Wetherill Canyon, Cathedral Canyon, Reflection Canyon and the Escalante River. All will have a chance to fish and view Indian ruins by day as we camp along sandy shores by night. The other half will be flown from Page, Utah by chartered plane to the Navajo Mountain Trading Post for three days on horseback. We'll ride through spectacular Cha Canyon, Surprise Valley and Hell's Gate. At night, camp will be pitched below massive rock cliffs and along cool flowing streams. On the fourth day, both groups will meet at the Rainbow Bridge National Monument, the world's highest natural bridge. We will enjoy a restful layover by swimming, hiking and dining on a shared feast. The next morning, the parties will switch. Horseback riders will don cut-offs and halters and climb aboard the houseboat for three days. The others will pull on boots and cowboy hats and mount their trusty steeds. The horse group will be flown back to Page on the sixth day to rejoin the others and bid farewell to a great week.

LENGTH OF TRIP: 6 days/5 nights **DEPARTURE DATES:** May 12 and 19

TOTAL COST: $750 per person **TYPE OF PAYMENT ACCEPTED:** Check, MC, Visa

RESERVATIONS/DEPOSIT: $100 deposit at least 30 days prior to trip

CANCELLATION POLICY: Loss of deposit and balance

DEPARTURE LOCATION: Page, AZ **NEAREST AIRPORT:** Page, AZ

TRANSPORTATION INFORMATION: Page motels offer free shuttle service from airport.

HEALTH, FITNESS OR AGE REQUIREMENTS: Good physical condition

TYPE OF WEATHER TO EXPECT: Warm and dry

BEST TYPE OF CLOTHING AND FOOTWEAR: Horseback: boots. Houseboat: sneakers.

PERSONAL GEAR REQUIRED: Personal duffle, sleeping bag

SPECIAL GEAR/EQUIPMENT REQUIRED: None

WHAT NOT TO BRING: Firearms, pets

PHOTO POSSIBILITIES: Fantastic

FISHING POSSIBILITIES: Fantastic **LICENSE REQUIREMENTS:** Utah $15

BEST TYPE OF FISHING TACKLE: Spinning lures, #1 or #2 Mepps, Daredevils

REPRESENTATIVE MENU—BREAKFAST: Eggs, bacon, juice, coffee

LUNCH: Fruit, cold cuts and cheese, chocolate bars

DINNER: Steak or chicken, Dutch oven biscuits, salad, potatoes, coffee, pie or cake

CHORES/DUTIES GUESTS ARE EXPECTED TO HELP WITH: Setting up personal sleeping area, keeping area clean.

ADDITIONAL SPECIAL INFORMATION: At the Navajo Trading Post, guests have the opportunity to purchase authentic Navajo rugs, blankets, etc.

NAME OF OUTFITTER: American Wilderness Experience, Inc.

ADDRESS: P.O. Box 1486 **CONTACT:** Dave Wiggins

CITY: Boulder **TITLE:** President

STATE: Colorado **ZIP:** 80306 **TELEPHONE:** (303) 444-2632

NUMBER OF YEARS IN BUSINESS: 13 **NUMBER OF STAFF:** 5

SPECIALIZING IN: Unique backcountry vacations. Horsepacking, whitewater rafting, canoeing, backpacking, sailing, guest ranching, combination adventures.

SPECIAL PHILOSOPHY, CREDO, GOALS BEHIND BUSINESS: Develop an appreciation and understanding of America's most precious resource—its wilderness.

Photo: American Wilderness Experience

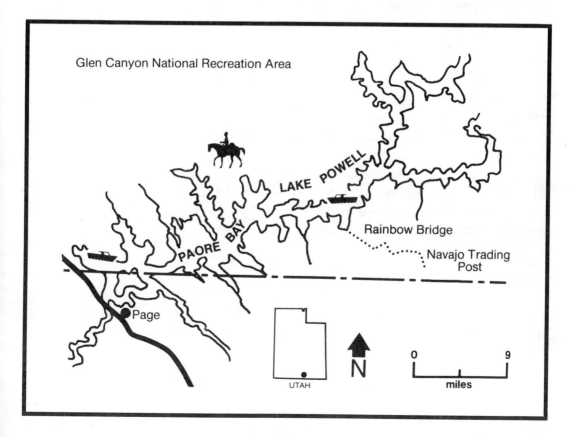

Glen Canyon National Recreation Area

LAKE POWELL

PAORE BAY

Rainbow Bridge

Navajo Trading Post

Page

UTAH

N

0 ─── 9

miles

COLORADO RIVER/CANYONLANDS

You straddle the front snout of the raft, your hands in a tight grip, as the boatman makes a final correction. Suddenly you are inside a swirling, roaring cascade of whitewater as the tube beneath you bucks and tosses. You are drenched and breathless, but you've just punched right through one of the biggest snarliest holes on the Colorado River. Cataract Canyon is four thrilling days of freedom and adventure in the wild beauty of Utah's Canyonlands National Park. This expedition is a combination of relaxation and action. For the first day and a half you float on the calm, warm waters of the Colorado through the soaring redrock canyons. There is plenty of time for swimming, hiking and exploring. On the afternoon of the second day you encounter the first of the 26 rapids you will test, just enough to whet your appetite for the big action on day three when you will shoot the major rapids on the 10-passenger rafts. Later, on the shores of Lake Powell, you board one of the 4-wheel drive Land Cruisers and climb into cool forests high in the nearby Abajo Mountains for camping and a visit to Poncho Ridge, site of the most extensive Native American ruins in Utah. The grand finale is arrival at the remote Needles section of Canyonlands National Park.

LENGTH OF TRIP: 7 days

DEPARTURE DATES: Every Sun. May 1–Oct. 15

TOTAL COST: $762

TYPE OF PAYMENT ACCEPTED: Check, Visa, MC, AMEX

RESERVATIONS/DEPOSIT: $50 when booking

CANCELLATION POLICY: Forfeit deposit

DEPARTURE LOCATION: Moab, Utah   **NEAREST AIRPORT:** Moab, Utah

TRANSPORTATION INFORMATION: Tag-A-Long Tours shuttle van $10

HEALTH, FITNESS OR AGE REQUIREMENTS: 8 years old minimum

TYPE OF WEATHER TO EXPECT: Hot, sunny

BEST TYPE OF CLOTHING AND FOOTWEAR: Cotton shorts and t-shirt, tennis shoes

PERSONAL GEAR REQUIRED: Personal duffle

SPECIAL GEAR/EQUIPMENT REQUIRED: None

WHAT NOT TO BRING: Too much clothing

PHOTO POSSIBILITIES: Good

FISHING POSSIBILITIES: Poor

REPRESENTATIVE MENU—BREAKFAST: Western omelette, coffee, juice, toast

LUNCH: Sandwiches, juice, cookies

DINNER: Chicken cordon bleu, cowboy potatoes, beans almondine, salad, strawberry shortcake

CHORES/DUTIES GUESTS ARE EXPECTED TO HELP WITH: Load and unload

NAME OF OUTFITTER: Tag-A-Long Tours

ADDRESS: P.O. Box 1206/ 452 N. Main

CONTACT: Bob Jones

CITY: Moab

TITLE: President

STATE: Utah   **ZIP:** 84532

TELEPHONE: (801) 259-8946 Utah (800) 453-3292 US and Canada

NUMBER OF YEARS IN BUSINESS: 22   **NUMBER OF STAFF:** 7-50

SPECIALIZING IN: 4-wheel drive & river expeditions, Canyonlands & Arches National Park, Colorado & Green Rivers, Indian country tours

Photo: Tag-A-Long Tours

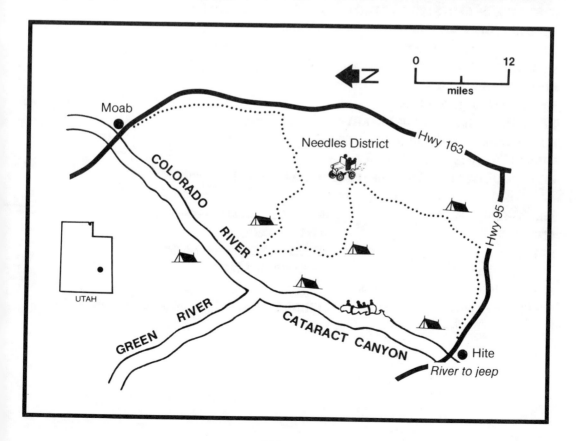

 # 12-DAY/FOUR ISLAND ADVENTURE

Hawaii is a tropical paradise whose landscape erupts in riotous colors, fragrances and vistas to enrapture the senses and entice the soul. This 12-day adventure follows ancient coastal paths and traps the tropical tradewinds in billowing sails as we visit four islands in this Pacific chain. Wake up with the sun atop volcanic summits and explore the secrets of Kauai, the Big Island, Maui and Lanai. On each island we explore Hawaii's most unique natural areas through a wide assortment of outdoor activities. Your senses may be overwhelmed by this collage of glistening sands, crystal waters, fecund forests, stark volcanoes and exciting outdoor pursuits, but what a way to tempt your wanderlust! Your appetite will be sated by barbequed fish, omelettes, fruit and other fresh island foods. Your body will be exercised by hiking, snorkeling, scuba diving, swimming and working the sails, a sure route to capturing the spirit and excitement of Hawaii. Participants will also set up their own tents and help break camp as you move from paradise to utopia.

LENGTH OF TRIP: 12 days

DEPARTURE DATES: Varies

TOTAL COST: $975

TYPE OF PAYMENT ACCEPTED: Check, money order

RESERVATIONS/DEPOSIT: $100 deposit at least two months before trip

CANCELLATION POLICY: No refund once trek under way

DEPARTURE LOCATION: Lihue, Kauai   **NEAREST AIRPORT:** Lihue, Kauai

TRANSPORTATION INFORMATION: N/A

HEALTH, FITNESS OR AGE REQUIREMENTS: Good health; under 16 years old must be accompanied by adult

TYPE OF WEATHER TO EXPECT: Rainy season Dec.-Feb.

BEST TYPE OF CLOTHING AND FOOTWEAR: Equipment list available

PERSONAL GEAR REQUIRED: Equipment list available

SPECIAL GEAR/EQUIPMENT REQUIRED: None

WHAT NOT TO BRING: Frame packs and radios

PHOTO POSSIBILITIES: Fantastic

FISHING POSSIBILITIES: Poor

REPRESENTATIVE MENU—BREAKFAST: Omelettes, sausage, fresh fruit

LUNCH: Pack lunch, sandwich, fruit, trail mix

DINNER: BBQ'd fish, potatoes, salad, fruit, dessert

CHORES/DUTIES GUESTS ARE EXPECTED TO HELP WITH: Set up own tent

NAME OF OUTFITTER: Pacific Quest, Inc.

ADDRESS: P.O. Box 205

CONTACT: Mary Jo Nuccio

CITY: Haleiwa

TITLE: Director

STATE: Hawaii   **ZIP:** 96712

TELEPHONE: (808) 638-8338

NUMBER OF YEARS IN BUSINESS: 4   **NUMBER OF STAFF:** 4

SPECIALIZING IN: Day hikes, skindiving, sailing, scuba diving

SPECIAL PHILOSOPHY, CREDO, GOALS BEHIND BUSINESS: To capture the spirit and excitement of Hawaii through a wide variety of outdoor activities.

Photo: Dave DePuy

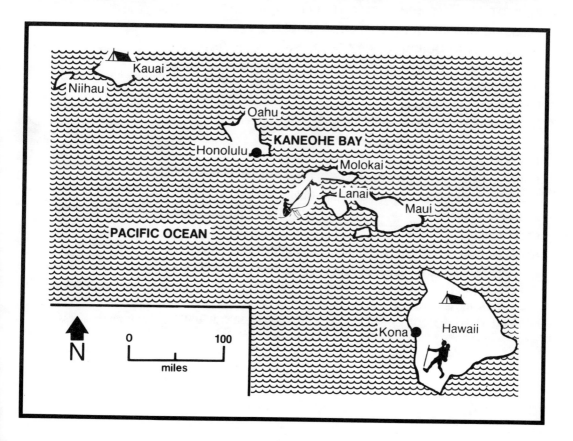

Kauai

Niihau

Oahu

Honolulu · KANEOHE BAY

Molokai

Lanai

Maui

PACIFIC OCEAN

Kona · Hawaii

N

0   100

miles

KACHEMAK TRAVERSE

An open skiff transports us and our dog team from Homer, Alaska to the south side of Kachemak Bay. After hiking along a salmon stream we ascend to an alpine lake where we find our personal equipment, including tents, packs, food, dog sled, harnesses, skis, poles and ropes cached by a bush pilot. After ferrying loads a short distance, we camp at another alpine lake adjacent to the icefield upon which we will be skiing in the upcoming days. Proceeding along the glacier's edge, we are likely to see mountain goats on meadows high above. By day's end, we camp at the glacier's firn line. Letting the dogs pull our packs, we leave the flowered alps and push off into the brilliance of the high glacier. What adventures we will encounter in the next three days of skiing can only be imagined. If it is sunny, expect to tan! After surmounting a high and exciting pass, we descend on skis into a beautiful valley with waterfalls, a lake and lush greenery. We will find rafts cached at the lake and spend our last two days leisurely floating to the coast where we will be picked up by sailboat for the return to Homer.

LENGTH OF TRIP: 7-8 days

DEPARTURE DATES: Open schedule

TOTAL COST: $575

TYPE OF PAYMENT ACCEPTED: Check

RESERVATIONS/DEPOSIT: Half due one month before trip

CANCELLATION POLICY: Return half of deposit if 2 weeks before trip

DEPARTURE LOCATION: Homer, AK   **NEAREST AIRPORT:** Homer, AK

TRANSPORTATION INFORMATION: Provided

HEALTH, FITNESS OR AGE REQUIREMENTS: Generally fit; 10 years old minimum

TYPE OF WEATHER TO EXPECT: Hope for the best; prepare for the worst

BEST TYPE OF CLOTHING AND FOOTWEAR: Equipment list available

PERSONAL GEAR REQUIRED: Boots, sleeping bag and pad, pack, eating utensils

SPECIAL GEAR/EQUIPMENT REQUIRED: Skis, seat harness, life vest

WHAT NOT TO BRING: If possible, use synthetic sleeping bag, not down

PHOTO POSSIBILITIES: Fantastic

FISHING POSSIBILITIES: None

REPRESENTATIVE MENU—BREAKFAST: Tea, toast, granola, oatmeal

LUNCH: Cheese, crackers, gorp, sweet drink

DINNER: Fresh salmon, vegetables

CHORES/DUTIES GUESTS ARE EXPECTED TO HELP WITH: Personal

NAME OF OUTFITTER: Kachemak Alpine Guides Service

ADDRESS: SRA #31   **CONTACT:** George Ripley

CITY: Homer   **TITLE:** Owner

STATE: Alaska   **ZIP:** 99603   **TELEPHONE:** (907) 235-6094

NUMBER OF YEARS IN BUSINESS: 4   **NUMBER OF STAFF:** 2-6 as needed

SPECIALIZING IN: Alpine activities of all kinds. Wildlife viewing, family hikes, technical rock climbing, glacier skiing, dogsledding, rafting.

SPECIAL PHILOSOPHY, CREDO, GOALS BEHIND BUSINESS: Wilderness is our business.

Photo: George Ripley

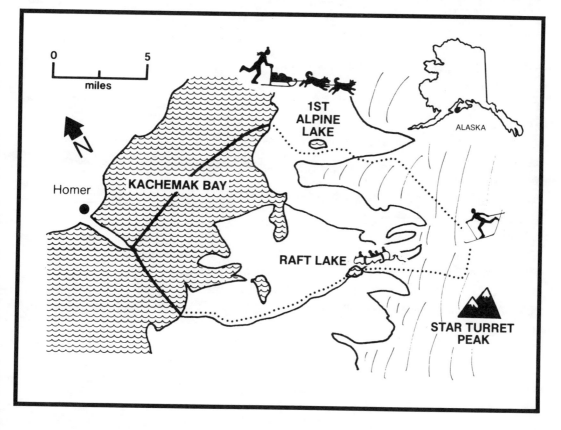

THE GREAT WHITE BEARS

Each year in late October, hundreds of 1,000-pound polar bears migrate in northern Manitoba toward the shore of Canada's vast Hudson Bay and wait for the coming of the winter sea ice. This unique expedition is limited to 15 participants who will be comfortably housed in the town of Churchill and will make forays from it by vehicles and helicopter to see and be able to photograph the remarkable and stirring sight of these magnificent wild carnivores roaming free. We allow two days for our forays to search for and photograph the bears in massive tracked vehicles. We then board chartered helicopters for flights to Cape Churchill where we photograph from the air and after we set down near—but never too close to—the bears. For a bonus, we also see large bands of graceful caribou racing across the tundra, arctic foxes who travel with the polar bears, ptarmigan in flocks of hundreds, snowy owls, gyrfalcons and occasionally moose and wolves. Apart from providing unusually expert leadership, we are the only company which goes to the considerable expense of positioning a helicopter at Churchill, which assures excellent viewing of the bears and other arctic wildlife in their natural habitat.

LENGTH OF TRIP: 7 days

TOTAL COST: $2,685 U.S.

RESERVATIONS/DEPOSIT: $300 with reservation

CANCELLATION POLICY: Never had any

DEPARTURE LOCATION: Winnipeg

DEPARTURE DATES: October 21, 1984

TYPE OF PAYMENT ACCEPTED: Check

NEAREST AIRPORT: Winnipeg, Manitoba

TRANSPORTATION INFORMATION: Hotel courtesy car

HEALTH, FITNESS OR AGE REQUIREMENTS: None

TYPE OF WEATHER TO EXPECT: Very cold

BEST TYPE OF CLOTHING AND FOOTWEAR: Warm winter clothes, hooded parka, boots

PERSONAL GEAR REQUIRED: None

SPECIAL GEAR/EQUIPMENT REQUIRED: None

WHAT NOT TO BRING: Good city clothes

PHOTO POSSIBILITIES: Fantastic

FISHING POSSIBILITIES: None

REPRESENTATIVE MENU—BREAKFAST: Full American

LUNCH: Three course

DINNER: Three course

CHORES/DUTIES GUESTS ARE EXPECTED TO HELP WITH: None

NAME OF OUTFITTER: Hanns Ebensten Travel Inc.

ADDRESS: 513 Fleming St.

CITY: Key West

STATE: Florida   **ZIP:** 33040

NUMBER OF YEARS IN BUSINESS: 12

SPECIALIZING IN: Wildlife, trekking

CONTACT: Mr. Hanns Ebensten

TITLE: President

TELEPHONE: (305) 294-8174

NUMBER OF STAFF: 8

Photo: Joseph Daniel

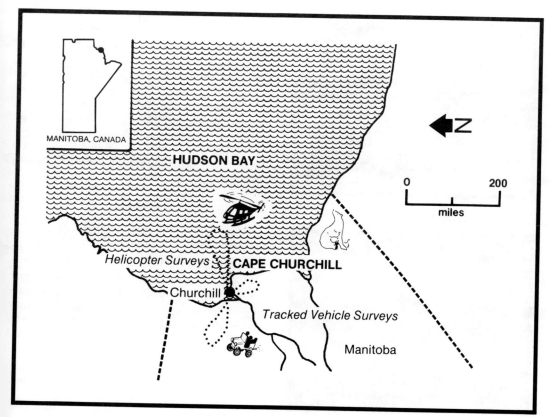

MANITOBA, CANADA

HUDSON BAY

Helicopter Surveys

CAPE CHURCHILL

Churchill

Tracked Vehicle Surveys

Manitoba

N

0   200
    miles

WILDERNESS OUTFITTERS DIRECTORY

If you are looking for an opportunity to learn a specific wilderness skill such as rock climbing or kayaking or if you would like to feel more confident in the wild by testing yourself in a wilderness survival course there are several good "schools" that can satisfy your need. I've presented a selection of 15, each with a specific course they offer. However, since most of these schools have a broad curriculum of courses, they should be contacted for a current list of offerings. Following the schools is a directory of outfitters arranged by type of adventure. Any one of them will be happy to send a current brochure outlining what specific trips they offer.

WILDERNESS SCHOOLS

Photo: Arizona Outdoor Institute

ARIZONA OUTDOOR INSTITUTE
6737 N. 18th Pl., Phoenix, AZ 85016; (602) 266-7585

The AOI offers courses in desert and mountain survival. The **BASIC DESERT APPRECIATION AND SURVIVAL COURSE** is oriented toward those who want a good background in the geography and natural history of the dry lands, combined with a two-day, overnight field experience, simulating an actual emergency survival situation. The four-day course costs $295, featuring classroom activities, and a two-day hands-on survival trek.

Photo: Canyonland Tours

CANYONLAND TOURS
P.O. Box 460, Flagstaff, AZ 86002; (602) 774-7343

The 7-day **INDIANLANDS PHOTOGRAPHY WORKSHOP** allows participants a chance to spend a week photographing the Wupatki National Monument's prehistoric pueblos, the Painted Desert, the Hopi Indian Mesas, Canyon de Chelly National Monument, Natural Bridges National Monument and Monument Valley Tribal Park. The workshop costs $695 and guests should bring a sample of their photography to share with the instructor.

Photo: Bill Roos

COLORADO OUTWARD BOUND SCHOOL
945 Pennsylvania St., Denver, CO 80203; (303) 837-0880

The **ADULT 10-DAY COURSE** takes participants into the Colorado Rockies to learn basic outdoor skills, such as climbing, orienteering and compass reading. A solo midway through the course gives participants a chance to be totally alone to reflect and gain new perspective on their lives. This physically strenuous and mentally challenging course costs $650.

Photo: Bob Elliott

EAST/WEST WILDERNESS SCHOOL
Box 611, Bethel, ME 04217; (207) 875-5255

Wilderness skills and environmental awareness are developed on the **WILDERNESS EXPERIENCE I** trip. Eight days in the deep forests of Maine will be home to participants as they bushwhack trails and learn map, compass, and camping skills that help people become competent no-trace backcountry travellers. Health and injury insurance is required. The course costs $380.

Photo: Kachemak Bay Wilderness Institute

KACHEMAK BAY WILDERNESS LODGE
Box 956, China Poot Bay, Homer, AK 99603; (907) 235-8910

Study marine and animal wildlife, observe birds and learn from natural history tours on the **ALASKAN NATURAL HISTORY TRIP.** This experience lasts two to ten days and teaches you a better understanding of the great outdoors and its ways as you explore a glacial moraine, deep forests, tidepools and beaches. Much time is spent on foot and in boats. This expedition costs $525-2,250.

Photo: Kachemak Alpine Guides

MOUNTAINEERING SCHOOL OF VAIL, INC.
P.O. Box 3034, Vail, CO 81658; (303) 476-4123

An intensive **6-DAY MOUNTAINEERING COURSE,** this program shows first time climbers "the ropes" as they are educated on the sport of rock climbing. Bowling balls and radios are unwelcomed during this expedition where participants learn to climb in the Rocky Mountains. The graduation climb conquers 12,620-foot-high Graduation Peak. The $300 course specializes in homemade and home-dried food as well as rock climbing.

Photo: Nolichucky Expeditions

NOLICHUCKY EXPEDITIONS, INC.
P.O. Box 460, Erwin, TN 37650; (615) 743-3221

No experience is necessary to sign up for the **10-DAY WILDERNESS SKILLS COURSE.** The adventure comes from learning the proper use of equipment, safety techniques and skills needed to whitewater raft/canoe, backpack, rock climb and cave. Base camp is located on 10 acres between the Appalachian Trail and the Nolichucky River. The course costs $400.

Photo: Barry Rosan

NORTH CAROLINA
OUTWARD BOUND SCHOOL
121 North Sterling St., Morganton, NC 28655; (704) 437-6112

The **ADULT INTENSIVE COURSE** is an educational program designed to increase understanding of self, others and the environment through challenging activities in a wilderness setting. It is based on Kurt Hahn's philosophy of four pillars: physical fitness, craftsmanship, self-reliance and compassion. The nine-day experience includes backpacking, rock climbing, canoeing and a solo for a $600-800 fee. (Financial aid is available.)

Photo: Arnor Larson

NORTHERN LIGHTS ALPINE RECREATION
Box 399, Invermere, B.C. V0A 1K0, Canada; No telephone

The **MOUNTAINEERING-SNOW & ICE COURSE** is for people of both sexes seriously interested in learning proper mountaineering skills. High in the mountains of British Columbia's Purcell Range, a small group will practice glacier travel, snow and ice climbing, rapelling, belaying, prussiking out of a crevasse and using the ice axe. Total cost for the eight days is $425 Canadian funds.

Photo: SEE

SCENIC AND EDUCATIONAL EXPEDITIONS
2715 Parklake Ct., Fort Collins, CO 80525; (303) 484-0808

Educational workshops in nature photography and mountain ecology (academic credit available through Colorado State University) are the focus of the **NATURE PHOTOGRAPHY WORKSHOP**. The five-day course costs $300 and takes place in the Never Summer Wilderness Area of Colorado. Gear is packed in on horses. Subject matter ranges from close-ups of wildflowers to telephoto shots of bighorn sheep, elk, moose and eagles.

Photo: Sierra Wilderness Seminars

SIERRA WILDERNESS SEMINARS
P.O. Box 707, Arcata, CA 95521; (707) 822-8066 summer; (619) 876-5384 winter

The three-day **WINTER MOUNTAINEERING SEMINAR** offers backpacking, mountaineering, cross-country skiing, and rock climbing seminars that incorporate relaxed learning experiences. We utilize mountain travel skills including rock climbing, snow camping, extended mountain travel, route finding, energy conservation and environmental awareness seminars led by qualified instructors. The course costs $120.

Photo: Southwest Wilderness Center

SOUTHWEST WILDERNESS CENTER
P.O. Box 2840, Santa Fe, NM 87501; (505) 982-3126

This is a mobile intensive course on backcountry travel in the isolated area of Big Bend National Park in southwestern Texas, and all our gear is on our backs. **THE DESERT COURSE** lasts nine days and costs $549. The basics of desert camping, backpacking, route finding, rock climbing and canyoneering are learned to earn the revered title of Desert Rat.

Photo: Sundance

SUNDANCE EXPEDITIONS, INC.
14894 Galice Rd., Merlin, OR 97532; (503) 479-8508

Nine days of on-beach camping and on-river paddling will completely immerse participants in kayaking. The **SUNDANCE OLYMPIC KAYAK SCHOOL** holds morning chalkboard discussions, on-river practice sessions, and evening slide and video presentations in its education process. The $675 fee covers meals and all kayak gear necessary for course.

Photo: Beckler Trip

WILDERNESS CHALLENGE OUTDOOR SURVIVAL SCHOOL
Box 2135, Montrose, CO 81402; (303) 249-5929

This **SURVIVAL SKILLS WORKSHOP** will teach primitive survival skills over a six-day period. While based at a camp in the San Juan Mountains, you will learn methods of building fires, primitive pottery, wilderness cookery, edible and useful plants, finding water, tracking, traps and snares, making tools and implements from stone and other natural materials, hide tanning, building shelters, wilderness first aid and other skills. The course costs $275.

Photo: Wilderness Southwest

WILDERNESS SOUTHEAST
711 Sandtown Rd., Savannah, GA 31406; (912) 897-5108

Participants on the **COASTAL INCREDIBLE EDIBLES** course will catch, trap, gather and forage food for all meals. The fare will include shrimp, blue crabs, oysters, fresh fish, clams, berries, marsh plants (succulents), marsh greens, flower petals of the yucca and "darn near anything else that is edible." The three-day course costs $125.

Photo: Colorado Daily

HIKING & TREKKING

ALASKA

Alaska Back Country Guides Cooperative
P.O. Box 81533, College, AK 99701, 907/456-8907

Alaska Discovery, Inc.
P.O. Box 26, Gustavus, AK 99826, 907/697-3431

Alaska Fish and Trails Unlimited
S.R. Box 20154-X, Fairbanks, AK 99701, 907/455-6012

Alaska Travel
200 N. Franklin St., Juneau, AK 99801, 907/586-6245

Arctic Treks
Box 73452, Fairbanks, AK 99707, 907/455-6502

Brooks Range Wilderness Trips
Bettles Field, Bettles, AK 99726, 907/692-5312

Genet Expeditions
Talkeetna, AK 99676, 907/376-5120

Kachemak Bay Wilderness Lodge
Box 956, Homer, AK 99603, 907/235-8910

Katmailand, Inc.
455 H. Street, Anchorage, AK 99501, 907/277-4314

Kenai Guide Service
Box 40-1, Kasilof, AK 99610, 907/262-5496

Northern Discoveries
200 W. 34th Ave. Suite 304, Anchorage, AK 99503,
907/272-5394

Outdoor Alaska
Box 7814, Ketchikan, AK 99901, 907/225-6044 or 225-8444

Sourdough Outfitters
Box 18-A, Bettles, AK 99726, 800/544-2203 or 907/692-5252

ARIZONA

Caiman Expeditions
3449 E. River Rd., Tucson, AZ 85718, 602/327-9293

Free Lance Expeditions
P.O. Box 1494, Wickenburg, AZ 85358, 602/684-3106

Grand Canyon Trail Guides
P.O. Box 2997, Flagstaff, AZ 86023, 602/526-0924 or
602/638-2391

Grand Canyon Youth Expeditions/Expeditions, Inc.
R.R. 4 Box 755, Flagstaff, AZ 86001, 602/774-8176 or
779-3769

Wild and Scenic Expeditions
P.O. Box 460, Flagstaff, AZ 86002, 602/774-7343 or
800/841-7317

CALIFORNIA

All-Outdoor Adventure Trips
2151 San Miguel Dr., Walnut Creek, CA 94596, 415/932-8993

American River Touring Assoc.
445 High Street, Oakland, CA 94601, 415/465-9355

Baja Expeditions
P.O. Box 3725, San Diego, CA 92103, 619/293-7465

Mountain Travel, Inc.
1398 Solano Ave., Albany, CA 94706, 800/227-2384 or
415/527-8100

Pacific Adventures
P.O. Box 5041, Riverside, CA 92517, 714/684-1227

Sierra Club Outings
530 Bush St., San Francisco, CA 94109, 415/981-8634

Sierra Wilderness Seminars
P.O. Box 707, Arcata, CA 95521, 707/822-8066

Sobek's International Explorers Society
Angels Camp, CA 95222, 800/344-3284 or 209/736-4524

Wilderness Journeys
P.O. Box 807, Bolinas, CA 94924, 415/868-1836 or
415/525-6578

Wilderness Travel
1760 Solano Ave., Berkeley, CA 94707, 415/524-5111

Wildwalk
P.O. Box 202, Homewood, CA 96718, 916/525-5506

COLORADO

American Wilderness Alliance
4260 East Avans Ave. #3, Denver, CO 80222, 303/758-5018

American Wilderness Experience
P.O. Box 1486, Boulder, CO 80306, 303/444-2632

Colorado Mountain School
Box 2106M, Estes Park, CO 80517, 303/586-5758

Colorado Outward Bound School
945 Pennsylvania, Denver, CO 80203-3118, 303/837-0880 x22

Crooked Creek Ski Touring
Box 3142, Vail, CO 81658, 303/949-5682

Ernest Outdoor Tours
3596 West Hwy. 160, Monte Vista, CO 81144, 303/852-3277

Outdoor Leadership Training Seminars
P.O. Box 20281, Denver, CO 80220, 303/333-7831 or
942-4362

Rocky Mountain Llama Treks
Sugar Loaf Star Rt., Boulder, CO 80302, 303/449-9941

Rocky Mountain Wilderness Experience, Inc.
Station 27, Box 63, Lakewood, CO 80215, 303/232-0371

Sunrise Adventures
Box 1790, Glenwood Springs, CO 81601, 303/945-1366

The Mountaineering School at Vail, Inc.
P.O. Box 3034, Vail, CO 81657, 303/476-4123

Trailhead Ventures
P.O. Box CC, Buena Vista, CO 81211, 303/395-8001

Ultimate Escape, Ltd.
P.O. Box 6445, Colorado Springs, CO 80934, 303/578-8383

University of the Wilderness
P.O. Box 1687, Evergreen, CO 80439, 303/674-9724

Western Walkabout
2576 Albion St., Denver, CO 80207, 303/355-8964

Wilderness Challenge
Box 2135, Montrose, CO 81402, 303/249-5929

Wind River Mountain Guides
6678 S. Arapahoe Dr., Littleton, CO 80120, 303/794-9518

FLORIDA

Florida Trail Association, Inc.
P.O. Box 13708, Gainesville, FL 32604, 904/378-8823

GEORGIA

Wilderness Southeast
9521 Whitfield, Ave., Savannah, GA 31406, 912/355-8008

HAWAII
Pacific Quest, Inc.
P.O. Box 205, Haleuva, HI 96712, 808/638-8338
Trek Hawaii
P.O. Box 1585, Kaneohe, HI 96744, 808/235-6614

IDAHO
Mystic Saddle Ranch
P.O. Box 165-AA, Mountain Home, ID 83647, 208/587-5937
Wilderness River Outfitters
P.O. Box 871, Salmon, ID 83467, 208/756-3959

IOWA
Iowa Mountaineers
30 Prospect Pl., Iowa City, IA 52240, 319/337-7163

MAINE
East/West Wilderness School
Box 611, Bethel, ME 04217, 207/875-5255

MASSACHUSETTS
Volunteer Vacations
P.O. Box 86, No. Scituate, MA 02060, 617/545-4819

MICHIGAN
Sequin Yacht Charters
1174 Alpine Dr., Grosse Pointe, MI 48236, 313/884-5323

MINNESOTA
Bear Track Outfitting Co.
Box 51, Grand Marais, MN 55604, 218/387-1162

MONTANA
Absaroka Outfitters
P.O. Box AM, Clyde Park, MT 59018, 406/686-4732
Bob Marshall Wilderness Ranch
Seeley Lake, MT 59868, 406/745-4466
High Country Holiday
Box 61, Big Sky, MT 59716, 406/995-4192
Lone Mountain Ranch
Box 145, Big Sky, MT 59716, 406/995-4644
Quality Outdoors
Rt. 2 Box 250, Libby, MT 59923, 406/293-6985
Sunburst Adventures
3038 Candy Lane, Bozeman, MT 59715, 406/586-3212

NEW HAMPSHIRE
Appalachian Mountain Club
Box 298, Gorham, NH 03581, 603/466-2721

NEW MEXICO
Southwest Wilderness Center
P.O. Box 2840, Santa Fe, NM 87501, 505/982-3126

NEW YORK
American Lung Association
1740 Broadway, New York, NY 10019, 212/245-8000
Mohonk Mountain House
New Paltz, NY 12561, 914/255-1000 or 212/233-2244

NORTH CAROLINA
Nantahala Outdoor Center
US 19 West Box 41, Bryson City, NC 28713, 704/488-2175
N.C. Greywolf Expeditions, Inc.
Rt. 8 Box 620G, Morganton, NC 28655, 704/584-3369
North Carolina Outward Bound School
121 N. Sterling St., Morganton, NC 28655, 704/437-6112

OHIO
Missoula Bicycle Club
P.O. Box 23111, Columbus, OH 43223, 614/461-6648

OREGON
Eclipse Expeditions, Inc.
Rt. 1, Cove, OR 97824, 503/568-4663 or 252-6413
Wilderness Freighters
2166 S.E. 142nd, Portland, OR 97233, 503/761-7428

TENNESSEE
Nolichucky Expeditions, Inc.
P.O. Box 460, Erwin, TN 37650, 615/743-3221

TEXAS
Outback Expeditions
P.O. Box 44, Terlingua, TX 79852, 915/371-2490

WASHINGTON
Liberty Bell Alpine Tours
Mazama, WA 98833, 509/996-2490
Wilderness: Alaska/Mexico
Bissel Rd., Hunters, WA 99137, 509/772-6104

WYOMING
L. D. Frome
RFD, Afton, WY 83110, 307/886-5240
National Outdoor Leadership School
Box AA, Lander, WY 82520, 307/332-6973
Old West Tours, Inc.
P.O. Box 3322, Jackson, WY 83001, 307/733-7131
Valley Ranch
Valley Ranch Rd., Cody, WY 82414, 307/587-4661
Wild Horizon Expeditions
Box 2348-A, Jackson, WY 83001, 307/733-5343

CANADA
Iskut Trail and River Adventures
1103-207 W. Hastings St., Vancounver, B.C. V6B 1H7,
604/669-5175
Kootenai Wilderness Recreation
Argenta, B.C. V0G 1B0, 604/366-4480 or 366-4287
Northern Lights Alpine Recreation
Box 399, Invermere, B.C. VOA 1K0, 604/342-6042
Skoki Lodge
P.O. Box 5, Lake Louise, Alta T0L 1E0, 403/522-3555
**Strathcona Park Lodge and
Outdoor Education Center**
Box 2160, Cambell River, B.C. V9W 5C9, 604/N693546 or
604/286-3122
Willard's Backpacking Expeditions
107 Dunlop St. E.—Box 10, Barrie, Ont. L4M 1A6,
705/737-1881 or 728-4787

Photo: Colorado Daily

CLIMBING

ALASKA

Alaska Discovery, Inc.
P.O. Box 26, Gustavus, AK 99826, 907/697-3431

Alaskan Back Country Guides Cooperative
P.O. Box 81533, College, AK 99701, 907/456-8907

Genet Expeditions
Talkeetna, AK 99676, 907/376-5120

Katmailand, Inc.
455 H. Street, Anchorage, AK 99501, 907/277-4314

Northern Discoveries
200 W. 34th Ave. Suite 304, Anchorage, AK 99503,
907/272-5394

Prism Ski Touring
Box 136, Girdwood, AK 99587, 907/783-2945

Sourdough Outfitters
Box 18, Bettles, AK 99726, 907/692-5252

CALIFORNIA

Climbing Unlimited
P.O. Box 2000-186, South Lake Tahoe, CA 95705,
916/577-7750

Mountain Travel, Inc.
1398 Solano Ave., Albany, CA 94706, 800/227-2384 or
415/527-8100

Pacific Adventures
P.O. Box 5041, Riverside, CA 92517, 714/684-1227

Palisade School of Mountaineering
P.O. Box 694, Bishop, CA 93514, 619/935-4330

Sierra Club Outings
530 Bush St., San Francisco, CA 94109, 415/981-8634

Sierra/Nevada Ski Adventures
P.O. Box 1751, Bishop, CA 93514, 619/935-4325

Sierra Summit Mountain Guides
P.O. Box 7345, Mammoth Lake, CA 93546, 619/648-7616

Sierra Wilderness Seminars
P.O. Box 707, Arcata, CA 95521, 707/822-8066

Yosemite Mountaineering School
Yosemite National Park, CA 95389, 209/372-1335,
Sept.-June 209/372-1244

COLORADO

Colorado Mountain School
Box 2106-A, Estes Park, CO 80517, 303/586-5758

Colorado Outward Bound School
945 Pennsylvania, Denver, CO 80203-3118,
303/837-0880 X22

Crooked Creek Ski Touring
Box 3142, Vail, CO 81658, 303/949-5682

Fantasy Ridge Mountain Guides
Box 206, Woody Creek, CO 81656, 303/925-9581

International Alpine School
Eldorado Springs, CO 80025, 303/494-4904

Lankford Mountain Guides
333 Fairfax St., Denver, CO 80220, 303/393-0400

Outdoor Leadership Training Seminars
P.O. Box 20281, Denver, CO 80220, 303/333-7831

Rocky Mountain Llama Treks
Sugar Loaf Star Rt., Boulder, CO 80302, 303/449-9941

Rocky Mountain Wilderness Experience, Inc.
Station 27, P.O. Box 63, Lakewood, CO 80215, 303/232-0371

Sunrise Adventures
Box 1790, Glenwood Springs, CO 81601, 303/945-1366

The Mountaineering School at Vail, Inc.
P.O. Box 3034, Vail, CO 81657, 303/476-4123

Ultimate Escapes, Ltd.
P.O. Box 6445, 2506 W. Colorado Ave., Colorado Springs, CO
80934, 303/578-8383

Uncompahgre Mountain Guides
Box 313, Ridgway, CO 81432, 303/626-5776

Wind River Mountain Guides
6678 S. Arapahoe Dr., Littleton, CO 80120, 303/794-9518

IDAHO

Teton Mountain Touring
Box 514, Driggs, ID 93422, 208/354-2768

IOWA

Iowa Mountaineers
30 Prospect Pl., Iowa City, IA 52240, 319/337-7163

MARYLAND

North Country Mountaineering, Inc.
1602 Shakespeare St., Historic Falls Point, MD 21231,
301/327-8194

MONTANA

Bob Marshall Wilderness Ranch
Seeley Ranch, MT 59868, 406/745-4466

Sunburst Adventures
3038 Candy Lane, Bozeman, MT 59715, 406/586-3212

NEW HAMPSHIRE

International Mountain Climbing School, Inc.
Box 1277, North Conway, NH 03860, 603/356-5287

NEW MEXICO

Southwest Wilderness Center
P.O. Box 286, Santa Fe, NM 87501, 505/982-3126

NORTH CAROLINA

Nantahala Outdoor Center
U.S. 19 West, Box 41, Bryson City, NC 28713, 704/488-2175

N. C. Greywolf Expeditions, Inc.
Rt. 8 Box 620 G, Morganton, NC 28655, 704/584-3369

North Carolina Outward Bound School
121 N. Sterling St., Morganton, NC 28655, 704/437-6112

OREGON

Timberline Mountain Guides
Box 464, Terrebonne, OR 97760, 503/548-1888

TEXAS

Outback Expeditions
P.O. Box 44, Terlingua, TX 79852, 915/371-2490

UTAH
World Wide River Expeditions, Inc.
175 E. 7060 S., Midvale, UT 84047, 801/566-2662

WASHINGTON
American Alpine Institute & North Cascades
Alpine School, 1212 24th T-2, Bellingham, WA 98225,
206/671-1505
Liberty Bell Alpine Tours
Mazama, WA 98833, 509/996-2250
Rainier Mountaineering
Paradise, WA 98397, 206/569-2227, Sept.-May:
201 St. Helens, Tacoma, WA 98402, 202/627-6242

WEST VIRGINIA
Class VI River Runners, Inc.
Box 78, Lansing, WV 25862, 304/574-0704

WYOMING
Exum Mountain Guides
Grand Teton National Park, Moose, WY 83012, 307/733-2297
Exum Mountain Guides
Box 580, Wilson, WY 83014, 307/733-2297
Jackson Hole Mountain Guides
Box 547, Teton Village, WY 83025, 307/733-4979
Old West Tours, Inc.
P.O. Box 3322, Jackson, WY 83001, 307/733-7131
Parkland Expeditions
P.O. Box 371, Jackson, WY 83001, 307/733-3379
Skinner Brothers
Box B-G, Pinedale, WY 82941, 307/367-2270

CANADA
Northern Lights Alpine Recreation
Box 399, Invermere, BC V0A 1K0, 604/342-6042
Strathcona Park Lodge
Box 2160, Cambell River, B.C. V9W 5C9, 604/N693546 or
604/286-3122

Photo: Liz Hymans

SPELUNKING

CALIFORNIA
Baja Expeditions
P.O. Box 3725, San Diego, CA 92103, 619/293-7465
California Caverns at Cave City
P.O. Box 78, Vallecito, CA 95251, 209/736-2708

NORTH CAROLINA
North Carolina Outward Bound School
121 N. Sterling St., Morganton, NC 28655, 704/437-6112

OHIO
Missoula Bicycle Club
P.O. Box 23111, Columbus, OH 43223, 614/461-6648

WEST VIRGINIA
Transmontane Outfitters, Ltd.
P.O. Box 325, Davis, WV 26260, 304/259-5117

CANADA
**Strathcona Park Lodge and
Outdoor Education Centre**
Box 2160, Cambell River, B.C. V9W 5C9, 604/N693546 or
604/286-3122

Photo: Arnor Larson/Northern Lights Alpine Recreation

PACKSTOCK HIKING

ALASKA
Kenai Guide Service
Box 40-A, Kasilof, AK 99610, 907/262-5496
Northern Discoveries
200 W. 34th Ave. Suite 304, Anchorage, AK 99503,
907/272-5394

CALIFORNIA
McGee Creek Pack Station
Rt. 1, Box 162, Mammoth Lakes, CA 93546, 619/935-4324
Nov.-May: Star Rt. 1, Box 100, Independence, CA 93526,
619/872-6071, unit 234
Rock Creek Pack Station
Box 248, Bishop, CA 93514, 714/935-4493; Oct.-June:
714/872-8331
Shasta Llamas
P.O. Box 1137, Mt. Shasta, CA 96067, 916/926-3959 or
415/635-0286
Trinity Pack Trains
P.O. Box 277, Trinity Center, CA 96091, 916/226-3305
Nov.-June: Rt. 1-89 McCoy Rd., Red Bluff, CA 96080,
916/527-5550

COLORADO
American Wilderness Alliance
4260 E. Evans Ave. #3, Denver, CO 80222, 303/758-5081

IDAHO
Mystic Saddle Ranch
Stanley, ID 83340, 208/774-3591; Nov.-May: Box 165

MONTANA

Circle Eight Guest Ranch
P.O. Box 729A, Choteau, MT 59422, 406/466-5564
Double Arrow Wilderness Outfitters
Drawer E, Seeley Lake, MT 59868, 406/667-2204 or
667-2411 or 667-2317
Seven Lazy P Guest Ranch
Box 178-A, Choteau, MT 59422, 406/466-2044
Wild Country Outfitters
213 Poplar, Helena, MT 59601, 406/442-7127

OREGON

Cal Henry
Box 26-A, Joseph, OR 97846, 502/432-9171
Wilderness Freighters
2166 S.E. 142nd Ave., Portland, OR 97233, 503/761-7428

WASHINGTON

Cascade Corals
Box A, Stehekin, WA 98852

WYOMING

Game Hill Ranch
Box A, Bondurant, WY 82922, 307/733-4120
L. D. Frome Outfitter
Box G, Afton, WY 83110, 307/886-5240

Photo: Peter Nichols

LLAMA TREKKING

CALIFORNIA

Mama's Llamas ESD
P.O. Box 655, El Dorado, CA 95623, 916/622-2566
Shasta Llamas
Box 1137-M, Mt. Shasta, CA 96067, 916/926-3959
Sobek's International Explorers Society
Angels Camp, CA 95222, 209/736-4524

COLORADO

Rocky Mountain Llama Treks
Sugar Loaf Star Rt., Boulder, CO 80302, 303/449-9941
San Juan Llama Co.
P.O. Box 5110, Durango, CO 81301
The Home Ranch
Box 822-K, Clark, CO 80428, 303/879-1780

NORTH CAROLINA

Noah Llama Treks, Inc.
412 Blowing Rock Road, Boone, NC 28607

OREGON

G. Jelineks Oregon Wilderness Llama Tours
P.O. Box 7515, Eugene, OR 97401, 503/995-6208
Oregon Llamas
Box 96, Brownsville, OR 97327, 503/466-5976

Photo: Mystic Saddle Ranch

HORSE PACKING

ALASKA

Alaskan Back Country Guides Cooperative
P.O. Box 81533, College, AK 99701, 907/456-8907
Kachemak Bay Horse Trips
P.O. Box 2004, Homer, AK 99603, 907/235-7850
Northern Discoveries
200 34th Ave., Suite 304, Anchorage, AK 99503,
907/272-5394

ARIZONA

Free Lance Expeditions
P.O. Box 1494, Wickenburg, AZ 85358, 602/684-3106
Honeymoon Trail Co.
Moccasin, AZ 86022, 602/643-5584
Price Canyon Ranch
P.O. Box 1065, Douglas, AZ 85607, 602/558-2383
Wild and Scenic Expeditions
P.O. Box 460, Flagstaff, AZ 86002, 602/774-7343 or
800/841-7317

CALIFORNIA

Alisal Ranch
P.O. Box 26, Solvang, CA 93463, 805/688-6411
McGee Creek Pack Station
Rt. 1, Box 162, Mammoth Lakes, CA 93546, 619/935-4324;
Nov.-May: Star Rt. 1, Box 100, Independence, CA
93526, 619/872-6071 unit 234
Pacific Adventures
P.O. Box 5041, Riverside, CA 92517, 714/684-1227
Rock Creek Pack Station
Box 243, Bishop, CA 93514, 714/935-4493; Oct.-June:
714/872-8331
Sierra Club Outings
530 Bush Street, San Francisco, CA 94109, 415/918-8634
Trinity Pack Train
P.O. Box 277, Trinity Center, CA 96091, 916/266-3305;
Nov.-June: Rt. 1-89 McCoy Road, Red Bluff, CA 96080,
916/527-5550
Trinity Trail Rides
Coffee Creek Ranch, P.O. Star Rt. 2, Box 4940, Trinity Center,
CA 96091, 916/266-3343

COLORADO

American Wilderness Alliance
4260 E. Evans Avenue, #3, Denver, CO 80222, 303/758-5018

American Wilderness Experience, Inc.
P.O. Box 1486, Boulder, CO 80306, 303/444-2632

Colorado Back Country Pack Trips
P.O. Box 110-E, La Jara, CO 81140, 303/274-5655

Crooked Creek Ski Touring
Box 3142, Vail, CO 81658, 303/949-5682

Delby's Triangle 3 Ranch
Box 14, Steamboat Springs, CO 80477, 303/879-1257

Range Tours
1540 S. Holly, Denver, CO 80222, 303/759-1988

San Juan Outfitting, Inc.
120 Beaver Meadows Rd., Bayfield, CO 81122, 303/884-2731

Scientific Educational Expeditions
2715 Parklake Ct., Fort Collins, CO 80525, 303/223-3720

711 Ranch
Parlin A, CO 81239, 303/641-0666

Sid Simpson Guide Service
R.R. 1, Paonia, CO 81428, 303/527-3486

Ultimate Escapes, Ltd.
2506 W. Colorado Ave., Colorado Springs, CO 80904, 303/578-8383

IDAHO

Elvin & Bret Hincks
P.O. Box 594, Palasades, ID 83437, 208/483-2545

Fourth of July Creek Outfitters, Inc.
Box 307, Mountain Home, ID 83647, 208/587-7646 or 464-2858

Happy Hollow Camps
Star Rt. Box 14-A, Salmon, ID 83467, 208/756-3954

Mackay Bar—Idaho's Wilderness Co.
3190 Airport Way, Boise, ID 83705, 800/635-5336 or 208/344-1881

Mystic Saddle Ranch
Stanley, ID 83340, 208/777-3591; Nov.-May: Box 165, Mountain Home, ID 83647, 208/587-5937

Teton Expeditions, Inc.
P.O. Box 218, Rigby, ID 83442, 208/523-4981 or 745-6476

MONTANA

Absaroka Outfitters
P.O. Box AM, Clyde Park, MT 59018, 406/686-4732

Bob Marshall Wilderness Ranch
Seeley Lake, MT 59868, 406/754-2285

Circle Eight Guest Ranch
P.O. Box 729-A, Choteau, MT 59422, 406/466-5564

Double Arrow Wilderness Outfitters
Drawer E, Seeley Lake, MT 59868, 406/677-2204 or 677-2411 or 677-2317

Gary Duffy
Box 863, Corwin Springs, MT 59021, 406/848-7287

Glacier Outfitters
East Glacier, MT 59434, 406/226-4442, Sept.-May: Box 219, Ronan, MT 59864, 406/675-2142

Great Adventures West, Inc.
820 Central Avenue, Great Falls, MT 59401, 406/761-1677

JJJ Wilderness Ranch
P.O. Box 383, Augusta, MT 59410, 406/562-3653

Lone Mountain Ranch
P.O. Box 145, Big Sky, MT 59716, 406/995-4644

Seven Lazy P Guest Ranch
Box 178-A, Choteau, MT 59422, 406/466-2044

Sixty-Three Ranch
Box 979, Livingston, MT 59047, 406/222-0570

Sunburst Adventures
3038 Candy Lane, Bozeman, MT 59715, 406/586-3212

Wild Country Outfitters
713 Poplar, Helena, MT 59601, 406/442-7127

Wilderness Outfitters
2800 Rattlesnake Drive, Missoula, MT 59802, 406/549-2820

NEW MEXICO

Wilderness Pack Trips
Rt. 3, Box 8, Tererro, NM 87573, 505/757-6213

NEW YORK

Cold River Trail Rides, Inc.
Coreys, Tupper Lake, NY 12986, 518/359-7559

NORTH CAROLINA

N. C. Greywolf Expeditions, Inc.
Rt. 8, Box 620, Morganton, NC 28655, 704/584-3369

OREGON

Cal Henry
Box 26-A, Joseph, OR 97846, 503/432-9171

Eclipse Expeditions, Inc.
Rt. 1, Cove, OR 97824, 503/568-4663 or 252-6413

High Country Outfitters, Inc.
Box 26, Joseph, OR 97846, 503/432-9171

TEXAS

Far Flung Adventures
Box 31, Terlingua, TX 79852, 915/371-2489

UTAH

Cache Valley Guide & Outfitters
252 South 2nd West, Hyrum, UT 84319, 801/245-3896

Piute Creek Outfitters
Rt. 1-A, Kamas, UT 84036, 801/783-4317 or 486-2607

Western Frontier Adventures
P.O. Box 6145, Salt Lake City, UT 84106, 801/484-4421

WASHINGTON

Cascade Corrals
Box A, Stehekin, WA 98852, no telephone

Wilderness: Alaska/Mexico
Bissel Rd., Hunters, WA 99137, 509/722-6164

WYOMING

Bar-T-Five Outfitters
Box 2140, Jackson, WY 83001, 307/733-5386

Boulder Lake Lodge
Pinedale, WY 82941, 307/367-2961

Box K Ranch
Moran, WY 83103, 307/543-2407

Cross Mill Iron Ranch
Crowheart, WY 82512, 307/486-2279

Crossed Sabres Ranch
Wapiti, WY 82450, 307/587-3750

Fall Creek Guide Service
Box 132, Boulder, WY 82923, 307/537-5262

Game Hill Ranch
Box A, Bondurant, WY 82922, 307/733-4120

Grizzley Ranch
North Fork Rt. A, Cody, WY 82414, 307/587-3966

L. D. Frome, Outfitter
Afton, WY 83110, 307/886-5240

Mad River Boat Trips
Box 2222, Jackson, WY 83001, 307/733-6203

National Outdoor Leadership School
Box AA, Lander, WY 82520, 307/332-6973

Old West Tours, Inc.
P.O. Box 3322, Jackson, WY 83001, 307/733-7131

Open Creek Outfitting
Box 3199, Jackson, WY 83001, 307/733-7924

Parklands Expeditions
Box 3055, Jackson, WY 83001, 307/733-3379; Oct.-May:
    930 Nobs Hill Rd., Redwood City, CA 94601, 415/366-8246

Rimrock Dude Ranch
Box FS, Northfork Rt., Cody, WY 82414, 307/587-3970

Skinner Brothers
Box B-G, Pinedale, WY 82941, 307/367-4675

Teton Trail Rides
Box 183, Moose, WY 83012, 307/733-2108; Oct.-May:
    Box 173, Rt. 2, St. Anthony, ID 83445, 208/624-7956

Toqwotee Mountain Lodge
Box 91-D, Moran, WY 83013, 307/543-2847

Triangle X Ranch
Box 120, Moose, WY 83012, 307/733-2183

Valley Ranch Inc.
Valley Ranch Rd. V, Cody, WY 82414, 307/587-4661

CANADA

Amethyst Lakes Pack Trips, Ltd.
Box 508, Jasper, Alberta T0E 1E0, 403/866-3980, Oct.-
    May: Brule, Alberta T0E 1E0, 403/866-3946

Holiday on Horseback
The Trail Rider Store, Box 2280, Banff, Alberta
    T0L 0C0, 403/762-4551

Iskut Trail and River Adventures
1103-207 W. Hastings St., Vancouver, B.C. V6B 1H7,
    604/669-5175

McKenzie's Trails West
Box 971, Rocky Mountain House, Alberta
    T0M IT0, 403/845-6708

Trail Riders of the Canadian Rockies
Box 6742, Station D, Calgary, Alberta T2P 2E6,
    403/287-1746

Warner and MacKenzie Guiding and Outfitting
Box 2280, Banff, Alberta T0L 0C0, 403/762-4551

Photo: Karen Schulenburg

CATTLE & HORSE DRIVES

CALIFORNIA
McGee Creek Pack Station
Rt. 1, Box 162, Mammoth Lakes, CA 93546, 619/935-4324
    Nov.-May: Star Rt. 1, Box 100, Independence, CA 93526,
    619/872-6071 unit 234

Rock Creek Pack Station
Box 248, Bishop, CA 93514, 714/935-4493

COLORADO
Canyon Ranch
Rt. 1, Box 61-A, Olathe, CO 81425, 303/323-5288

NEW YORK
Adventures on Horseback
Box E, 36 E. 57th St., New York, NY 10022, 212/355-6334

WASHINGTON
Cascade Corrals
Box A, Stehekin, WA 98852

WYOMING
Schively Ranch
1062 Rd. 15, Lovell, WY 82431, 307/548-6688

TX Tillett Ranch
Box 453, Lovell, WY 82431

Photo: Country Cycling

BICYCLE TOURING

ARIZONA
Bicycle Detours
P.O. Box 44078-X, Tucson, AZ 85733, 602/326-1624

CALIFORNIA
Action Adventures Wet-N-Wild
Box 1500, Woodland, CA 95695, 916/662-5431

All-Outdoor Adventure Trips
2151 San Miguel, Dr., Walnut Creek, CA 94596, 415/932-8993

Backroads Bicycle Touring Co.
P.O. Box 5534, Berkeley, CA 94705, 415/652-0786

Pacific Adventures
P.O. Box 5041, Riverside, CA 92517, 714/684-1227

Sierra Club Outings
530 Bush St., San Francisco, CA 94109, 415/981-8634

COLORADO
American Wilderness Alliance
4260 E. Evans Ave. #3, Denver, CO 80222, 303/758-5018

Colorado Adventure Network
194 S. Franklin St., Denver, CO 80209, 303/722-6482

Colorado Bicycle Tours
P.O. Box 45-A, Pitkin, CO 81241, 303/641-4240

Colorado Outward Bound School
945 Pennsylvania, Denver, CO 80203-3118, 303/837-0880 x22

Range Tours
1540 S. Holly, Denver, CO 80222, 303/759-1988

Trailhead Ventures
P.O. Box 2023, Buena Vista, CO 81211, 303/395-8001

Ultimate Escapes, Ltd.
2506 W. Colorado Ave., Colorado Springs, CO 80904,
303/578-8383
Wind River Mountain Guides
6678 S. Arapahoe Dr., Littleton, CO 80120, 303/794-9518

DISTRICT OF COLUMBIA
American Youth Hostels, Inc.
Travel Dept., 1332 "I" N.W., Washington, DC 20005,
202/783-6161

FLORIDA
Swannee Country Tours, Inc.
P.O. Box 247, White Springs, FL 32096, 904/397-2347

IOWA
Ragbrai 12
P.O. Box 10333, Des Moines, IA 50306

MARYLAND
Bicycle USA
Box 988, Baltimore, MD 21203, 301/727-2022

MASSACHUSETTS
Cape Cod Bicycle Tours
Box 189, Orleans, MA 02653, 800/451-1833 or 451-1818

MICHIGAN
Bicycle Touring Network
Box 7559, Ann Arbor, MI 48107, 313/ONE-TOUR
Christian Adventures
Calvin College Commons, Grand Rapids, MI 49506,
616/957-6492
Michigan Bicycle Touring
3512 Red School #D4-A, Kingsley, MI 49649, 616/263-5885

MONTANA
Bikecentennial, Inc.
113 W. Main, Missoula, MT 59802, 406/721-1776

NEVADA
Sierra Bicycle Touring Co.
P.O. Box 5453, Incline Village, NV 89450, 702/831-3576

NEW HAMPSHIRE
Appalachian Mountain Club
Box 298, Gorham, NH 03581, 603/466-2721
The Biking Expedition
Box 547, Henniker, NH 03242, 603/428-7500

NEW MEXICO
Bicycle Detours
535 Cordova Rd., #463, Santa Fe, NM 87501, 505/984-0856

NEW YORK
American Lung Association
1740 Broadway, New York, NY 10019, 212/245-8000
Breakaway Bicycle Tours
Box 3713, Kingston, NY 12401, 914/339-4836
Country Cycling Tours
140 W. 83rd St., New York, NY 10024, 212/874-5151
Freewheeling Adventures
84K Durand Dr., Rochester, NY 14622, 716/323-2657
Raquette River Bike and Boat Co., Inc.
Box 6530, Tupper Lake, NY 12986, 518/359-3228

NORTH CAROLINA
Nantahala Outdoor Center
U.S. 19 West, Box 41, Bryson City, NC 28713, 704/488-2175

OHIO
Missoula Bicycle Club
P.O. Box 23111, Columbus, OH 43223, 614/461-6648

OREGON
R. Marriner Orum
2384 Floral Hill Dr., Eugene, OR 97403, 503/342-4527
Trailwind Bicycle Touring Outfitters
1275 N.W. 180th Ave., Beaverton, OR 97006, 503/645-2526

TEXAS
Bike Dream Tours, Inc.
P.O. Box 20653, Houston, TX 77225-0653, 915/783-9526

VIRGINIA
American Automobile Association
8111 Gatehouse Rd., Falls Church, VA 22047, 202/222-6000

VERMONT
Bike Vermont
P.O. Box 75A, Grafton, VT 05146, 802/843-2259
Vermont Bicycle Touring
Box 711-BV, Bristol, VT 05443, 802/453-4811
Vermont Country Cyclers
P.O. Box 14, Waterbury Center, VT 05677, 802/244-5215

WASHINGTON
Liberty Bell Alpine Tours
Mazama, WA 98833, 509/966-2250

CANADA
Northwest Bicycle Tours
14556 104th Ave., Surrey, B.C. V3R 1M2, 604/589-3328
Rocky Mountain Cycle Tours
Box 895, Banff, Alta T0L 0C0, 403/762-3477, 403/762-3477

Photo: Wyoming Travel Commission

SNOWMOBILING

COLORADO
Lichen Guest Ranch
Box C, Kremmling, CO 80459, 303/724-3450

MAINE
Northern Outdoors, Inc.
P.O. Box 100, The Forks, ME 04985, 207/663-2271

MICHIGAN
Merle's Kasino
P.O. Box 225, Southfield, MI 48037, 313/353-2240

Photo: Joseph Daniel

Photo: Colorado Daily

DOG SLEDDING

ALASKA
Alaskan Back Country Guides Cooperative
P.O. Box 81533, College, AK 99701, 907/456-8907
Alaska Fish and Trails Unlimited
S.R. Box 20154-X, Fairbanks, AK 99701, 907/455-6012
Brooks Range Wilderness Trips
Bettles Field, Bettles, AK 99726, 907/692-5312
Denali Dog Tours and Wilderness Freighters
Box 1, McKinley Park, AK 99755, 907/683-2314 or 683-2321
Genet Expeditions
Talkeetna, AK 99676, 907/376-5120
Prism Ski Touring
Box 136, Girdwood, AK 99587, 907/783-2945
Sourdough Outfitters
Box 18, Bettles, AK 99726, 800/544-2203 or 907/692-5252

ARIZONA
Wild and Scenic Expeditions
P.O. Box 460, Flagstaff, AZ 86002, 800/841-7317 or
    602/774-7343

CALIFORNIA
Sobek's International Explorers Society
Angels Camp, CA 95222, 209/736-4524

COLORADO
Krabloonik
P.O. Box 5517, Snowmass Village, CO 81615, 303/923-3953

MINNESOTA
Bear Track Outfitting Co.
Box 51, Grand Marais, MN 55604, 218/387-1162
Snow Trails Winter Adventure
130 Country Rd. 7, Finland, MN 55603, 218/353-7744

OREGON
Wilderness Freighters
2166 S.E. 142nd Ave., Portland, OR 97233, 503/761-7428

WYOMING
Old West Tours, Inc.
P.O. Box 3322, Jackson, WY 83001, 307/733-7131

CROSS-COUNTRY SKIING & SNOWSHOEING

ALASKA
Alaska Discovery
P.O. Box 26, Gustavus, AK 99826, 907/697-3431
Alaskan Back Country Guides Cooperative
P.O. Box 81533, College, AK 99701, 907/456-8907
**Alaskan Rivers Touring Co., Inc.
and Yentna Station Roadhouse**
P.O. Box 1884, Anchorage, AK 99510, Attn: Daniel Gabryszak
Brooks Range Wilderness Trips
Bettles Field, Bettles, AK 99726, 907/692-5312
Denali Dog Tours and Wilderness Freighters
Box 1, McKinley Park, AK 99755, Attn: Dennis Kogl,
    907/683-2314 or 683-2321
Genet Expeditions
Talkeetna, AK 99676, 907/376-5120
PRISM Ski Touring
Box 136-M, Girdwood, AK 99587, Attn: Bill Glude,
    907/783-2945
Sourdough Outfitters
Box 18, Bettles, AK 99726, 907/692-5252

ARIZONA
Wild and Scenic Expeditions
P.O. Box 460, Flagstaff, AZ 86002, 800/841-7317 or
    602/774-7343

CALIFORNIA
Backroads Bicycle Touring Co.
P.O. Box 5534, Berkeley, CA 94705, Attn: Tom Hale,
    415/652-0786
Coffee Creek Ranch
P.O. Star Rt. 2, Box 4940, Trinity Center, CA 96091, Attn:
    Ruth & Mark Hartman, 916/266-3343
Montecito-Sequoia Cross Country Ski Center
1485 Redwood Dr., Los Altos, CA 94022, Attn: Dr. Virginia C.
    Barnes, 415/967-8612
Pacific Adventures
P.O. Box 5041, Riverside, CA 92517, 714/684-1227
Rock Creek Winter Lodge
Rt. 1, Box 5, Mammoth Lakes, CA 93546, 619/935-4464
Royal Gorge Nordic Ski Resort
P.O. Box 178, Soda Springs, CA 95728, 916/426-3871
Sierra Club Huts
c/o Dick Simpson, 3326 Kipling, Palo Alto, CA 94306,
    415/494-9272

Sierra Club Outings
530 Bush Street, San Francisco, CA 94109, 415/981-8634
Sierra/Nevada Ski Adventures
P.O. Box 1751, Bishop, CA 93514, 619/935-4325
Sierra Ski Touring
Box C9, Mammoth Lakes, CA 93546, 619/834-4495 or 935-4606
Sierra Wilderness Seminars
P.O. Box 707, Arcata, CA 95521, 707/822-8066
Sobek's International Explorers Society
Angels Camp, CA 95222, 209/736-4524
Yosemite Mountaineering School
Yosemite National Park, CA 95389, Attn: Lloyd Price, 209/372-1244 (June-Sept.: 209/372-1335)

COLORADO
Aspen/Alfred A. Braun Hut System
U.S. Ski Educational Assoc., 702 W. Main St., Aspen, CO 81611, 303/925-7162
Colorado Adventure Network
194 S. Franklin St., Denver, CO 80209, 303/722-6482
Colorado Mountain School
Box 2106M, Estes Park, CO 80517, 303/586-5758
Colorado Outward Bound School
945 Pennsylvania, Denver, CO 80203-3118, 303/837-0880
Crooked Creek Ski Touring
Box 3142, Vail, CO 81658, 303/949-5682
Devil's Thumb Ranch
3530 Grand County Rd. 83, Frasier, CO 80442
Ernest's Outdoor Tours
3596 West Hwy. 160, Monte Vista, CO 81144, Attn: Ernest Wilkinson, 303/852-3277
John Harlin Guiding
2705 Spruce St., Boulder, CO 80302, 303/440-4894
Lichen Guest Ranch
Box C, Kremmling, CO 80459, 303/724-3450
Mountaineering School at Vail, Inc.
P.O. Box 3034, Vail, CO 81658, 303/476-4123
Outdoor Leadership Training Seminars
P.O. Box 20281, Denver, CO 80220, Attn: Rick Medrick, 303/333-7831
Rocky Mountain Outdoor Center
Star Rt. Box 323, Howard, CO 81233, 303/942-3214 or 494-3494
Rocky Mountain Wilderness Experience, Inc.
Station 27, P.O. Box 63, Lakewood, CO 80215, 303/232-0371
Soda Springs Ski Ranch
Grand Lake, CO 80447
Tenth Mountain Division Trail Hut System
P.O. Box 9000, Aspen, CO 81612, 303/925-7625
The Home Ranch
Box 822-K, Clark, CO 80428, 303/879-1780
Tumbling River Ranch
Grant, CO 80448, 303/838-5981
Ultimate Escapes, Ltd.
2506 W. Colorado Ave., Colorado Springs, CO 80904, Attn: Jim Miller, 303/578-8383
Uncompahgre Mountain Guides
Box 313-O, Ridgway, CO 81432, 303/626-5776
Vista Verde Ranch
Box 465, Steamboat Springs, CO 80477, Attn: Frank & Winton Brophy, 303/879-3858
Wilderness Challenge
Box 2135 Montrose, CO 81402, 303/249-5929

IDAHO
Busterback Ranch
Star Route, Ketchum, ID 83340, 208/774-2217

Sun Valley Trekking Co.
P.O. Box 2200, Sun Valley, ID 83353, 208/726-9595
Teton Mountain Touring
P.O. Box 514, Driggs, ID 83422, 208/354-8295
Wilderness River Outfitters and Trail Expeditions
P.O. Box 871, Salmon, ID 83467, 208/256-3959
Wilderness Trails
P.O. Box 9252, Moscow, ID 83843, 208/882-1955

MAINE
East/West Wilderness School
Box 611, Bethel, ME 04217, 207/875-5255
North Country Outfitters
Moosehead Lake, Rockwood, ME 04478, 207/534-2242
The Birches Ski Touring Center
North Country Outfitters
P.O. Box 81-O, Rockwood, ME 04478, 207/534-7305

MASSACHUSETTS
Foxhollow
Box 777 Rt. 7, Lenox, MA 01240, 413/637-2000

MINNESOTA
Bear Track Outfitting Co.
Box 51, Grand Marais, MN 55605, Attn: David & Cathi Williams, 218/387-1162
Bearskin Lodge
Gunflint Trail, Box 10, Grand Marais, MN 55604, Attn: Dave Tuttle, 218/388-2292
Gunflint Northwoods Outfitters
Box 100, Grand Marais, MN 55604, Attn: Bruce & Sue Kerfoot, 218/388-2294
Maplelag
Rt. 1, Callaway, MN 56521, 218/375-4466

MONTANA
Adventures West
820-D Central Ave., Great Falls, MT 59401, 406/761-1677
Bob Marshall Wilderness Ranch
Seeley Lake, MT 59868, 406/745-4466
Great Adventures West, Inc.
820 Central Ave., Great Falls, MT 59401, 406/761-1677
Lone Mountain Ranch
P.O. Box 145, Big Sky, MT 59716, Attn: Bob & Viv Schaap, 406/955-4644
Sunburst Adventures
3038 Candy Lane, Bozeman, MT 59715, 406/586-3212
Valhalla Expeditions
P.O. Box 272, Gardiner, MT 59030, 406/848-7346

NEW HAMPSHIRE
Appalachian Mountain Club
Reservations Secretary, P.O. Box 298, Gorham, NH 03581, 603/466-2727
Balsams/Wilderness
Dixville Notch, NH 03576, 603/255-3400; 617/227-8288; 212/563-4383
Franconia Inn
Rt. 116, Franconia, NH 03580, Attn: Alec Morris, 603/832-5542
Jackson Ski Touring Foundation
Box 216AA, Jackson, NH 03846, 603/383-9355

NEW MEXICO
Southwest Wilderness Center
P.O. Box 2840, Santa Fe, NM 87501, 505/982-3126

NEW YORK

Adirondack Hut-to-Hut Tours
RD 1, Box 85, Ghent, NY 12075, 518/499-5098

Adirondack Lodge-to-Lodge Tours
Box 139, Keene, NY 12942, 518/576-2221

Adirondack Wilderness Tours
Box 52-A, Canoga Lake, NY 12032, 518/835-4193

American Lung Association
1740 Broadway, New York, NY 10019, 212/245-8000

Cold River Trail Rides, Inc.
Coreys, Tupper Lake, NY 12986, Attn: John Fontana,
518/359-7559

Garnet Hill Lodge & Ski Touring Center
North River, NY 12856, Attn: George & Mary Heim,
518/251-2821

Mohawk Mountain House
New Paltz, NY 12561, 914/255-1000 or 212/233-2244

The Bark Eater
Alstead Mill Rd., Keene, NY 12942, Attn: Joe-Pete Wilson,
518/576-2221

OHIO

Missoula Bicycle Club
P.O. Box 23111, Columbus, OH 43223, 614/461-6648

OREGON

Crater Lake Ski Service
4605 Jump Off Joe Creek Rd., Grants Pass, OR 97526,
503/476-8734 (Winter: Crater Lake National Park, Crater
Lake, OR 97604, 503/594-2361)

Morrisons Lodge
8500 Galice Rd., Merlin, OR 97532-9799, 503/476-3825

R. Marriner Orum
2384 Floral Hill Dr., Eugene, OR 97403, 503/342-4527

PENNSYLVANIA

Suequehannock Lodge
Box 120, Ulysses Rd. 1 (on Rt. 6), PA 16948, Attn: Wil and
Betty Ahn, 814/435-2163

The Inn at Starlight Lake
Starlight, PA 18461, Attn: Jack & Judy McMahon,
717/798-2519

UTAH

Piute Creek Outfitters
Rt. 1-A, Kansas, UT 84036, Attn: Barbara & Arch Arnold,
801/783-4317 or 486-2607

VERMONT

Burke Mt. Touring Center
E. Burke, VT 05832, 802/626-3305

Edson Hill Manor
Edson Hill Rd., Stowe, Vt 05672, 802/253-7371

Green Trails Country Inn
Dept. A, Brookfield, VT 05036, Attn: Joyce Butler,
802/276-3412

Ski Tours of Vermont
RFD 1, Chester, VT 05143, 802/875-3631

Trapp Family Lodge
Stowe, VT 05672, 802/253-8511

WASHINGTON

Cascade Corals
Box A, Stehekin, WA 98852, Attn: The Courtneys

Liberty Bell Alpine Tours
Mazana, WA 98833, Attn: Eric Sanford, 509/996-2250

Methow Valley Ski-Touring Assoc.
P.O. Box 147, Winthrop, WA 98862, 509/996-2334

Scottish Lakes Cross-Country Area
P.O. Box 312, Leavenworth, WA 98826, 509/548-7330

WISCONSIN

Eagle River Nordic
Box 936, Eagle River, WI 54521, 715/479-7285

WYOMING

Game Hill Ranch
Box A, Bondurant, WY 82922, Attn: Pete & Holly Cameron,
307/733-4120

Jackson Hole Karhu Cross-Country Ski Center
Box 269, Teton Village, WY 83025, Attn: Wayne Hanson,
307/733-3560 (May-Dec.: 307/733-7950)

National Outdoor Leadership School
Box AA, Lander, WY 82520, 307/332-6973

Old West Touring, Inc.
P.O. Box 3322, Jackson, WY 83001, 307/733-7131

Pahaska Tepee Resort
Box 2370, Cody, WY 82414, 307/587-5536

Togwotee Mountain Lodge
Box 91-D, Moran, WY 83103, Attn: Dave & Julie Helgeson,
307/543-2847

Triangle X Ranch
Box 120, Mooje, WY 83012, Attn: The Turner Brothers,
307/733-2183

CANADA

Banff National Park
Superintendent, Box 900, Banff, Alberta T0L 0C0,
403/762-3324

Northern Lights Alpine Recreation
Box 399, Invermere, British Columbia V0A 1K0, Attn: Arnor
Larson, 604/342-6042

Ptarmigan Tours
160 Higgins St., Kimberley, British Columbia Y1A 1K6,
604/427-4029

Skoki Lodge
P.O. Box 5, Lake Louise, Alberta T0L 1E0 Canada,
Attn: John M. Worrall, 403/522-3555

**Strathcona Park Lodge and
Outdoor Education Centre**
Box 2160, Cambell River, B.C. V9W 5C9, 604/N693546 or
604/286-3122

Wanapitei
Box A, 7 Engleburn Pl., Peterborough, Ontario K9H 1C4,
705/743-3774

Wildwaters
R.R. 13, Lakeshore Drive, Thunder Bay, Ontario P7B 5E4,
Attn: Bruce T. Hyer, 807/683-3151

Photo: Colorado Daily

Photo: Canadian Mountain Holidays

OUT-OF-BOUNDS SKIING

ALASKA
Northern Discoveries
200 W. 34th Ave. Suite 304, Anchorage, AK 99503,
907/272-5394

CALIFORNIA
Sierra Nevada Ski Adventures
P.O. Box 1751, Bishop, CA 93514, 619/935-4325

COLORADO
Colorado Outward Bound School
945 Pennsylvania, Denver, CO 80203-3118, 303/837-0880 x22
Crooked Creek Ski Touring
Box 3142, Vail, CO 81658, 303/949-5682
Golconda Resort
P.O. Box 95, Lake City, CO 81235, 303/944-2256
John Harlin Guiding
2705 Spruce St., Boulder, CO 80302, 303/440-4894
Mountaineering School at Vail, Inc.
P.O. Box 3034, Vail, CO 81658, 303/476-4123

IDAHO
Teton Mountain Touring
Box 514, Driggs, ID 83422, 208/354-2768
Wilderness Trails
P.O. Box 9252, Moscow, ID 83843, 208/882-1955

MONTANA
Lone Mountain Ranch
Box 145, Big Ski, MT 59716, 406/995-4644

WYOMING
National Outdoor Leadership School
Box AA, Lander, WY 82520, 307/332-6973

HELI-SKIING

ALASKA
Alaska Discovery
P.O. Box 26, Gustavus, AK 99826, 907/697-3431

ARIZONA
Wild and Scenic Expeditions
P.O. Box 460, Flagstaff, AZ 86002, 800/841-7317 or
602/774-7343

CALIFORNIA
Sierra/Nevada Ski Adventures
P.O. Box 1751, Bishop, CA 93514, 619/935-4325
Sobek's International Explorers Society
Angels Camp, CA 95222, 209/736-4524

COLORADO
Colorado Adventure Network
194 S. Franklin St., Denver, CO 80209, 303/722-6482
Golconda Resort
P.O. Box 95, Lake City, CO 81235, 303/944-2256
Wilderness Challenge
Box 2135, Montrose, CO 81402, 303/249-5929

IDAHO
Wilderness Trails
P.O. Box 9252, Moscow, ID 83843, 208/882-1955

MONTANA
Bob Marshall Wilderness Ranch
Seeley Ranch, MT 59868, 406/745-4466

WASHINGTON
Liberty Bell Alpine Tours
Star Rt., Mazama, WA 98830, 509/996-2250

WYOMING
Old West Tours
P.O. Box 3322, Jackson, WY 83001, 307/733-7131

Photo: Dave DePuy

SCUBA SCHOOLS

CALIFORNIA
Baja Expeditions
P.O. Box 3725, San Diego, CA 92103, 619/293-7465
Bay Travel Diving Adventures
2435 East Coast Highway, Corona Del Mar, CA,
800/854-9303 or 714/675-4320
New England Divers
398 5th St., San Francisco, CA 94107, 415/434-3614
Ocean Voyages
1709 Bridgeway, Sausalito, CA 94965, 415/332-4681
Pacific Adventures
P.O. Box 5041, Riverside, CA 92517, 714/684-1227
S. Steele's Scuba, Inc.
2350 El Camino Real, Santa Clara, CA 95051, 408/984-5819

COLORADO
A-1 Diving Co.
4730 S. Lipan, Englewood, CO 80111, 303/789-2450
Colorado Diving Center Ltd.
909 S. Oneida, Denver, CO, 303/388-DIVE (3483)
Divers Supply Denver
557 Milwaukee, Denver, CO, 303/399-2877
Diversified Marine-Air Products
8921 E. Union Ave., Englewood, CO 80111, 303/740-7623
High Country Divers Inc.
60 S. Havana, Unit #611, Aurora, CO 80012, 303/341-5735
Lichen Guest Ranch
Box C, Kremmling, CO 80459, 303/724-3450
Mile High Divers
5025 Ward Rd., Wheatridge, CO, 303/422-1017
Rocky Mountain Diving & Sailboard Center
1737 15th Street, Boulder, CO 80302, 303/449-8606
Rocky Mountain Diving Center Ltd.
1920 Wadsworth Blvd., Lakewood, CO 80215, 303/232-2400
Scuba Den
5055 W. 44th Ave., Denver, CO, 303/458-0376
Scuba Shoppe Ltd.
10101 E. Hampden Ave., Denver, CO, 303/750-2997 and
85 S. Union Blvd., Lakewood, CO, 303/988-6725
Sunrise Adventures
Box 1790, Glenwood Springs, CO 81601, 303/945-1366
Weaver's Dive Center
623-A S. Broadway, Boulder, CO 80303, 303/499-0963

CONNECTICUT
International Scuba Center Ltd.
758 Main St., Rt. 10, Plantsville, CT 06479, 203/621-8265

Jack's Dive Center, Inc.
466 East St., Rt. 10, Plainville, CT 06062, 203/747-3170

FLORIDA
Capt. Slate's Atlantis Dive Center
51 Garden Cove Dr., Key Largo, FL 33037, 305/451-3020
Diving Trips, Inc.
4565 S.W. 37th Ave., Fort Lauderdale, FL 33312,
305/989-5813
Ginnie Springs
Rt. 1, Box 153, High Springs, FL 32643, 904/454-2202
Island Sport-Divers
98474 Overseas Hwy., Key Largo, FL 33037, 305/852-2586
Key West Pro Dive Shop, Inc.
1605 N. Roosevelt Blvd., Key West, FL 33040, 305/296-3823
Mac's Diving Charts, Inc.
2126 Drew St., Clearwater, FL 33515, 813/442-9931
Plantation Inn Marina
P.O. Box 1093, Crystal River, FL 32629, 904/795-5797
Scuba Key West/Reef Raiders Dive Shop
US #1, Stock Isle, Key West, FL 33040, 305/294-0660
The Diving Site & Coral Lagoon Resort
12399 Overseas Hwy., Marathon, FL 33050, 305/289-1021
The Reef Shop, Dive Center and Charter Service
Rt. 2, Box 7, Islamorada, FL 33036, 305/664-4385
Watersport People
508 South St., Key West, FL 33040, 305/296-4546

GEORGIA
Wilderness Southeast
9521 Whitfield Ave., Savannah, GA 31406, 912/355-8008

HAWAII
Aloha Dive Shop
Koko Marina Shopping Center, Honolulu, HI 96825,
808/395-5922
Fathom Five Professional Divers
Box 907, Kaloa, HI 96756, Attn: Terry O'Halloran,
808/742-6991
Fun in the Sun
Kaanapali Beach Hotel, Lahaina, Maui, HI 96761
Maui Dive Shop
Azeka Place, Kihei, HI 96753, 808/879-3388
Pacific Quest, Inc.
P.O. Box 205, Haleiwa, HI 96712, 808/638-8338
Sea Sage
4544 Kukui St., Kapaa, Kauai, HI 96746
Skindiving Hawaii
1651 Ala Moana Blvd., Honolulu, HI 96815
Trek Hawaii
P.O. Box 1585, Kaneohe, HI 96744, 808/235-6614

IOWA
Mac's Marine & Dive Shop Inc.
3808 S. Concord, St., Davenport, IA 52802, 319/324-8771

ILLINOIS
Blue Hole Dive Shop
Div. of BHI Companies, 4817 W. Farmington Rd., Peoria, IL
61604, 309/676-1852
Underseas Scuba Center
626 N. Addison Rd., Villa Park, IL 60181, 312/833-8383

MASSACHUSETTS
Inland Divers
100 S. Main St. (Rt. 9), Leicester, MA 01524, 617/892-3323

Underwater Safaris
Capt. Fred Calhoun, Yankee Fleet, 7 Essex Ave., Gloucester,
MA 01930, 617/532-5431

MAINE
Skin Diver's Paradise
RFD #3, Turner Rd. Box 817, Auburn, ME 04210,
207/782-7739

MICHIGAN
Scuba North, Inc.
13258 W. Bayshore Dr., Traverse City, MI 49684,
616/947-2520

MINNESOTA
The Superior Diver, Inc.
4833 Hanover Rd., Mound, MN 55364, 612/472-1845

MISSOURI
West End Diving Center
11215 Natural Bridge Rd., Bridgeton, MO 65044, Attn:
Douglas & Catherine Goergens, 314/731-5003

NEW HAMPSHIRE
LaPorte's Skindiving Shop
Box 53, Rt. 103, Newbury, NH 03255, 603/763-5353
North Country Scuba Diving Schools
Main St., Wolfeboro, NH 03894, 603/569-2120 AND
57 Elm St., Laconia, NH 03246, 603/524-8606

NEW JERSEY
East Coast Diving Service
340 F. Spring Valley Road, Morganville, NJ 07751, Attn:
W. J. Cleary, 201/591-9374

NEW YORK
Niagara Scuba Sports
2048 Niagara St., Buffalo, NY 14207, 716/875-6528
7Z's—Hampton Bays Divers, Inc.
1140 Flanders Rd., Riverhead, NY 11901, 516/727-2642
Westchester Dive Center
62 Westchester Ave., Port Chester, NY 10573, 914/937-2685

OHIO
Buckeye Diving Schools
46 Warrensville Center Rd., Bedford, OH 44146, Attn: Paul
Reynolds, 216/439-3677

PENNSYLVANIA
Diving Bell, Inc.
681 North Broad St., Philadelphia, PA 19123, Attn: Howard
Pruyn, 215/763-6868
Harrisburg Scuba Center, Inc.
991-A Peiffers Lane, Harrisburg, PA 17109, 717/561-0517

TEXAS
Sport Diver's
2402 Bay Area Blvd., Houston, TX 77058, 713/486-1844

WASHINGTON
Wilderness: Alaska/Mexico
Bissel Rd., Hunters, WA 99137, 509/722-6164

BRITISH COLUMBIA
**Strathcona Park Lodge and
Outdoor Education Center**
Cambell River, B.C. V9W 5C9, 604/N693546 or
604/286-3122

Photo: Vern Walker

SAILING SCHOOLS

CALIFORNIA
California Sailing Academy
14025 Panay Way, Marina Del Rey, CA 90291, 213/821-3433

HAWAII
Trek Hawaii
P.O. Box 1585, Kaneohe, HI 96744, 808/235-6614

FLORIDA
Watersport People
508 South Street, Key West, FL 33040, 305/296-4546

MAINE
Maine Waterways Camps
Deer Isle Sailing Center, Box 62, Deer Isle, ME 04627,
207/348-2339

MARYLAND
Annapolis Sailing School
P.O. Box 3334, Annapolis, MD 21403, 800/638-9192 or
301/267-7205

MINNESOTA
Sailboats Inc.
P.O. Box 412, Excelsior, MN 55331, 612/474-5156

NEW YORK
Cruise Away Sailing School, Inc.
P.O. Box 390, Drawer G, Mameroneck, NY 10543,
914/472-3894
Offshore Sailing School, Ltd.
East Schofield St., City Island, NY 10464, 800/221-4326 or
212/885-3200

Photo: Nicholson Yacht Charters

CHARTERS & CRUISES

ALASKA
Alaskan Wilderness Sailing Safaris
Box 701, Whittier, AK 99693, 907/338-2134
Northern Discoveries
200 W. 34th Ave. Suite 304, Anchorage, AK 99503,
907/272-5394
Outdoor Alaska
Box 7814, Ketchikan, AK 99901, 907/247-8444 or
225-6044 or 225-3498

CALIFORNIA
American River Touring Assoc.
445 High St., Oakland, CA 94601, 415/465-9355
Fraser Charters, Inc.
2353 Shelter Island Dr., San Diego, CA 92106, 741/225-0588
Nature Expeditions International
599 College Ave., Palo Alto, CA 94306, 415/494-6572
Ocean Voyages
1709 Bridgeway, Sausalito, CA 94965, 415/332-4681
Pacific Adventures
P.O. Box 5041, Riverside, CA 92517, 714/684-1227
Sierra Club Outings
530 Bush St., San Francisco, CA 94109
Sobek's International Explorers Society
Angels Camp, CA 95222, 209/736-4524

COLORADO
Adrift Adventures Ltd.
Box 577 Dept. J, Glenwood Springs, CO 81602, 303/945-2281
American Wilderness Alliance
4260 E. Evans Ave. #4, Denver, CO 80222, 303/758-5018
American Wilderness Experience
P.O. Box 1486, Boulder, CO 80306, 303/444-2632

CONNECTICUT
Russell Yacht Charter
2750 Black Rock Trnpk. #72, Fairfield, CT 06430, 203/372-6633

GEORGIA
Wilderness Southeast
9521 Whitfield Ave., Savannah, GA 31406, 912/355-8008
Windward Bound Bareboat Charters
1535 Snapfinger Rd., Dept 0, Decatur, GA 30032,
404/288-1259

HAWAII
Pacific Quest, Inc.
P.O. Box 205, Haleiwa, HI 96712, 808/638-8338

LOUISIANA
The Moorings, Ltd.
U.S. Agents, Box 24459, New Orleans, LA 70184,
800/535-7289 or 504/834-0785

MAINE
Glad Tidings Charters
Box 394, Oakland, ME 04963, 207/465-7372
Maine Windjammer Cruises, Inc.
Box 617, Camden, ME 04843, 207/236-2938

MARYLAND
Eastern Shore Yachts
P.O. Box 216, Oxford, MD 21654, 301/266-5571
Stevens Yacht of Annapolis, Inc.
P.O. Box 129, Stevensville, MD 21666, 800/638-7044

MASSACHUSETTS
Nicholson Yacht Charter
9A Chauncy St., Cambridge, MA 02138, 617/661-8174

MINNESOTA
Pigeon River Expeditions
Box 547 Hwy. 61, Hovland, MN 55606, 218/475-2359
Sailboats, Inc.
P.O. Box 412, Excelsior, MN 55331, 612/474-5156

NEW JERSEY
Caribbean Sailing Yachts, Ltd.
Box 491, Tenafly, NJ 07670, 800/631-1593 or 201/568-0390

VIRGIN ISLANDS
Blue Water Cruises
P.O. Box 758-A, St. Thomas, VI 00801, 800/524-2020
Trimarine Boat Co. Ltd.
Homeport, St. Thomas, VI 00801, 809/494-2490

WASHINGTON
Northwest Marine Charters, Inc.
2400 Westlake Ave., Suites 1 & 2, Box 10, Seattle, WA 98109,
206/283-3040

WYOMING
National Outdoor Leadership School
Box AA, Lander, WY 82520, 307/332-6973

CANADA
Strathcona Park Lodge and Outdoor Education Centre
Box 2160, Cambell River, B.C. V9W 5C9, 604/N693546 or
286-3122

Photo: Maine Windjammers

WINDJAMMING

ALASKA
Alaskan Wilderness Sailing Safaris
Box 701, Whittier, AK 99693, 907/338-2134

CALIFORNIA
American River Touring Assoc.
455 High St., Oakland, CA 94601, 415/465-9355
Ocean Voyages, Inc.
1709 Bridgeway, Sausalito, CA 94965, 415/332-4681
Pacific Adventures
P.O. Box 5041, Riverside, CA 92517, 714/684-1227
Sobek's International Explorers Society
Angels Camp, CA 95222, 209/736-4524

COLORADO
American Wilderness Experience, Inc.
P.O. Box 1486, Boulder, CO 80306, 303/444-2632

CONNECTICUT
Dirigo Cruises
39 Waterside Lane, Clinton, CT 06413, 203/669-7068

GEORGIA
Wilderness Southeast
9521 Whitefield Ave., Savannah, GA 31406, 912/355-8008

HAWAII
Pacific Quest, Inc.
P.O. Box 205, Haleiwa, HI 96712, 808/638-8338
Trek Hawaii
P.O. Box 1585, Kaneohe, HI 96744, 808/235-6614

MAINE
Coasting Schooner Heritage
Box 482, Rockland, ME 04841, 207/594-8007
Maine Windjammer Cruises, Inc.
P.O. Box 617-CA, Camden, ME 04843, 207/236-2938
Schooner Isaac H. Evans
Schooner J & E Riggin
Box 571, Rockland, ME 04841, 207/594-2923
Schooner Lewis R. French
Box 482, Rockland, ME 04841, 207/594-8007
Schooner Nathaniel Bowditch
Res. Dept., Harborside, ME 04642, 207/326-4822
Schooner Stephen Tabor
70 Elm St., Camden, ME 04843, 207/236-3520
Schooner Timberwind
P.O. Box 247, Rockport, ME 04856, 207/236-9063

Sylvina W. Beal Schooner Cruises
Box 509 N, Belfast, ME 04915, 207/548-2972
Yankee Schooner Cruises
Box 696, Camden, ME 04843, 207/236-4449
Yankee Packet Company
Box 736, Camden, ME 04843, 207/236-8873

MASSACHUSETTS
Nicholson Yacht Charters
9 Chauncy St., Cambridge, MA 02138, 617/661-8174

MINNESOTA
Pigeon River Expeditions
Box 547, Hwy 61, Hovland, MN 55606, 218/475-2359

NEW YORK
Appledore
P.O. Box 1414, Southhampton, NY 11968, 516/283-6041

VIRGIN ISLANDS
Kimberly Cruises
Box 5086, St. Thomas, VI 00801, 809/774-4811

CANADA
**Strathcona Park Lodge and
Outdoor Education Centre**
Box 2160, Cambell River, B.C. V9W 5C9, 604/N693546 or
604/286-3122
Whitewater Adventures, Ltd.
105 West 6th, Vancouver, B.C. V6B 1H7, 604/879-6701

Photo: Vern Walker

WINDSURFING

CALIFORNIA
Bay Windsurfing
853 G. Industrial Way, San Carlos, CA 94070, 415/595-2285
International Windsurfer Sailing Schools
Box 2950, Torrance, CA 90509, 213/515-4900

CONNECTICUT
Longshore Sailing School
Longshore Club Park, Westport, CT 06880, 203/226-4646

ILLINOIS
Viking Boardsailing School
3422 W. Fullerton Ave., Chicago, IL 60647, 312/276-1222

NEW YORK
Great South Bay Charters
5510 Merrick Rd., Massapequa, NY 11758, 516/799-5968

Photo: Del E. Webb

Photo: Whitewater, Inc.

HOUSEBOAT RENTALS

ARIZONA
Lake Powell Marinas
c/o Del Webb, Box 29040, Phoenix, AZ 85038,
800/528-6154 or 602/278-8888

CALIFORNIA
Herman and Helen's Marina
Venice Island Ferry, Stockton, CA 95209, 209/951-4634
Paradise Point Marina
8095 Rio Blanco Rd., Stockton, CA 95209, Attn: Bob Breese,
John Ohanesian, 209/952-1000

COLORADO
American Wilderness Experience, Inc.
P.O. Box 1486, Boulder, CO 80306, 303/444-2632

FLORIDA
Sebastian Houseboat Rentals
Indian River Dr., Sebastian, FL 32958; Attn: Raymond &
Ellen Workman, 305/589-7575
Shanty Boat Cruises
Rt. 29, Box 434-CT, Fort Meyers, FL 33905, Attn: Cap'n
Stan & Jenny, 813/694-3401
Sunshine Line Inc.
P.O. Box 3558, Holly Bluff Marina, Deland, FL 32720, Attn:
T. W. Adolph, 904/736-9422

NEW YORK
Reman Rentals, Inc.
510 Theresa St., Clayton, NY 13624, Attn: Robert V.
Lashomb, 315/686-3579

TENNESSEE
Dale Hollow Dock
Rt. 1, Box 94, Celina, TN 38551, Attn: Swan Stove,
615/243-2211

WISCONSIN
Upper Mississippi Cruises
1919 Rose St., La Crosse, WI 54601, Attn: Larry Disbrow &
Sue Chandler, 608/781-6800

RIVER RUNNING

ALASKA
Alaska Discovery
P.O. Box 26, Gustavus, AK 99826, 907/697-3431
Alaskan Back Country Guides Cooperative
P.O. Box 81533, College, AK 99701, 907/456-8907
**Alaskan River Touring Co., Inc. and
Yentna Station Roadhouse**
P.O. Box 1884, Anchorage, AK 99510, no telephone
Arctic Treks
Box 73452, Fairbanks, AK 99707, 907/455-6502
Brooks Range Wilderness Trips
Bettles Field, Bettles, AK 99726, 907/692-5312
Genet Expeditions
Talkeetna, AK 99676, 907/376-5120
Kachemak Bay Wilderness Lodge
Box 956, Homer, AK 99603, 907/235-8910
Nova Riverrunners of Alaska
P.O. Box 444, Eagle River, AK 99577, 907/694-3750
Sourdough Outfitters
Box 18, Bettles, AK 99726, 800/544-2203 or 907/692-5252

ARIZONA
Arizona Raft Adventures, Inc.
P.O. Box 697, Flagstaff, AZ 86002, 602/526-8200
Canyoneers, Inc.
P.O. Box 2997, Flagstaff, AZ 86003, 602/526-0924 or
800/525-0924
Del Webb River Adventures
Box 29040, Phoenix, AZ 85038, 800/528-6154 or
602/278-8888
Diamond River Adventures
P.O. Box 1316, Page, AZ 86040, 602/645-8866
Free Lance Expeditions
P.O. Box 1494, Wickenburg, AZ 85358, 602/684-3106
Grand Canyon Youth Expeditions/Expeditions Inc.
R.R. 4 Box 755, Flagstaff, AZ 86001, 602/774-8176 or
779-3769
Wild and Scenic Expeditions
P.O. Box 460, Flagstaff, AZ 86002, 800/841-7317 or
602/774-7343
Wilderness World
Box 310, Flagstaff, AZ 86002, 602/774-6468

CALIFORNIA
Action Adventures Wet n Wild, Inc.
Box 1500, Woodland, CA 95695, 916/662-5431

All-Outdoor Adventure Trips
2151 San Miguel Dr., Walnut Creek, CA 94596, 415/
932-8993 or 932-6334

American River Touring Association
445 High Street, Oakland, CA 94601, 415/465-9355

ECHO: The Wilderness Company
6529 Telegraph Ave., Oakland, CA 94609, 415/652-1600

Grand Canyon Dories
Box 3029, Stanford, CA 94305, 415/851-0411

**Henry & Grace Falany's White Water
River Expeditions, Inc.**
P.O. Box 1249-D, Turlock, CA 95381, 209/667-7714

Kern River Tours/Wild Wild West
P.O. Box 1884, 636 Mary Ann St., Ridgecrest, CA 83555
619/375-5598 Oct-Mar.: 714/375-5732

Libra Expeditions
11017 Seven Hills Drive, Tujunga, CA 91042, 213/353-7469

Mountain Travel, Inc.
1398 Solano Ave., Albany, CA 94706, 800/227-2384 or
415/527-8100

O.A.R.S., Inc.
P.O. Box 67-G, Angels Camp, CA 95222, 209/736-4677

Outdoor Adventures
3109 Fillmore St., San Francisco, CA 94123, 415/346-8700
or 213/688-1188

Outdoors Unlimited
P.O. Box 22513, Sacramento, CA 95822, 916/452-1081

Pacific Adventures
P.O. Box 5041, Riverside, CA 92517, 714/684-1227

Salmon River Outfitters
P.O. Box 307, Columbia, CA 95310, 209/532-2766

Sierra Club Outings
530 Bush St., San Francisco, CA 94109, 415/981-8634

Sobek's International Explorers
Angels Camp, CA 95222, 800/344-3284 or 209/736-4524

White Water Expeditions, Inc.
P.O. Box 1269, Mariposa, CA 95338, 209/742-6633

Wilderness Journeys
P.O. Box 807, Bolinas, CA 94924, 415/868-1836 or
415/525-6578

World of Whitewater
Box 708, Big Bar, CA 96010, 916/623-6588

Zephyr River Expeditions
P.O. Box 3607, Sonora, CA 95370, 209/532-6249

COLORADO

Adrift Adventures, Inc.
P.O. Box 577, Glenwood Springs, CO 81601, 303/945-2281

Adventure Bound, Inc
122 S. 8th St., Grand Junction, CO 81501, 800/525-7084,
303/245-0024

American Wilderness Alliance
4260 E. Evans Ave. #3, Denver, Co 80222, 303/758-5018

American Wilderness Experience, Inc.
P.O. Box 1486, Boulder, CO 80306, 303/444-2632

Colorado Outward Bound School
945 Pennsylvania, Denver, CO 80203-3118, 303/837-0880 x22

Echo Canyon River Expeditions
P.O. Box 1002, Colorado Springs, CO 80901, 303/632-3684

Four Corners Expeditions
P.O. Box 1032, Buena Vista, CO 81211, 303/395-8949

Outdoor Leadership Training Seminars
P.O. Box 337, Cotopaxi, CO 81223, 303/942-4362

Partners River Program
1260 W. Bayaud, Denver, CO 80223, 303/777-7000

Range Tours
1540 S. Holly, Denver, CO 80222, 303/759-1988

Roaring Fork River Company
6805D East Arizona, Denver, CO 80224, 303/759-9599

Rocky Mountain River Expeditions
1260 S. Inca, Denver, CO 80223, 303/698-0058

Roughriders Unlimited, Inc.
314 Charles Street Square, Buena Vista, CO 81211,
303/395-6988

Ultimate Escapes, Ltd.
2605 W. Colorado Ave., Colorado Springs, CO 80904,
303/578-8383

Viking River Experience
P.O. Box 383, Greeley, CO 80632, 303/737-2930

Wilderness Aware
5104 Greenview Court, Ft. Collins, CO 80525, 303/223-8924

GEORGIA

Southeastern Expeditions, Inc.
1955 Cliff Valley Way N.E., Suite 220-B, Atlanta, GA 30329,
404/329-0433

IDAHO

Frontier Expeditions, Inc.
Box 839, Dept. 201, North Fork, ID 83466, 208/865-2200
Sept.-May: 877 Eagle Hills Way, Eagle, ID 83616,
208/939-7110

Happy Hollow Camps
Star Rt. Box 14-A, Salmon, ID 83467, 208/756-3954

High Adventure River Tours, Inc.
Box 1434, Twin Falls, ID 83301, 208/324-1191

Idaho Adventures, Inc.
P.O. Box 834, Salmon, ID 83467, 208/756-2986

Mackay Bar—Idaho's Wilderness Co.
3190 Airport Way, Boise, ID 83705, 800/635-5336 or
208/344-1881

Middle Fork Rapid Transit
P.O. Box 285, Twin Falls, ID 83301, 208/734-2260

Middle Fork River Co.
P.O. Box 233-A, 220 Lewis St., Sun Valley, ID 83353

Middle Fork River Expeditions
Box 199, Stanley, ID 83278, 208/774-3659; Sept.-May:
1615 21st E., Seattle, WA 98112, 206/324-0364

Northwest Voyagers, Ltd.
Box 1734, McCall, ID 83638, 208/634-2274

Rocky Mountain River Tours, Inc.
P.O. Box 126, Hailey, ID 83333, 208/788-9300

Salmon River Adventures
400 North St. Charles, Salmon, ID 83467, 208/756-3556

Salmon River Challenge
Salmon River Route, Riggins, ID 83549, 208/628-3264

Teton Expeditions, Inc.
P.O. Box 218, Rigby, ID 83442, 208/523-4981 or 745-6476

Wilderness River Outfitters
P.O. Box 871, Salmon, ID 83467, 208/756-3959

MAINE

Eastern River Expeditions
Box 1173, Greenville, ME 04441, 207/695-2411

Maine Whitewater, Inc.
Suite 454, Bingham, ME 04920, 207/672-4814
Oct.-May: 207/622-2260

North Country Outfitters
Moosehead Lake, Rockwood, ME 04478, 207/534-2242

Northern Whitewater Expeditions
P.O. Box 100, The Forks, ME 04985, 207/663-2271

Rolling Thunder River Co.
P.O. Box 291-A, Kingfield, ME 04947, 207/628-2121

Unicorn Rafting Expeditions, Inc.
Box 50, The Forks, ME 04985, 207/663-2258

MONTANA
Double Arrow Outfitters
Drawer E, Seeley Lake, MT 59868, 406/677-2204 or 2411 or 2317
Glacier Raft Company
P.O. Box 264, West Glacier, MT 59936, 406/888-5541
Great Adventures West, Inc.
820 Central Ave., Great Falls, MT 59401, 406/761-1677
Missouri River Outfitters
Box 1212-A, Fort Benton, MT 59442, 406/622-3295

NEVADA
Fastwater Expeditions
Box 365-A, Boulder City, NV 89005, 702/293-1406
Georgies Royal River Rats
P.O. Box 12057, Las Vegas, NV 89112, 702/451-5588

NEW HAMPSHIRE
Downeast Rafting Co., Inc.
c/o Saco Bound, Box 113, Rt. 302, Center Conway, NH 03813, 603/447-3002

NEW MEXICO
Southwest Wilderness Center
P.O. Box 2840, Santa Fe, NM 87501, 505/982-3126

NEW YORK
Adirondack Wildwater, Inc.
Box 801, Corinth, NY 12822, 518/654-2640
Bob Lander's Delaware River Raft Trips
RD-2, Dept. A, Narrowsburg, NY 12764, 914/252-3925

NORTH CAROLINA
Nantahala Outdoor Center
U.S. 19 West, Box 41, Bryson City, NC 28713, 704/488-2175

OHIO
Missoula Bicycle Club
P.O. Box 23111, Columbus, OH 43223, 614/461-6648

OREGON
Cascade Whitewater Adventure
P.O. Box 1511, Eugene, OR 97440, 503/345-5536
Don Merrell's Northwest Whitewater Expedition
P.O. Box 3765, Portland, OR 97208, 503/236-9706
Eclipse Expeditions, Inc.
Rt. 1, Cove, OR 97824, 503/568-4663 or 252-6413
Hells Canyon Navigation
P.O. Box 159-A, Oxbow, OR 97840, 503/785-3352
Lute Jerstad Adventures, LJA, Inc.
P.O. Box 19537, Portland, OR 97219, 503/244-4364, Telex: 36-0484 Wilderness PTL
Orange Torpedo, Inc.
P.O. Box 1111, Grants Pass, OR 97526, 503/479-5061
Ray Bakers Whitewater Guide Service
P.O. Box 5586, Eugene, OR 97405, 503/343-7514
River Trips Unlimited
900 Murphy Rd., Medford, OR 97501, 503/779-3798
Rogue Excursions Unlimited, Inc.
P.O. Box 855, Medford, OR 97501, 503/773-5983
Rogue River Raft Trips
8500 Galice Rd., Merlin, OR 97532, 503/476-3825
Sundance Expeditions, Inc.
14894 Galice Rd., Merlin, OR 97532, 503/479-8508

Sunrise Scenic Tours
3791 Rogue River Hwy., Gold Hill, OR 97525, 503/582-0202
Walker River Expeditions
Rt. 1, Enterprise, OR 97828, 503/426-3307

PENNSYLVANIA
Pocono Whitewater Rafting
Rt. 903, Jim Thorpe 43, PA 18229, 717/325-3656
White Water Adventures
Box 31-A, Ohiopyle, PA 15470, 412/329-8850 or 5986
Whitewater Challengers, Inc.
Star Rt. #6A1, White Haven, PA 18661, 717/443-9532
Wilderness Voyagers, Inc.
P.O. Box 97, Ohiopyle, PA 15470, 412/329-4752 or 329-5517

SOUTH CAROLINA
Wildwater, Ltd.
Dept. A, Long Creek, SC 29658, 803/647-5336

TENNESSEE
Nolichucky Expeditions, Inc.
P.O. Box 460, Erwin, TN 37650, 615/743-3221
Sunburst Wilderness Adventure
P.O. Box 329A, Benton, TN 37307, 615/338-8388

TEXAS
Far Flung Adventures
Box 311, Terlingua, TX 79852, 915/371-2489
Outback Expeditions
P.O. Box 44, Terlingua, TX 79852, 915/371-2490
Texas Canoe Trails, Inc.
121 River Terrace, New Braunfels, TX 78130, 512/625-3375

UTAH
Adventure River Expeditions, Inc.
P.O. Box 96, Green River, UT 84525, 801/564-3648
Don Hatch River Expeditions
Dept. B, Box C. Vernal, UT 84078, ofc 801/789-4316, hm 801/789-4715
Grand Canyon Expeditions
P.O. Box O, Kanab, UT 84741, 801/644-2691
Holiday River Expeditions
519 Malibu Dr., Salt Lake City, UT 84107, 801/266-2087
Mark P. Sleight Expeditions, Inc.
P.O. Box 118, LaVerkin, UT 84745, 801/635-2177
Moki Mac River Expeditions, Inc.
P.O. Box 21242, Salt Lake City, UT 84121, 801/943-6702
Sierra Western River Guides
P.O. Box 7129, University Station, Provo, UT 84602, 800/453-1482 or 801/377-9750
Tag-A-Long Tours
P.O. Box 1206, 452 N. Main St., Moab, UT 84532, 800/453-3292 or 801/259-8946
Western River Expeditions, Inc.
7258 Racquet Club Dr., Salt Lake City, UT 84121, 800/453-7450 or 801/942-6669
Western River Guides Association, Inc.
994 Denver St., Salt Lake City, UT 84111, 801/355-3388

WASHINGTON
Liberty Bell Alpine Tours
Star Rt., Mazama, WA 98833, 509/996-2250
Pacific Northwest Float Trips
P.O. Box 287, Burlington, WA 98233, 206/855-0535
Wilderness: Alaska/Mexico
Bissel Rd., Hunters, WA 99137, 509/722-6164

WEST VIRGINIA

Appalachian Wildwaters, Inc.
P.O. Box 126, Albright, WV 26537, 800/624-8060 or
304/329-1665

Blue Ridge Outfitters
P.O. Box 456 Rt. 340, Harpers Ferry, WV 25425,
304/724-3444

Cheat River Outfitters
Box 196, Albright, WV 26519, 304/392-9816; July-Feb.:
301/461-2554

Class VI River Runners, Inc.
P.O. Box 78, Lansing, WV 25862, 304/574-0704

Mountain River Tours, Inc.
P.O. Box 88CA, Hico, WV 25854, 304/658-5817

North American River Runners, Inc.
P.O. Box 81, Hico, WV 25854, 304/658-5276

Passages to Adventure, Inc.
Box 71, Fayetteville, WV 25840, 304/658-4219

Wildwater Expeditions Unlimited, Inc.
1 Riverfront St., Thurmond, WV 25936, 304/469-2551

WISCONSIN

River Forest Rafts
St. Rt., White Lake, WI 54491, 715/882-3351

Whitewater Specialty
P.O. Box 157, Whitelake, WI 54491

WYOMING

Barker-Ewing, Inc.
Box 1243, Jackson, WY 83001, 307/733-3410

Dave Hansen Whitewater
Box 328, Jackson, WY 83001, 307/733-3273 or 6295

Fort Jackson Float Trips
310 West Broadway, Jackson, WY 83001, 307/733-2583

Grand Teton Lodge Co.
P.O. Box 250, Moran, WY 83013, 307/543-2811

Heart Six Guest Ranch
Box 70, Moran, WY 83013, 307/543-2477 or 733-7742

High Adventure Float Trips
P.O. Box 625, Jackson, WY 83001, 307/733-6886

Lewis and Clark Expeditions
Box 720, Jackson, WY 83001, 307/733-4022 or 6858

Mad River Boat Trips, Inc.
P.O. Box 2222-A, 60 E. Broadway, Jackson, WY 83001,
307/733-6203

National Park Float Trip
P.O. Box 411, Jackson, WY 83001, 307/733-6445

Old West Tour, Inc.
P.O. Box 3322, Jackson, WY 83001, 307/733-7131

Osprey Float Trips
Triangle X Ranch, Box 120, Moose, WY 83012, 307/733-5500

Parkland Expeditions
Box 3055, Jackson, WY 83001, 307/733-3379; Oct.-May:
930 Nobs Hill Rd., Redwood City, CA 94601, 415/366-8246

Sands Float Trips
P.O. Box 848, Wilson, WY 83014, 307/733-4410 or
543-2545

Signal Mountain Lodge
Moran, WY 83013, 307/543-2831

Snake River Park Float Trips
Star Rt. 14A, Jackson, WY 83001, 307/733-7078

Solitude Float Trips
Box 112, Moose, WY 83012, 307/733-2871 or 543-2522

CANADA

Iskut Trail and River Adventures
1103-207 W. Hastings St., Vancouver, B.C. V6B 1H7

North Country River Trips
Berens River, Man R0B 0A0, 204/382-2284 or 2379

Quebec Whitewater World
Box 148, Calumet, P.Q. J0V 1B0, 819/242-6084

Whitewater Adventures, Ltd.
105 West 6th, Vancouver, B.C., 604/879-6701

Wilderness Tours
Box 89, Beachburg, Ont. K0T 1C0, 613/582-3351

Photo: Colorado Daily

CANOES & KAYAKS

ALASKA

Alaska Discovery
P.O. Box 26, Gustavus, AK 99826, 907/697-3431

Alaska Travel
200 N. Franklin St., Juneau, AK 99801, 907/586-6245

Alaskan Back Country Guides Cooperative
P.O. Box 81533, College, AK 99701, 907/456-8907

Brooks Range Wilderness Trips
Bettles Field, Bettles, AK 99726, 907/692-5312

Genet Expeditions
Talkeetna, AK 99676, 907/376-5120

Katmailand, Inc.
455 H. Street, Anchorage, AK 99501, 907/277-4314

Northern Discoveries
200 W. 34th Suite 304, Anchorage, AK 99503, 907/272-5394

Outdoor Alaska
Box 7814, Ketchikan, AK 99901, 907/225-6044 or 225-8444

Sourdough Outfitters
Box 18, Bettles, AK 99726, Attn: David Ketscher, 800/544-2203
907/692-5252

ARIZONA

Arizona Raft Adventures
P.O. Box 697, Flagstaff, AZ 86002, 602/526-8200

Wild and Scenic Expeditions
P.O. Box 460, Flagstaff, AZ 86002, 800/841-7317 or
602/774-7343

ARKANSAS

Barnes Buffalo River Canoe Service
Rt. A, Yellville, AR 72687, Attn: Bill Fagen, 501/449-6235
(Nov.-Feb.: 501/449-6064)

CALIFORNIA

California Rivers
P.O. Box 468, 21001 Geyserville, CA 95441, Attn: Ann Dwyer,
707/857-3872

Mountain Travel, Inc.
1398 Solans Ave., Albany, CA 94706, 800/227-2384,
   415/527-8100

National Outdoor College
Box 962A, Fair Oaks, CA 95628, 916/338-3600

Otter Bar Lodge
Forks of Salmon, CA 96031, 707/442-7312

Pacific Adventures
P.O. Box 5041, Riverside, CA 92517, 714/684-1227

Salmon River Outfitters
P.O. Box 307, Columbia, CA 95310, 209/532-2766

Sierra Club Outings
530 Bush Street, San Francisco, CA 94109, 415/981-8634

Sierra Nevada Ski Adventures
P.O. Box 1751, Bishop, CA 93514, 619/935-4325

Sobek's International Explorers Society
Angels Camp, CA 95222, 209/736-4524

Wilderness Journey
P.O. Box 807, Bolinas, CA 94924, 415/868-1836 or
   415/525-6578

World of Whitewater
Box 703, Big Bar, CA 96010, Attn: O.K. & Glenna Goodwin,
   916/623-6588

Zephyr River Expeditions
P.O. Box 3607, Sonora, CA 95370, Attn: Robert Ferguson,
   209/532-6249

COLORADO

American Wilderness Alliance
4260 East Evans Ave. #3, Denver, CO 80222, 303/758-5018

American Wilderness Experience, Inc.
P.O. Box 1486, Boulder, CO 80306, 303/444-2632

Aspen Kayak School
P.O. Box 1520A, Aspen, CO 81011, 303/925-4433

Boulder Kayak School
P.O. Box 3155, Boulder, CO 80307, 303/494-2061

Boulder Whitewater Supply
2510 N. 47th St., Boulder, CO 80301, 303/444-8420

Escalante Canyon Outfitters Deer Creek Ranch
Box 325, Boulder, CO 84716, No Telephone

Four Corners Marine
Box 379, Durango, CO 81301, 303/259-3893

Partners River Program
12460 W. Bayaud, Denver, CO 80223, 303/777-7000

Quetico Canoe Adventures, Inc.
194 S. Franklin St., Denver, CO 80209, Attn: Brooke & Eric
   Durland, 303/722-6482

Ultimate Escapes, Ltd.
2506 W. Colorado Ave., Colorado Springs, CO 80904,
   303/578-8383

White Water Canoe Co., Inc.
2675 65th Ave., Greeley, CO 80634, Attn: Bernie Kendall, Jim
   Barrington, 303/330-7124 or 686-7816

Wind River Mountain Guides
6678 S. Arapahoe Dr., Littleton, CO 80120, 303/794-9518

FLORIDA

Everglades Canoe Outfitters, Inc.
39801 Ingraham Hwy., C-6, Homestead, FL 33034,
   305/246-1530

Everglades Canoe Trips
7241 S.W. 57th Ct., South Miami, FL 33143, 305/665-7832

Florida Trail Assoc., Inc.
P.O. Box 13708, Gainesville, FL 32604, Attn: Margaret Scruggs,
   904/378-8823

Mangrove Wilderness Outfitters, Inc.
17241 S.W. 57th Ct., S. Miami, FL 33143, 305/665-7832

Suwannee Country Tours
Box 247A, White Springs, FL 32096, 904/397-2347

GEORGIA

High Country Inc.
6300 Powers Ferry Rd., Atlanta, GA 30339, 404/955-1866

Wilderness Southwest
9521 Whitfield Ave., Savannah, GA 31406, Dick Murlless,
   912/355-8008

IDAHO

Salmon River Challenge
Salmon River Route, Riggins, ID 83549, 208/628-3264

IOWA

American Outdoor Learning Center
Box 150 Maywood, Milford, IA 51351, 712/262-5630

LOUISIANA

Natchez Canoe Park
1729 Filmore St., Morgan City, LA 70380, Attn: Albert G. Sens,
   504/384-1725; 601/262-7573

MAINE

Allagash Canoe Trips
P.O. Box 713, Greenville, ME 04441, Attn: Warren & Beverly
   Cochrave, 207/695-3668

Allagash Wilderness Outfitters
Frost Pond, Star Route 76-A, Greenville, ME 04441, Attn:
   Rick Givens, 207/695-2821
Dec.-April: 36-A Minuteman Dr., Millinocket, ME 04462,
   207/723-6622

Chewonki Foundation
RFD 3, Wiscasset, ME 04578, Attn: Tim Ellis, 207/882-7323

East/West Wilderness School
Box 611, Bethel, ME 04217, 207/875-5255

Eastern River Expeditions
Box 1173, Greenville, ME 04441, Attn: John M. Connelly III
   207/695-2411

Maine Wilderness Canoe Basin
Springfield, ME 04487, Attn: Carl W. Selin, 207/989-3636
   Ext. 631; Sept.-June: Box 62, Deer Isle, ME 04627,
   207/348-2339

North County Outfitters
Moosehead Lake, Rockwood, ME 04478, 207/534-2242

Northern Outdoors, Inc.
P.O. Box 100, The Forks, ME 04985, 207/663-2271

Northern Rivers
Box 326, Orono, ME 04473, 207/866-4341

Northern Whitewater Expeditions, Inc.
Box 100, The Forks, ME 04985, 207/663-2271 or 663-2249

Sunrise Country Canoe Expeditions, Inc.
Cathance Lake, Grove Post, ME 04638, Attn: Martin Brown,
   207/454-7708

Taiga Outfitters
Box 312, Ashland, ME 04732, 207/435-6851

MASSACHUSETTS

Riverrun North
Rt. 7, Sheffield, MA 01257, Attn: John F. Pogue, 413/528-1100

MICHIGAN

Keweenaw Waterway Resort
Rt. 1, Box 241, Houghton, MI 49931, Attn: Bruce A. Barna,
   906/482-1109

MINNESOTA

Anderson's Canoe Outfitters
Box 74, Crave Lake, MN 55725, Attn: Bob Anderson

Bear Track Outfitting Co.
Box 51, Grand Marais, MN 55604, Attn: David & Cathi Williams,
218/387-1162
Bill Rom's Canoe Country Outfitters, Inc.
Box 30, Ely, MN 55731, Attn: Bob Olson, 218/365-4046
Bill Zup's Fishing Lodge
Crane Lake, MN 55725, 807/599-2710 (Jan.-May: Ely,
MN 55731, 218/365-4018)
Border Lakes Outfitters
P.O. Box 8, Winton, MN 55796, Attn: Jack Niemi, 218/365-3783
Gunflint Northwoods Outfitters
Box 100GT, Grand Marais, MN 55604, Attn: Bruce & Sue Kerfoot,
218/388-2296
Pigeon River Expeditions
P.O. Box 547, Hovland, MN 55606, Attn: H. F. Drabik,
218/475-2359
Quetico-Superior Canoe Outfitters
Box 80, Ely, MN 55731, Attn: Bernice Carlson, 218/365-5480
Superior-North Canoe Outfitters
Box 141GT, Grand Marais, MN 55604, Attn: Jerry Mark
Tip of the Trail
Box 147, Grand Marais, MN 55604, 218/388-2225
Tom & Woods Moose Lake Wilderness Canoe Trips
Box 358, Ely, MN 55731, Attn: Woods Davis, 218/365-5837
Tuscarora Canoe Outfitters
Gunflint Trail Box 110, Grand Marais, MN 55604, 218/388-2221

MISSOURI
Akers Ferry Canoe Rental
Cedar Grove Rt., Salem, MO 65560, Attn: G. E. Maggard,
314/858-3224 or 858-3228
Big M. Resort
R. 7, Licking, MO 65542, Attn: Daniel & Alicia Kuhn,
314/674-3488
The Last Resort
Rt. 1, Box 115, Duke, MO 65461, Attn: Richard Sphar,
314/435-6669
Wild River Canoe Rental
Gladden Star Rt., Box 60, Salem, MO 65560, Attn: Jack Patton,
314/858-3230

MONTANA
Great Adventures West Inc.
820 Central Ave., Great Falls, MT 59401, 406/761-1677
Missouri River Outfitters
Box 1212 A, Fort Benton, MT 59442, Attn: Bob Singer,
406/622-3295
Sunburst Adventures
3038 Candy Lane, Bozeman, MT 59715, 406/586-3212

NEBRASKA
Adventures Unlimited
903 Mercer Blvd., Omaha, NE 68131, 402/558-0210

NEVADA
Fastwater Expeditions
Box 365, Boulder, City, NV 89005, 702/293-1406

NEW HAMPSHIRE
Appalachian Mountain Club
Box 298, Gorham, NH 03581, 603/466-2721
Saco Bound/Northern Waters
Box 113, Center Conway, NH 03813, Attn: Ned McSherry,
603/447-2177

NEW MEXICO
Vision Quest
P.O. Box 9109, Santa Fe, NM 87504, 505/473-3106

NEW YORK
Bob Lander's Delaware River Canoe Trips
RD 2, Narrowsburg, NY 12764, Attn: Bob Lander, 914/252-3925
Jerry's Three River Canoe Corp.
P.O. Box 7, Pond Eddy, NY 12270, Attn: Jerry Lovelace,
914/557-6078
Jon Ross Guiding
5 River Rd., New Paltz, NY 12561, 914/658-9811

NORTH CAROLINA
Nantahala Outdoor Center
U.S. 19 West, Box 41, Bryson City, NC 28713, 704/488-2175
North Carolina Outward Bound
121 N. Sterling St., Morganton, NC 28655, 704/437-6112

OHIO
Loudonville Canoe Livery
424 W. Main St., Loudonville, OH 44842, Attn:
Dick Schafrath, 419/994-4161
Missoula Bicycle Club
P.O. Box 23111, Columbus, OH 43223, 614/461-6648

OREGON
Eclipse Expeditions, Inc.
Rt. 1, Cove, OR 97824, 503/568-4663 or 252-6413
Get Wet River Trips
P.O. Box 698, Ashland, OR 97520, 503/482-1254
Northwest Waters
P.O. Box 212, Portland, OR 97207, 503/242-0838
Orange Torpedo Trips, Inc.
P.O. Box 1111, Grants Pass, OR 97526, 503/479-5061
Sundance Expeditions, Inc.
14894 Galice Rd., Merlin, OR 97532, Attn: Judo Patterson,
503/479-8508
Sunrise Scenic Tours
3791 Rogue River Hwy., Gold Hill, OR 97525, Attn: Ted &
Sheri Birdseye, 503/582-0202

PENNSYLVANIA
Kittatinny Canoes
Dept. AT, Dingmans Ferry, PA 18328, Attn: Frank & Ruth Jones,
717/828-2700 or 828-2338
Point Pleasant Canoe Outfitters
P.O. Box 6, Point Pleasant, PA 18950, Attn: Tom A. McBrien,
215/297-8400 or 297-8949

TENNESSEE
Nolichucky Expeditions
P.O. Box 484 N, Erwin, TN 37650, 615/743-3221, 743-5400

TEXAS
Far Flung Adventures
Box 31, Terlingua, TX 79852, 915/371-2489
Outback Expeditions
P.O. Box 44, Terlingua, TX 79852, Attn: Larry G. Humphreys,
915/371-2490
Texas Canoe Trails, Inc.
121 River Terrace, New Braunfels, TX 78130, 512/625-3375

UTAH
Holiday River Expeditions
519 Malibu Dr., Salt Lake City, UT 84107, 801/266-2087
Slickrock Kayaks
P.O. Box 1400, Moab, UT 84532, Attn: Cully Erdman
Tag-A-Long Tours
P.O. Box 1206/452 N. Main, Moab, UT 84532, 801/259-8946 or
800/453-3292

VIRGINIA
Downriver Canoe Co.
Rt. 1, Box 256-A, Bentonville, VA 22610, Attn: John Gibson
703/635-5526

Shenandoah River Outfitters
RFD 3, Luray, VA 22835, Attn: Joe Sottosanti, 703/743-4159

WASHINGTON
Liberty Bell Alpine Tours
Mazama, WA 98833, Attn: Erick Sanford, 509/996-2250

Wilderness: Alaska/Mexico
Bissel Rd., Hunters, WA 99137, 509/772-6164

WEST VIRGINIA
Appalachian Wildwaters, Inc.
P.O. Box 126, Albright, WV 26537, 800/624-8060 or
304/329-1665

Blue Ridge Outfitters
P.O. Box 456, Rt. 340, Harpers Ferry, WV 25425, Attn: Bill Rolle,
304/725-3444

Class VI River Runners, Inc.
P.O. Box 78, Lansing, WV 25862, 304/574-0704

WISCONSIN
Whitewater Specialty
Box 157, White Lake, WI 54491, 715/882-5400

CANADA
Algonquin Outfitters
RR 1A, Dwight, Ont. P0A 1H0, 705/635-2243

Arctic Edge Canoe Expedition Outfitting
Box 4896, Whitehorse, Yukon Y1A 4N6, 403/633-2443

Canoe Arctic, Inc.
Box 130A, Fort Smith,ᐧ Northwest Territories, Canada X0E 0P0

Canoe Canada Outfitters
P.O. Box 1810-A, Atikokan, Ontario P0T 1C0, Attn: Bud Dickson
or Jim Clark, 807/597-6418

Caribou Wilderness Canoe Outfitters
Box 1390, Atikokan, Ont. P0T LC0, Attn: JoAnne or Bob
Bigwood, 807/597-6888

Ecosummer Canada
Dept. O, 1516 Duranlean St., Vancouver, B.C. V6H 3S4,
604/669-7741

Madawaska Kanu Camp
Box 635, Barry's Bay, Ont. K0J 1B0, 613/756-3620

Nordick Ski Institute
Box 1050, Cannoe, Alberta T0L 0M0, 403/678-4102

Ottawa River Whitewater Rafting Ltd.
(Whitewater Rafting—Kayak and Canoe School), Box 179,
Beachburg, Ont. K0J 1C0, 613/646-2501

**Strathcona Park Lodge and Outdoor
Education Center**
Box 2160, Cambell River, B.C. V9W 5C9, 604/N693546 or
286-3122

Wanapite:
Box A, 7 Engleburn Pl., Peterborough, Ont. K9H 1C4,
705/743-3774

Wild Waters
R.R. 13, Lakeshore Drive, Thunder Bay, Ont. P7B 5E4, Attn:
Bruce T. Hyer, 807/683-3151

Photo: Colorado Daily

FLYFISHING

ALASKA
Alaska Travel Adventures
200 N. Franklin St., Juneau, AK 99801

Alaskan Hospitality: Quiet
Hornberger, Box 69A, Iliamma, AK 99606

Stephan Lake Lodge
Jim Bailey, P.O. Box 695, Eagle River, AK 99577,
907/688-2163

COLORADO
American Wilderness Alliance
4260 E. Evans Ave. #3, Denver, CO 80222, 303/758-5018

Lichen Guest Ranch
Box C, Kremmling, CO 80459, 303/724-3450

MAINE
L. L. Bean Fly Fishing Schools
924 Main St., Freeport, ME 04033, 207/865-4761

MONTANA
Absaroka Outfitters
P.O. Box AM, Clyde Park, MT 59018, 406/686-4732

Beartooth Wilderness Expeditions
High Country Expeditions, Nye, MT 59061, 406/328-8429

Yellowstone Angler
124 N. Main St., Livingston, MT 59047, 406/222-7130

WYOMING
Coy Wilderness Outfitting
P.O. Box 393, Lander, WY 82520, 307/332-5539

Valley Ranch
Valley Ranch Rd., Cody, WY 82414, 307/587-4661

Photo: Jerry Cleveland

COVERED WAGON TRIPS

ARIZONA
Honeymoon Trail Inc.
Box A, Moccasin, AZ 86022, 602/643-5584

KANSAS
Flint Hills Overland Wagon Trips, Inc.
Box 1076, El Dorado, KS 67042, 316/321-6300
Wagons Ho
Box 75-A, Main St., Quinter, KS 67752, 913/754-3347;

NEBRASKA
Oregon Trail Wagon Train
Rt. 2 Box 200-B, Bayard, NE 69334, 308/586-1850

NORTH DAKOTA
Fort Seward Wagon Train
Box 244, Jamestown, ND 58401, 701/252-6844

WYOMING
Bar-T-Five Outfitters
P.O. Box 2140S, Jackson, WY 83001, 307/733-5386
Wagons West
L. D. Frome, Outfitters, Box G, Afton, WY 83110,
   307/886-5240

Photo: River Runners

JEEP EXPEDITIONS

ARIZONA
Wild and Scenic Expeditions
P.O. Box 460, Flagstaff, AZ 86002, 800/841-7317 or
   602/774-7343

CALIFORNIA
American River Touring Association
445 High Street, Oakland, CA 97601, 415/465-9355
Sierra Club Outings
530 Bush, San Francisco, CA 94109, 415/981-8634
Sobek's International Explorers
Angels Camp, CA 95222, 209/736-4524
White Water River Expeditions
P.O. Box 1269, Mariposa, CA 95338, 209/742-6633

COLORADO
Canyon Ranch
Rt. 1, Box 61-A, Olathe, CO 81425, 303/323-5288
Ghost Town Jeep Tours
11150 U.S. Hwy 50, Salida, CO 81201, 303/539-2144
The Mountain Men
11100 East Dartmouth 219, Denver, CO 80014, 303/750-0090
Vail Jeep Guides
1000 Lionshead Loop, Vail, CO 81657, 303/476-5387

FLORIDA
Everglades Canoe Outfitters, Inc.
39801 Ingraham Hwy, Homestead, FL 33034, 305/246-1530

UTAH
Lin Ottinger Tours
137 North Main St., Moab, UT 84532, 801/259-7312
Tag-A-Long Tours
P.O. Box 1206, 425 N. Main St., Moab, UT 84532,
   800/453-3292 or 801/259-8946

WYOMING
Old West Tours, Inc.
P.O. Box 3322, Jackson, WY 83001, 307/733-7131

Photo: Tom Bishop

GOLD PROSPECTING

CALIFORNIA
Gold Prospecting Expeditions
P.O. Box 974, Jamestown, CA 95327, 209/984-4162

Photo: Doug Conarroe

BUSH FLYING

ALASKA
Alaska Travel Adventures
200 N. Franklin St., Juneau, AK 99801, 907/586-6245
Katmailand, Inc.
455 H. Street, Anchorage, AK 99501, 907/277-4314
Northern Discoveries
200 W. 34th Suite 304, Anchorage, AK 99503, 907/272-5394
Prism Ski Touring
Box 136, Githwood, AK 99587, 907/783-2945
Sourdough Outfitters
Box 18, Bettles, AK 99726, 907/692-5252

FLORIDA
Hanns Ebensten Travel, Inc.
513 Fleming Street, Key West, FL 33040, 305/294-8174

NEW MEXICO
Southwest Safaris
Box 945, Santa Fe, NM 87504

Photo: Joseph Daniel

PARACHUTING

CALIFORNIA
Adventure Aloft Travel
14526 Sherman Way #1023, Van Nuys, CA 91405,
213/785-0396
Perris Valley Parachute Center
2091 Goetz Rd., Perris, CA 92370, 714/657-3904 or
657-8727

FLORIDA
Deland Sport Parachute Center, Inc.
1360 Flightline Blvd., Deland, FL 32720, 904/736-3141
Paragaters, Inc.
Star Rt. Box 462, Eustis, FL 32726, 904/357-7800
Zephyrhills Parachute Center, Inc.
P.O. Box 1101, Zephyrhills, FL 33599, 813/788-5591

HAWAII
Paradise Paracenter
P.O. Box 700, Haleiwa, HI 96712, 808/637-4677 or 4942

ILLINOIS
Skydiver Sandwich
Rt. 34, Sandwich, IL 60548, 815/786-8200 or 9988

INDIANA
Parachute and Associates, Inc.
State Rd. 28 W., Frankfort, IN 46041, 317/654-6188

KENTUCKY
Green County Sport Parachute Center of Kentucky
Rt. 2, Box 140, Bardstown, KY 40004, 502/348-9981 or 9531

MASSACHUSETTS
Orange Parachuting Center
P.O. Box 96, Orange, MA 01364, 617/544-6911

NEW JERSEY
Lakewood Skydiving Center
Cedar Bridge Ave., P.O. Box 517, Lakewood, N.J., 08701,
201/367-8264

NEW YORK
Albany Skydiving Center
P.O. Box 131, Duanesburg, NY 12056, 518/895-8140

NORTH DAKOTA
Valley Parachuting Inc.
630 7th St. W, West Fargo, ND 58078, 701/282-5072

PENNSYLVANIA
Southern Cross Parachute Center
3506 Airport Rd., Chambersburg, PA 17201, 717/264-1111

WASHINGTON
Issaquah Parachute Center
2617 271st S.E., Issaquah, WA 98027, 206/392-2121

TEXAS
Skydivers of Texas Inc.
2553 Valley View Lane, Dallas, TX 75234, 214/484-1234

Photo: Joseph Daniel

SOARING

ARIZONA
Arizona Soaring, Inc.
P.O. Box 27427, Tempe, AZ 85282, 602/568-2318

CALIFORNIA
Adventure Aloft Travel
14526 Sherman Way #1023, Van Nuys, CA 91405,
  213/785-0393
Calistoga Soaring Center
1546 Lincoln Ave., Calistoga, CA 94515, 707/942-5592
Pacific Adventures
P.O. Box 5041, Riverside, CA 92517, 714/684-1227
Sailplane Enterprise
P.O. Box 1678, Hemet, CA 92343, 714/658-6577
Skylark North Gliderport
P.O. Box 918, Tehachapi, CA 93561, 805/822-5267

COLORADO
Black Forest Gliderport
9990 Gliderport Rd., Colorado Springs, CO 80908,
  303/495-4144
Shadow Mountain Soaring
Box 485, Granby, CO 80446, 303/530-2208
The Cloud Base, Inc.
Airport Rd., Boulder, CO 80301, 303/530-2208

FLORIDA
Lenox Flight School
Rt. 4, Box 4639, Arcadia, FL 33821, 813/494-3921
Seminole Flying & Soaring
1600 West Hwy 419, Chuluota, FL 32766, 305/365-3201

ILLINOIS
Hinckley Soaring, Inc.
Hinckley Airport, U.S. Hwy 30, Hinckley, IL 60520,
  815/286-7200

NEVADA
Desert Soaring
1499 Nevada Hwy, Boulder City, NV 89005, 702/293-4577

NEW HAMPSHIRE
Northeastern Gliderport
Brady Ave., Salem, NH 07938, 603/898-7919

PENNSYLVANIA
Kutztown Aviation Service, Inc.
Rt. 1, Box 1, Kutztown, PA 19530, 215/683-3821 or 8389

Posey Aviation, Inc.
P.O. Box 41, Ervinna, PA 18920, 215/847-2770

VIRGINIA
Warrenton Soaring Center, Inc.
P.O. Box 796, Warrenton, VA 22186, 703/347-0054

WYOMING
Old West Tours
P.O. Box 3322, Jackson, WY 83001, 307/733-7131

Photo: Doug Conarroe

HANG GLIDING

CALIFORNIA
Adventure Aloft Travel
14526 Sherman Way #1023, Van Nuys, CA 91405,
  213/785-0393
Chandelle San Francisco
198 Los Banos Ave., Daly City, CA 98014, 415/756-0650
Hang Flight Systems
1202-M E. Walnut, Santa Ana, CA 92701, 714/542-7444
Hang Glider Emporium
613 N. Milpas, Santa Barbara, CA 93103, 805/965-3733
Hang Gliders West
20 Pamaron Way, Ignacio, CA 94947, 415/883-3494
Kitty Hawks Kites—West
P.O. Box 828, Marina, CA 93933, 408/384-2622
Mission Soaring Center
43551 Mission Blvd., Fremont, CA 90405, 415/656-4745
San Francisco Windsports
3620 Wawona, San Francisco, CA 94116, 415/731-7766
U.S. Hang Gliding Association
Box 6630, Los Angeles, CA 90066
Windsports International
16145 Victory Blvd., Van Nuys, CA 91406, 818/789-0836

GEORGIA
Lookout Mountain Flight Park
Rt. 2 Box 215H, Rising Fawn, GA 30738, 404/398-3541

NEW YORK
Mountain Wings
Main Street, Kerhonkson, NY 12446, 914/629-5555

NORTH CAROLINA
Kitty Hawk Kites, Inc.
P.O. Box 386, Nags Head, NC 27959, 919/441-4124

TENNESSEE
Crystal Air Sports
Rt. 4 Cummings Hwy., Chattanooga, TN 37409, 615/825-1995

WYOMING
Old West Tours
P.O. Box 3322, Jackson, WY 83001, 307/733-7131

Photo: Doug Conarroe

HOT AIR BALLOONING

CALIFORNIA
Action Adventures Wet-N-Wild
Box 1500, Woodland, CA 95695, 916/662-5431
Adventure Aloft Travel
14526 Sherman Way #1023, Van Nuys, CA 91405,
213/785-0393
Balloon Aviation
Box 3298, Napa, CA 94558, 707/252-7067
Balloon Aviation of Napa Valley
P.O. Box 3298, 520 Ornduff St., Napa, CA 94558,
707/252-7067
Balloon Excelsior Inc.
1241 High St., Oakland, CA 94601, 415/261-4222
Farnham Enterprises
1033 Cranberry Dr., Capertino, CA 95014, 408/253-1031

Pacific Adventures
P.O. Box 5041, Riverside, CA 92517, 714/684-1227
Scorpion Balloons, Inc.
Box 1147, Perris, CA 92370, 714/657-6930

COLORADO
Ballon Ranch Adventure
Star Rt. Box 41, Del Norte, CO 81132, 303/754-2533
Colorado Adventure Network
194 S. Franklin St., Denver, CO 80209, 303/722-6482
Unicorn Balloon Co.
413 East Cooper Ave., Aspen, CO 81611, 303/925-5752

CONNECTICUT
Boland Balloon
Pine Drive R.F.D. #2, Burlington, CT 06013, 203/673-1307
New England Hot Air Balloons, Inc.
30 Yorktown Rd., Southington, CT 06489, 203/628-4093

IOWA
American Balloon Services, Inc.
1113 Park Ave., Muscatine, IA 52761, 319/264-1878

MICHIGAN
Captain Phogg's International School of Ballooning
P.O. Box 3039, Flint, MI 48502, 313/767-2120

MINNESOTA
Wiederkehr Balloon International, Inc.
1604 Euclid St., St. Paul, MN 55106, 612/776-5776 or
436-8172

VIRGINIA
Blue Ridge Balloonport
11010 Bristow Rd., Bristow, VA 22013, 703/631-0423 or
361-1690
Bombard Society
6727 Curran Street, McLean, VA 22101, 800/862-8537

WYOMING
Old West Tours, Inc.
P.O. Box 3322, Jackson, WY 83001, 307/733-7131